Human Resource Practices in
Multinational Companies in Ireland
A Contemporary Analysis

Edited by Jonathan Lavelle, Anthony McDonnell and Patrick Gunnigle

About the Editors

Jonathan Lavelle

Jonathan Lavelle is currently a Research Scholar in the Department of Personnel & Employment Relations, Kemmy Business School, University of Limerick. A former Government of Ireland Doctoral Scholar at UL, his main research interests are employment relations in multinational companies and international human resource management. He previously held the University of Limerick Alumni Scholarship and the Kemmy Business School Registrar's Scholarship.

Anthony McDonnell

Anthony McDonnell is a Research Fellow at the Centre for Institutional and Organisational Studies, Faculty of Business and Law, University of Newcastle (Autralia). He is a former Government of Ireland Doctoral Scholar at the University of Limerick, whose research interests focus on Irish-owned multinational companies, particularly organisational learning, management development and talent management. He previously held the CRH Ireland-Canada University Foundation scholarship and University of Limerick 'Advanced Scholar' award.

Patrick (Paddy) Gunnigle

Paddy Gunnigle is Professor of Business Studies and Head, Department of Personnel & Employment Relations, Kemmy Business School, University of Limerick. A graduate of University College Dublin and Cranfield School of Management, and a former Fulbright Scholar, he has authored or co-authored sixteen books and over one hundred refereed journal papers and book chapters.

July 2009

BAILE ÁTHA CLIATH
ARNA FHOILSIÚ AG OIFIG AN tSOLÁTHAIR

Deartha ag www.paulmartin.ie
Arna chlóbhualadh i bPoblacht na hÉireann ag Spectrum Print Logistics

Le ceannach díreach ón
OIFIG DHÍOLTA FOILSEACHÁN RIALTAIS,
TEACH SUN ALLIANCE, SRÁID THEACH LAIGHEAN,
BAILE ÁTHA CLIATH 2,

nó tríd an bpost ó
FOILSEACHÁIN RIALTAIS, AN RANNÓG POST-TRÁCHTA,
AONAD 20 PÁIRC MIONDÍOLA COIS LOCHA, CLÁR CHLAINNE MHUIRIS,
CONTAE MHAIGH EO
(Teil: 01 – 647 6834 nó 1890 213 434; Fax 094 - 937 8964 nó 01 – 647 6843)

nó trí aon díoltóir leabhar.

© An Coimisiún um Chaidreamh Oibreachais agus údair aonair

Iúil 2009

DUBLIN
PUBLISHED BY THE STATIONERY OFFICE

Designed by www.paulmartin.ie
Printed by Spectrum Print Logistics

To be purchased directly from the
GOVERNMENT PUBLICATIONS SALE OFFICE
SUN ALLIANCE HOUSE, MOLESWORTH STREET, DUBLIN 2,

or by mail order from
GOVERNMENT PUBLICATIONS, POSTAL TRADE SECTION,
UNIT 20 LAKESIDE RETAIL PARK, CLAREMORRIS, CO. MAYO
(Tel: 01 - 647 6834 or 1890 213 434; Fax: 094 - 937 8964 or 01 - 647 6843)

or through any bookseller.

© Labour Relations Commission and individual contributors

July 2009

ISBN 978–1–4064–2269–6
€10·00

Contents

Acknowledgements

This study of human resource management (HRM) and employment relations practice in multinational companies (MNCs) in Ireland would not have been possible without the cooperation of a large number of people and institutions.

First and foremost, we acknowledge the senior HRM executives in almost 300 MNCs (including the pilot surveys) and thank them all for their time and insights on HR and general management practice in their respective organisations. We also wish to thank the *Labour Relations Commission* (LRC) for their help at three critical junctures. Through their Research and Advisory Service, the LRC provided initial financial assistance to aid the fieldwork. They subsequently supported a national symposium on HRM in MNCs (June 2008) to disseminate the findings from both the Irish and parallel international studies among the practitioner community. And finally, the LRC were instrumental in the publication of this edited volume. We particularly wish to thank Kieran Mulvey (Chief Executive), and Larry O'Grady for their support and also for their observations and constructive comments as the project progressed. We also acknowledge the help of Assumpta McGill and Eddie Nolan (LRC) in helping bring this work to publication stage.

Possibly the greatest initial challenge in this project was to develop an accurate population list of MNCs operating in Ireland. A significant shortcoming in previous research stemmed from a lack of representativeness in the MNC populations utilised. This was largely due to the omission of certain categories, such as non-grant aided foreign MNCs or Irish-owned MNCs. We spent a full year on the painstaking process of reviewing and building our MNC population list using diverse sources. A strong base was provided by the industrial promotions agencies. We specifically wish to acknowledge the help of Marcus Breathnach, Michael Fitzgibbon and Debbie Quinn of *Forfás*, Jim Barry and Enda McDonnell of *Enterprise Ireland*, and Noirin Lynch, Siobhan Kelleher and Michelle O'Neill of *IDA Ireland*. We also wish to thank Bill Moss of *Bill Moss Partnership* Limited for his help in sourcing the best available external company databases. Other individuals and institutions provided additional intelligence and input on our MNC population listing. John Cullen and John Mangan of the *Irish Management Institute* provided particularly useful advice and direction, as did Eoin O'Malley of the *Economic and Social Research Institute* (ESRI). The help and advice of Aoife Geraghty of the *Library & Information Services, University of Limerick* in securing access to the various external databases is also acknowledged.

To help complete the fieldwork phase of this study, we engaged the *Economic and Social Research Institute* (ESRI). We are particularly indebted to Dr. Dorothy

Watson, then head of the ESRI Survey Unit, for her immense expertise, assistance and hard work throughout the fieldwork phase. We also acknowledge the input of various members of the ESRI team, notably Sylvia Blackwell, Shirley Gorby and Carley Cheevers.

A research project of this scale requires adequate finance. We thank the *University of Limerick Research Office,* particularly former Vice President (Research) Professor Vincent Cunnane and current incumbent Professor Brian Fitzgerald, for providing initial funding. As mentioned earlier, the *LRC* provided additional financial assistance to aid both the fieldwork and dissemination of the findings. Special thanks must also go to the *Irish Research Council for the Humanities and Social Sciences* (IRCHSS) which provided two *Government of Ireland Scholarships* to authors Anthony McDonnell and Jonathan Lavelle in the pursuit of their doctoral studies.

We are indebted also to the *Chartered Institute of Personnel and Development* (CIPD) in Ireland for their assistance. We particularly acknowledge the input of Michael McDonnell, Wendy Sullivan, Brid O'Brien and Don Hegarty in promoting the relevance of this study to the HR community in Ireland and for highlighting the importance of academic inquiry of this nature. We also acknowledge the help and insights provided by Michael Crowley (Pfizer), Bernard Delany (Golden Pages), Jack Golden (CRH), Declan Morrin (ILO), Alan O'Leary (SIPTU) and Professor Hugh Scullion (NUI, Galway).

Last, but certainly not least, we wish to thank our international partners. This project was conducted in parallel with similar studies in Canada, Mexico, Spain and the UK, while plans are afoot for studies in Australia, Argentina, Denmark and Norway, and Singapore. We particularly wish to thank the UK team for inviting us to participate in this study. Both the UK and Canadian teams provided invaluable assistance on instrument design. Subsequent meetings and exchanges with our international partners have proved both stimulating and constructive. At extreme risk of leaving somebody out, we therefore wish to thank the following:

- Australia: John Burgess (University of Newcastle)
- Canada: Gregor Murray, Pierre-Antoine Harvey, Patrice Jalette (University of Montreal), Jacques Bélanger (Laval University), Christian Lévesque (HEC Montréal)
- Mexico: Jorge Carrillo and Ismael Plascenia (El Colegio de la Frontera Norte, Tijuana)
- Spain: Javier Quintanilla, Lourdes Susaeta, Rocío Sánchez Mangas and María Jesús Belizon (IESE, University of Navarra)
- UK: Paul Edwards, Paul Marginson, Duncan Adam (Warwick University), Anthony Ferner, Olga Tregaskis (De Montfort University), Tony Edwards (King's College, London).

Abbreviations and Conventions

ATN = Above the Norm

CIPD = Chartered Institute of Personnel & Development

CSO = Central Statistics Office

CUL = Cranfield-University of Limerick

Double counting = where the same MNC is listed twice or more, often under differing registered or trade names.

EFILWC = European Foundation for the Improvement of Living and Working Conditions

EPOC = Employee Direct Participation in Organisational Change Study

ER = Employment Relations

ESRI = Economic and Social Research Institute

ETUI-REHS = European Trade Union Institute for Research, Education and Health and Safety

EU = European Union

EWC = European Works Council

FD = Forced Distribution (in performance appraisal rankings)

FDI = Foreign Direct Investment

HPWS = High Performance Work Systems

HR = Human Resource

HRIS = Human Resource Information System

HRM = Human Resource Management

ICTU = Irish Congress of Trade Unions

I&C = Information and Consultation

IBEC = Irish Business and Employers Confederation

IDA = Industrial Development Agency

IFSC = International Financial Services Centre

IHRM = International Human Resource Management

Irish operations = All the operations (subsidiary companies, business divisions, etc.) of an MNC within the Republic of Ireland

IT = Information Technology

JIT = Just in Time

KG = Key Group

LOG = Largest Occupational Group

MBA = Masters of Business Administration

MNC = Multinational Company

MSF = Manufacturing, Scinece and Finance Union

OECD = Organisation for Economic Trade and Development

PCN = Parent Country National

Contributors

David Collings is Lecturer in International Management at the National University of Ireland, Galway. Previously he was on the faculty at the University of Sheffield Management School and Visiting Research Fellow at Strathclyde International Business Unit, University of Strathclyde. He completed his Ph.D. at the University of Limerick where he was an Irish Research Council for the Humanities and Social Sciences (IRCHSS) Government of Ireland Doctoral Scholar. He has published six books and over 50 book chapters and journal articles. He is Editor of the Human Resource Management Journal.

Paddy Gunnigle is Professor of Business Studies and Head, Department of Personnel & Employment Relations, Kemmy Business School, University of Limerick. A graduate of University College Dublin and Cranfield School of Management, and a former Fulbright Scholar, he has authored or co-authored sixteen books and over one hundred refereed journal papers and book chapters.

Ryan Lamare is a Post-Doctoral Research Scholar in Work Research, Department of Personnel & Employment Relations, Kemmy Business School, University of Limerick. He completed his Ph.D. at Cornell University's School of Industrial and Labor Relations, and has research interests in HR practices in multinational companies, union influences on voting behaviour, alternative dispute resolution, and quantitative social science research methods.

Jonathan Lavelle is a Research Scholar in the Department of Personnel & Employment Relations, Kemmy Business School, University of Limerick. A former IRCHSS Government of Ireland Doctoral Scholar at UL, his main research interests are employment relations in multinational companies and international human resource management. He previously held the University of Limerick Alumni Scholarship and the Kemmy Business School Registrar's Scholarship.

Anthony McDonnell is a Research Fellow at the Centre for Institutional and Organisational Studies, Faculty of Business and Law, University of Newcastle, (Australia). He is a former IRCHSS Government of Ireland Doctoral Scholar at the University of Limerick, whose research interests focus on Irish-owned multinational companies, particularly organisational learning, management development and talent management. He previously held the CRH Ireland-Canada University Foundation scholarship and University of Limerick 'Advanced Scholar' award.

Michael Morley is Professor of Management and Head, Department of Management and Marketing, Kemmy Business School, University of Limerick. He has co-authored/edited some 18 books and over 130 refereed journal articles and book chapters. He currently serves as Associate Editor of the Journal of Managerial Psychology and Regional Editor of the European Journal of International Management.

Thomas Turner is a Senior Lecturer in the Department of Personnel and Employment Relations, Kemmy Business School, University of Limerick. His main areas of research and publication include social partnership in Ireland, trade unions, immigrant experiences in the workplace and occupational changes in the Irish labour market.

Joseph Wallace is a Senior Lecturer in Industrial Relations at the University of Limerick. He is a graduate of Trinity College, Dublin and the College of Europe, Bruges and has been a visiting lecturer at Michigan State University. He has conducted research for a number of national international bodies, including the International Labour Organisation, The European Foundation for the Improvement of Living and Working Conditions and the Labour Relations Commission. He is co-author of Industrial Relations in Ireland, published by Gill & Macmillan.

Foreword

Foreign direct investment by multinational companies (MNCs) has undoubtedly been a very significant contributor to economic growth in Ireland over recent decades. While the current economic crisis will curb the pace of globalisation, the internationalisation of business activity is likely to continue. Indeed, even in 2008 Ireland experienced high levels of new investment by MNCs while concurrently witnessing closures and disinvestment in the MNC sector.

This publication is particularly timely. Not only does it come at a time of immense challenge for the Irish and international economy but it also addresses key issues regarding employment practice in MNCs in Ireland. This publication is based on data gathered through a comprehensive and highly representative survey of HR practice in MNCs in Ireland. This survey forms part of a larger international project involving parallel surveys by research teams in Australia (University of Newcastle, Victoria University, University of Wollongong & La Trobe University), Canada (University of Montreal, HEC Montreal and Laval University), Denmark & Norway (Copenhagen Business School, University of Copenhagen & the Norwegian School of Economics and Business Administration), Mexico (El Colegio del Norte), Spain (IESE, University of Navarra) and the UK (De Montfort University, King's College, London and the University of Warwick).

Findings from the Irish and international studies were presented last June at an LRC National Symposium entitled Human Resource Management in MNCs: Employment Practice and Global Value Chains in the Croke Park Conference Centre, Dublin. This symposium involved presentations by some of the world's leading scholars in the field and considered the experience of MNCs in countries such as Australia, Canada, Mexico, Spain and the UK, in addition to Ireland. It also involved presentations from HR practitioners from both foreign and Irish owned MNCs including CRH, Golden Pages and Pfizer and contributions from trade union executives and from the ILO. This symposium attracted an attendance of some 150 HR practitioners from MNCs.

The Commission believes that this study makes a significant contribution to our knowledge of the human resource landscape in Ireland. It is a part also of our continuing "Best Practice" research programme on Irish industrial relations and human resource practices.

In the uncertain times ahead our collective ability to maximise the huge potential of a highly skilled and educated workforce will be a significant challenge for all the social partners and all sectors of our economy.

Kieran Mulvey, Chief Executive
July 2009

CHAPTER 1
Background and Objectives:
Multinationals Matter

Patrick Gunnigle, Jonathan Lavelle & Anthony McDonnell

Introduction

In spite of conflict in the Middle East, oscillating oil prices and extreme stock market volatility, globalisation has continued apace. The most recent *United Nations Conference on Trade and Development Report* (UNCTAD, 2008) indicates that there are almost 80,000 multinational companies (MNCs) worldwide employing a staggering 82 million people. The numbers employed in MNCs has more than doubled in less than two decades (MNCs employed 24 million in 1990). The impact of the current financial crisis remains to be seen. However, while it will likely temper the pace of globalisation, it is unlikely to stall it as a range of developments in information and communications technology (ICT), transportation and trade regulation encourage increased international business activity.

Ireland has been a major beneficiary of inward foreign direct investment (FDI) by MNCs. As FDI grew dramatically through the 1990s, MNCs were heralded as one of the principal reasons behind the country's rapid ascent towards becoming one of the world's most successful economies. However, times have clearly changed. Ireland has quickly transitioned from a high growth to a negative growth economy. More pertinently, much of the recent media spotlight has focused on cases of MNCs closing or downsizing their Irish operations. Concurrently some MNCs have increased employment whilst new organisations have also been attracted, although this position is worsening.

There has also been a change in the character of FDI. We have seen examples of the attraction of high-skilled activities, thus providing some support for the industrial policy objective of moving MNC operations in Ireland up their corporate 'value chain'. It is also clear that much recent FDI activity has been in services rather than manufacturing. Arguably though, the most dramatic development has been the surge in significance of Irish-owned MNCs. Ireland now boasts comparatively large numbers of indigenous firms operating on a global stage. In the period 2004-06, Ireland was a net exporter of FDI, with outflows exceeding inflows. The situation reversed in 2007 but the anticipated pattern is one of steady growth in FDI flows over future years.

The analysis of human resource management (HRM) and employment relations (ER) in MNCs has been historically limited by the lack of systematic data on employment policy and practice, and how these are influenced by organisational characteristics. In spite of the importance of MNCs to the Irish economy, thus far we have not had an authoritative study of management practice in MNCs. This book seeks to address this knowledge deficit. Drawing on the most representative empirical survey-based investigation of HRM and ER in MNCs in Ireland to date, we report key findings on the profile of MNCs in Ireland and on practice in regard to various aspects of HRM, specifically on issues such as the HR function, pay and performance, employee representation and consultation, employee involvement and communication, training and development, and issues of autonomy and control in the management of MNC subsidiaries. We also use the survey findings to test the impact of various organisational factors (principally nationality of ownership, sector and size) on variation in HRM practice among MNCs.

This chapter has two principal objectives. First, we outline the key role that MNCs play in the global economy, and particularly so in the Irish context. Second, we summarily outline the specific aims of the survey of HRM and ER practice in MNCs upon which this volume is based.

The role of multinational companies

Multinationals matter! On any measure of business activity, the sheer scale of MNC operations is quite phenomenal. As indicated above, the most recent UNCTAD report (2008) identifies approximately 79,000 MNCs worldwide that, in turn, operate some 790,000 affiliates. Despite the global economic downturn, MNCs remain one of the key drivers of the world economy. In 2007, FDI inflows reached an all time high of $1.8 trillion, surpassing the previous watershed of $1.3 trillion in 2000 (UNCTAD, 2001; 2008). And the influence of MNCs is not simply confined to the business sphere: MNCs also carry considerable economic and political clout. This is evidenced in the fact the revenues in many large MNCs significantly exceed the economic worth of most nation states. Of the world's largest 150 economic entities, 95 (63%) are corporations rather than countries (Butler, 2005). Whilst a diminution in growth in MNC activity is anticipated as a result of the current financial crisis, the general trend of increased globalisation shows no sign of abating. A number of the largest MNCs plan to increase their international investment expenditures, albeit at a more moderate level than heretofore (UNCTAD, 2008).

We now turn our focus to MNCs in Ireland by briefly reviewing the pattern of FDI (both inward and outward) by way of providing a backdrop for our subsequent investigation of HRM in MNCs in Ireland.

MNCs in Ireland

Multinationals matter, particularly in Ireland! Ireland is one of the world's most FDI-dependent economies. This is the product of a deliberate and consistent state policy of wooing foreign MNCs via a package of incentives, the most significant of which is a comparatively low level of corporation tax (cf. Gunnigle and McGuire, 2001; Barry, 2002; Gunnigle et al., 2005). This policy has its genesis in the late 1950s when the Government of the day abandoned the pre-existing strategy of protecting indigenous industry and decided that (i) Ireland should seek membership of the then European Economic Community (EEC) at the first opportunity[i] and (ii) the pace of industrialisation could be more effectively accelerated by encouraging foreign-owned MNCs to locate there. This policy of 'industrialisation by invitation' was underpinned by a generous incentive package to encourage inward FDI, the most significant of which then was zero tax on profits from exports. While the nature of these incentives have evolved over time (e.g. corporation tax is now 12.5 per cent), the policy of actively encouraging inward investment by foreign MNCs remains broadly intact to the present day.

This policy has met with remarkable success. For some time now Ireland has been hailed as one of the most successful FDI models in the world (te Velde, 2001), with the UNCTAD (2004) suggesting Ireland represents a leading example of economic development. *IDA Ireland*, the state agency primarily charged with attracting foreign investment, identifies in excess of 970 foreign MNCs with Irish operations and employing over 135,000 (IDA Ireland, 2008), a figure which could be a significant under-representation given that not all MNCs operating here receive financial or other assistance from bodies like *IDA Ireland* (cf. McDonnell et al., 2007). While this success has continued through the difficult trading conditions of recent years it is increasingly being eroded. In the early 1990s Ireland was ranked 50th in the UNCTAD inward FDI *performance and potential index* but by 2004 it had moved up to 4th position (Rios-Morales and Brennan, 2007). Ireland was one the major beneficiaries of the global FDI boom from the early 1990s. Over the period 1993-2003, it was the largest net recipient of FDI in the OECD, recording a cumulative balance of inflows over outflows of $71 billion and making it the world's 11th largest recipient of inward FDI[ii]. These figures represent an extraordinary performance, given that Ireland accounts for such a small fraction of the European Union (EU) population.

Table 1.1 FDI inflows 1970 – 2004 (millions of dollars)

	1970-79	%	1980-89	%	1990-99	%	2000-04	%
Ireland	1,370	0.76	2,210	0.31	39,225	1.41	100,419	3.24
Denmark	1,079	0.60	2,291	0.32	42,642	1.53	43,485	1.41
UK	32,572	18.06	103,919	14.37	324,769	11.65	294,114	9.49
Germany	14,364	7.96	15,140	2.09	124,615	4.57	263,915	8.51
Portugal	739	0.41	4,453	0.62	18,285	0.66	22,370	0.72
Italy	5,582	3.26	18,873	2.61	42,553	1.53	76,020	2.45

Adapted from UNCTAD (2005).

Table 1.1 outlines the growth in FDI inflows into Ireland over the period 1970-2004 in comparative perspective, and illustrates the significant growth in FDI inflows achieved by Ireland in that period. We can see that pre-1990 Ireland accounted for just 0.31 per cent of FDI inflows into Europe but by the 2000–2004 period this had risen to 3.24 per cent (Rios-Morales and Brennan, 2007)[iii].

Foreign-owned companies now account for approximately 50 per cent of all Irish manufacturing employment, well above the average figure of 23 per cent for the Western European Union (EU) member states and the 33 per cent for the three largest Central and Eastern European countries (Czech Republic, Hungary and Poland) (Barry, 2004; Buckley and Ruane, 2006; Barry, 2007). Ireland also boasts the highest levels of service sector employment in foreign-owned MNCs (OECD, 2005a). Furthermore, the proportion of employment in foreign-owned companies, as a percentage of total international trade related employment in Ireland, is the highest in the world (UNCTAD, 2007) .

Despite being the first 'euro-zone' member to fall into recession since the global economic slowdown (Central Statistics Office, 2008a), the most recent data indicate that Ireland continues to perform reasonably well in attracting FDI. Although the level of inward FDI peaked in 2000, the levels attained in 2002 and 2003 were equivalent to the totals attained by the full 10-member Central and Eastern European bloc, averaging $25 billion annually (Enterprise Ireland, 2005). Indeed only five countries (Luxembourg, China, France, Spain, United States) registered larger absolute FDI inflows in 2003 (Begley et al., 2005; Forfás, 2005). After three years of negative inflows, 2007 saw an increase to $31 billion (UNCTAD, 2008).

The United States (US) is, by considerable distance, Ireland's largest source of inward FDI. In the period 1990–1997, almost 25 per cent of all US manufacturing investment and 40 per cent of electronics investment to Europe located in Ireland (Economist, 1997). This significance has been enduring. The US corporate investment position in Ireland accounted to some $83 billion in 2006, larger than the combined US investment in the so called 'BRIC' economies (Brazil, Russia India and China) (Hamilton and Quinlan, 2008). Investment from the US in 2006 alone equated to $13.3 billion, almost double that of US FDI to all South American countries (Hamilton and Quinlan, 2008). Furthermore, the chemicals and information and communication technology (ICT) industries account for three quarters of goods exports from Ireland and these sectors are dominated by US owned MNCs (OECD, 2008). Of course this is also a 'double-edged sword': Ireland's dependence on inward FDI from America renders it particularly susceptible to economic downturns and, indeed, changes in MNC regulation in the US.

We also find evidence of a shift away from reliance on manufacturing. While manufacturing firms in the pharmaceutical, medical devices and computer hardware sectors constitute a very substantial proportion foreign-owned MNC activity in Ireland, particularly in terms of exports (Barry, 2004), the services sector is also significant. Employment in the international financial services and computer software sector is now on a par with that of the aforementioned manufacturing sectors (Barry and Van Welsum, 2005).

Challenging times

Without doubt, a large measure of Ireland's economic growth can be traced to its success in attracting inward FDI by foreign-owned MNCs. Indeed, many other countries have examined the 'Irish story' to establish if they can replicate it. Clearly recent developments in Ireland, and in the world economy, indicate a very different economic trajectory going forward. The international financial crisis and 'credit-crunch', combined with a very significant fall in property prices, growing unemployment and precarious public finances are likely to herald a reduction in economic and business activity, including lower levels of FDI. While the scale of the current economic crisis was not foreseen, there was recognition some time ago, particularly among the relevant state agencies, that the attractiveness of Ireland as a site for inward FDI was likely to diminish, particularly for manufacturing investment and that if the country was to continue to attract inward investment then it needed to re-position itself in this 'market'. Acknowledging that Ireland's success in securing new FDI was likely to recede in the face of more intense international competition for FDI and increased operating costs at home, the industrial promotions agencies (particularly *IDA Ireland*) initiated two notable changes in strategy (cf. Gunnigle et al., 2003):

1. Shifting the emphasis away from attracting new greenfield start-ups towards the retention of existing MNC facilities through facilitating the Irish subsidiary's move up their corporation's 'value chain' by securing the production of higher margin products or services and developing greater product development and research capacities in the Irish sites.
2. Placing a greater emphasis on regional balance in the geographic distribution of FDI (essentially encouraging FDI projects to locate outside of Dublin and major industrial centres into more economically disadvantaged regions).

The success or otherwise of this policy remains to be seen. Over recent years, there have been positive and negative developments. On the positive side, a number of new investments, often involving the creation of high quality jobs, have been announced in both start-ups and expansions. The most notable include the attraction of prominent internet based organisations such as *Google* and *Ebay* and expansions by established MNCs such as *Wyeth, Merck* and *Abbott Laboratories*. There have also been some significant closure and retrenchment decisions including those at *Dell, Celestica, Honeywell* and *Procter & Gamble*. Predictably, the majority of these job losses have been in manufacturing, a trend likely to continue over the foreseeable future. However, the fact that more recently the service sector has overtaken manufacturing as the major source of employment is an indicator of the changing profile of the FDI landscape in Ireland.

The service sector now accounts for almost 66 per cent of total employment (Eurostat, 2004). Of particular importance has been the role of the International Financial Services Centre (IFSC) which, in 2004, accounted for the majority of FDI into Ireland at €4.4 billion, compared to €1.5 billion for non-IFSC FDI (Forfás, 2006). Somewhat paradoxically, considering it represents one of the primary growth engines of the service sector, the retail sector has been under-represented in extant research on MNCs in Ireland (see McDonnell et al., 2007). The most recent census data show one in seven people now work in retail and wholesale outlets, making the sector the country's biggest employer (Kelly, 2007). Of the 1,930,042 employed people, a total of 13.3 per cent work in the retail sector compared with 12.6 per cent in manufacturing and 11.1 per cent in construction (Kelly, 2007). The arrival of retailers from the UK and further a field has played a major role in this growth and it is expected that more new entrants will establish in Ireland (Feeney, 2007). It is now a rare occurrence for a medium sized Irish town not to have a retail park comprising one or more multinational retail MNC such as a *Tesco, Penneys, LIDL* or *B&Q*.

Remarkable growth in outward FDI

A much less trumpeted but particularly significant development is the surge in outward FDI from Ireland and the growing importance of the 'Irish MNC'. Remarkably, over recent years, the scale of inward FDI is now more than rivalled by outward FDI by Irish-owned firms. In 2005, FDI outflows stood at $12,931 million, a significant increase from the 1997 level of $1,014 million (UNCTAD, 2006). Ireland now has a larger stock of outward FDI as a percentage of gross domestic product (GDP) than most EU countries, and substantially higher than the EU average (Forfás, 2007). Furthermore, outflows have grown more sharply than inflows in recent times, reflecting the increasing numbers and scale of Irish-owned MNCs (Barry et al., 2003; Everett, 2006). Interestingly cluster analysis of the most recent FDI figures for OECD countries places Ireland in the group of countries with the second largest level of FDI outflows, along with countries such as Japan, Germany, Canada and Sweden (UNCTAD, 2006).

Table 1.2 reveals some interesting findings, not least the variable nature of outflows. However, the most noteworthy aspect is the substantial increase in outward direct investment from Ireland over the past decade. While some volatility of FDI flows exists, the indications are that FDI outflows will continue to increase and that:

Ireland may be adopting the profile of a more typical developed economy in that it is becoming more important as a source rather than a destination of FDI
Forfás, 2006: 39.

Table 1.2 FDI outflows 1997-2005 ($million)[IV]

	1997	1998	1999	2000	2001	2002	2003	2004P	2005E
Ireland	1,013.7	3,902.1	6,109.1	4,629.6	4,066.1	11,035.2	5,554.7	15,813.1	12,930.6
Germany	41,794.1	88,837.2	108,691.6	56,567.5	39,691.1	18,963.5	6,179.5	1,884	45,606.1
Czech Republic	25.2	127.1	89.8	42.8	165.4	206.5	206.7	1,014.4	855.8
UK	61,620	122,861.2	201,436.7	233,487.7	58,885.2	50,346.5	62,493.3	94,928.5	101,079.8
US	104,803	142,644	224,934	159,212	142,349	154,460	140,579	244,128	9,072
Poland	45	316	31	16	-90	230	300	778.0	1,455
Sweden	12,647.5	24,379.4	21,928.6	40,667.3	6,374.9	10,630	21,259.8	11,947.2	26,028.8

Adapted from OECD (2006). p: projected; e: estimate

In summary, FDI has played a pivotal role in the turnaround of the Irish economy from the bleak economic and industrial climate in place for much of the twentieth century to the prosperity experienced over the past couple of decades. While foreign-owned MNCs have made a very substantial contribution, indigenous owned MNCs are now playing an important and ever more significant role in this success. Due to the global economic conditions, their future impact is hard to predict. A study that, for the first time, provides a representative depiction of HRM practice in MNCs in Ireland (both Irish- and foreign-owned) is both necessary and timely.

HRM in multinational companies - aims and objectives

This volume presents and discusses the main findings from a comprehensive survey of employment practice in MNCs operating in Ireland. This study covers all key areas of HRM and provides the first comprehensive portrait of HR policy and practice amongst MNCs here in Ireland. The Irish investigation forms part of a larger international project involving similar studies of MNCs by research teams from Australia, Canada, Denmark and Norway, Mexico, Singapore, Spain and the UK[iv]. The specific aims of the study are as follows:

- To carry out an innovative and comprehensive survey of employment practice in organisational context based on a representative sample of MNCs in Ireland, and thereby provide a template for future surveys of trends in Ireland and for similar surveys in other countries.
- To analyse employment practice across some of the main substantive HR and ER areas in relation to three distinct groups of staff ('largest occupational group', 'managers' and the 'key group', see greater detail below), and to relate variations in practice to organisational structure and strategy.
- To provide an accurate picture of the organisation and management practice in MNCs.
- To contribute to policy debates on the extent to which MNCs are pursuing common agendas and are able to impose these agendas on the countries in which they operate, as well as the debate on whether MNCs are able to identify and diffuse 'best practice' across their operations.

The primary objective is to map the HR practices of MNCs and to relate these to such organisational factors as nationality of ownership and sector of operation. The survey focuses on five key HR areas, namely: the HR function, pay and performance management, employee representation and consultation, employee communication and involvement, and training, development and organisational learning.

In addressing these five areas, the study focuses on HR practice relating to three groups of employees. The first group is the 'largest occupational group' (LOG) defined as, "the largest non-managerial occupational group among the employees in the 'headcount' in Ireland". The second group is 'managers', defined for the purpose of this study as "employees who primarily manage the organisation, or a department, subdivision, function, or component of the organisation and whose main tasks consist of the direction and coordination of the functioning of the organisation. In other words, managers are those above the level of first-line supervision". The final group, and a major innovation in studies of this nature, is the 'key group' defined as "those employees whom you might identify as critical to your firm's organisational learning and core competence. These might be research staff, product designers, major account handlers, developers of new markets, etc." In subsequent chapters dealing with

HR practice, reference normally relates to the LOG unless explicitly stated otherwise.

In the next chapter we set out the methodology employed in this study. This is of special significance since much previous research on MNCs has been criticised for its lack of representativeness (cf. Collinson and Rugman, 2005; Alfaro and Charlton, 2006; McDonnell et al., 2007; Edwards et al., 2008). In chapter three we attempt to answer the question "who are the MNCs in Ireland", by providing a profile of MNCs by size, ownership and sector. Chapters four through eight cover the substantive areas of HR practice (i.e. dealing, respectively, with the HR function, pay & performance, employee representation & consultation, employee involvement & communication, and training, development & organisation learning). Chapter nine focuses on a more generic and particularly significant aspect of management practice in MNCs, namely the issues of autonomy, coordination and control in regard to HRM in MNCs. Finally, in chapter ten, we present our conclusions.

ENDNOTES

[i] The Republic of Ireland joined the then European Economic Community in 1973.

[ii] Figures compiled from OECD International Direct Investment Statistics, http://www.oecd.org.

[iii] This is compared with the 17 EU member states, prior to the admission of the Central and Eastern European economies in 2004, and the US and Norway.

[iv] Where a negative figure is shown this reflects subsidiaries repaying loans to the parent company.

CHAPTER 2
Research Methodology: Providing a Representative of MNCS in Ireland[i]
Anthony McDonnell, Jonathan Lavelle & Patrick Gunnigle

Introduction

> Research methodology is essentially a decision-making process. Each decision made is affected by, and in turn, influences every other decision. It is a system of decisions, all of which are interrelated. The one decision that focuses, and to a large extent drives all the rest including theoretical development, philosophical approach, research strategy and data collection is the research question
> *Brannick and Coghlan, 2006: 6.*

This chapter outlines the research methodology employed in the overall research project. The purpose of the chapter is two-fold. First, it is important to provide the methodological approach adopted in any research as this provides detail on how the data were collected and analysed, which has obvious ramifications for the reliability and validity of the research. The second purpose of the chapter is to detail the methodological contribution that this research project has made, namely carrying out the first representative survey of MNCs operating in Ireland. In so doing, this chapter outlines the research approach adopted, namely a quantitative approach through a survey. We detail the research instrument and how it was developed and tested. We subsequently cover a critical aspect of any research, defining the population. We also provide details on how our sample was chosen, followed by an insight into how the questionnaire was administered in the field, including negotiating access and response rates. Finally we provide details on the data analysis.

Research strategy

As noted by Brannick and Coghlan (2006) above, it is the research aim and questions which essentially drive everything else in a research project. Consequently, it is worth revisiting these briefly before proceeding. The overarching research aim was:

- To carry out an innovative and comprehensive survey of employment practice in an organisational context based on a representative sample of MNCs in Ireland.

Having reviewed a number of methodological techniques, the most suited research strategy, to answer the research aims of the project, was the survey. The survey is the most commonly used strategy in management research (Baruch and Holtom, 2008) because of its ability to answer the 'who', 'what', 'where', 'how much' and 'how many' questions. Surveys provide the researcher with the opportunity to collect vast amounts of data from large populations in a relatively economical fashion. By collecting this quantitative data, descriptive and inferential statistics can be used to offer reasons for relationships found between variables and produce models highlighting these relationships (Saunders et al., 2007). Through the use of sampling, findings can be generalised to larger populations at a far lower cost than having to collect data for every case in the population. The quality and comprehensiveness of the both the total population and sample chosen will be a key determinant over the ability to generalise findings as being representative of the whole population. However, one is limited in collecting very wide-ranging data due to only being able to ask a limited number of questions. All things considered, the survey method was the preferred choice for satisfying this study's research aim and questions, due to the ability it allows for exploratory, descriptive and explanatory data to be gathered.

Reliability and validity

The credibility of the research findings is one of the most important considerations in a researcher's choice of methods. Consequently, attention must be paid to the study's reliability and validity. Although important for all research types, these issues are arguably of even greater importance when the generalisability of the findings is a key concern. In a nutshell, reliability means that if the same study was conducted again, using the same procedures, one would arrive at the same results. As such it "is a criterion that refers to the validity of the results" (Cresswell, 1994: 229). Easterby-Smith et al. (2002: 53) pose three questions that, if answered 'yes', suggest there is a high degree of reliability present:

1. Will the measures yield the same results on other occasions?
2. Will similar observations be reached by other observers?
3. Is there transparency in how sense was made from the raw data?

All reasonable efforts were made to ensure that if the study was conducted again the same results would occur. It has long been suggested that surveys are one of the most reliable methods due to their highly structured nature (Gill and Johnson, 2002). For example, a standardised instrument was used at all times during the research. Questions and necessary instructions were set out in the same order to improve consistency and reduce the possibility of errors as a result of carelessness. There is no reason to believe that the measures used should not yield similar results if conducted on a different occasion. One caveat to this is, however, that the results represent a 'picture in time'. Situations may change, meaning results may change. Through the detail set out in the data analysis of this chapter, transparency is brought to the analytical process. Thus, we are confident that the research study is reliable.

Validity refers to whether tests or measurements used in a study are what they say they are. In other words, do they measure what they should? There are two primary types of validity tests: internal validity and external validity (Gill and Johnson, 2002). Internal validity is concerned with whether the research design can eliminate bias and the effect of irrelevant variables. In other words it relates to whether you can be sure that the independent variable used brings about the variation in the dependent variable and not some other variable. Finally, external validity refers to the extent to which the results can be generalised (i.e., can they be generalised beyond the specific research sample). One of the strengths of survey-research is its high level of external validity. This is the case here as extensive efforts were made to develop a comprehensive population and ensure a high response rate.

Despite reliability and validity treated as two distinct terms, at the same time they are very much related because "if your measure is not reliable, it cannot be valid" (Bryman and Bell, 2003: 79).

The research instrument - questionnaire

The research method most commonly associated with the survey strategy is the questionnaire. Structured observation and structured interviews are other forms that fall under the survey strategy radar. Questionnaires are particularly useful for providing insights into individual opinions and beliefs and organisational policies and practices (Baruch and Holtom, 2008). Due to the research aims here, the questionnaire is particularly appropriate.

Questionnaire development

The questionnaire focused on five substantive areas of human resource management/employment relations (the HR function; pay and performance management; employee representation and consultation; employee involvement and communication; training, development and organisation learning) as well as encompassing a section on company background and other key attributes. The questionnaire was developed at the University of Limerick (UL) and was based in part on previous instruments developed by a team of UK and Canadian academics. Adopting and adapting questions used in other studies is one of the most common and popular means of questionnaire design as it can help the reliability and validity of the instrument (Saunders et al., 2007).

The process of questionnaire development commenced in March 2005 with a first draft completed in early September 2005. A series of meetings were held in order to discuss both the types of questions to be used in the questionnaire and also its layout and structure. These meetings were used as a means of improving the validity of the research. This was achieved through discussing and debating the merits of each question, what it intended to measure, its wording and so forth. A number of different types of questions were used throughout, including multiple choice, list, ranking, rating, quantity and dichotomous questions. A number of filter or contingency questions were also used (i.e., asking one question to determine if the respondent is qualified to answer a subsequent question or series of questions). To further improve the study's reliability a number of check questions were also used. Open-ended questions were kept to a minimum due to coding issues and for reliability and validity reasons. Yet in spite of this some respondents provided further information to what was asked, particularly after the instrument had been administered. This resulted in some useful qualitative data being gathered which is utilised, where appropriate, in each of the subsequent chapters.

Pilot testing

Undertaking a pilot study prior to the main fieldwork taking place is now regarded as essential practice (Gill and Johnson, 2002). By doing this, one is able to see and correct potential problems in the questionnaire before beginning the main fieldwork stage. This process is also said to help in improving the survey's reliability and validity (Roberts, 1999). "No matter how many times a questionnaire is re-drafted it can only be considered a usable document if it has been tested successfully in the field" (Murphy, 1997: 34).

Table 2.1 Pilot study interview schedule

Participant's Job Title	Nationality of participant MNC	Sector of participant MNC	Date interview	Location of interview
T&D manager	Ireland	Multi-sector	24/02/2006	Kerry
HR manager	United States	Manufacturing	14/03/2006	Limerick
HR manager	Ireland	Manufacturing	20/03/2006	Limerick
Senior HR officer	United States	Manufacturing	22/03/2006	Galway
HR Manager	United Kingdom	Manufacturing	24/03/2006	Cork

During March and April 2006, five pilot interviews were undertaken which proved extremely useful. These were conducted in two phases. The first phase incorporated two interviews in which it became apparent that there were a number of issues. Among the issues raised included difficulties in understanding some of the questions, the length of time to complete the questionnaire and the requirement for a number of 'missing' categories (i.e., a 'don't know' and/or 'not applicable' option). Furthermore, it was felt that some structural changes would improve the flow of the questionnaire. After making these alterations the questionnaire was re-piloted in phase two, with three more companies. These ran a lot smoother with the time required to complete reduced to 50 minutes or less. A minute number of alterations, primarily in ensuring greater clarity of questions, were made after these interviews. The instrument was then deemed ready to enter the main fieldwork stage.

Development of the MNC population

As noted in Chapter 1, much of the extant literature on MNCs is criticised due to its lack of representativeness (cf. Collinson and Rugman, 2005; Alfaro and Charlton, 2006; McDonnell et al., 2007; Edwards et al, 2008). For instance Collinson and Rugman (2005) note that much of the MNC literature focuses on a small number of, predominately large, well known, US-owned, MNCs which they outline presents an unrepresentative picture of management policies and practices in MNCs. Recent years have witnessed a marked interest in research on the activities of MNCs in Ireland and whilst there have been many interesting and informative studies (cf. Kelly and Brannick, 1985; Gunnigle et al., 1994; Turner et al., 1997a&b; Geary and Roche, 2001; Collings, 2003; Gunnigle et al., 2005), their representativeness is open to question. In particular these studies tend to neglect some important groups of MNCs, namely the non-grant aided service sector (e.g. retail) and indigenous-owned MNCs. The root cause of this is the incomplete coverage of company database sources much used by researchers and academics in identifying study populations. Most populations tend to have been derived from the listings provided by the main industrial development agencies. The common exclusion of non-grant aided firms is likely to bias findings on key aspects of practice and behaviours of MNCs. In an international context, Whitley (1999: 128) argues that 'the more dependent are foreign firms on domestic organizations and agencies, both within and across sectors, the less likely are they to change prevalent patterns of behaviour'. This is significant as it would suggest that those firms which have tenuous links to state agencies may be less restricted in implementing practices which are at odds with host traditions. Thus we may be getting a biased picture of 'excessive' conformity from research which draws on databases derived from the state agencies.

Relying solely on these 'traditional' listings is problematic due to the large numbers of firms they exclude. As a result, the development of populations from these conventional sources is both unreliable and likely to bias the results (cf. Murphy, 1997).

Redressing these issues so as to provide, for the first time, representative empirical evidence on the whole MNC sector was a critical concern. In order to satisfy this objective, a three-stage process was undertaken.

Phase 1 – Defining the MNC

As outlined in Chapter 1, MNCs are significant players in the Irish economy and thus it is of great surprise that a comprehensive list of MNCs in Ireland is not easily forthcoming. The magnitude of the process ahead to develop such a list could not have been foreseen in advance. A critical first step in identifying the total population was to clearly outline a definition of what constitutes an MNC. From the literature, it emerges that no universal definition of an MNC exists; key criteria used include percentage of foreign sales or operating profits, number of employees abroad or some combination of these variables (Shaked, 1986). For example, Bartlett and Ghoshal (1989: 14) define an MNC in terms of its 'portfolio of multiple national entities', while Vernon and Wells (1986: 2) provide a commonly used definition of an MNC as 'enterprises… characteristically made up of a parent firm located in one country and a cluster of affiliated firms located in a number of other countries'. Generally MNCs are further understood as firms which have internationalised through acquisition, mergers and joint ventures, or through 'greenfield' investments. This understanding is adopted here. Thus, whilst firms may also internationalise through other mechanisms, such as franchise arrangements, these are not of primary concern in this study. For the purposes of this study MNCs are referred to as organisations with a controlling interest in foreign companies (Daniels and Radebaugh, 1995). Moreover when looking at the nationality we are looking at 'this moment in time' e.g. where a long standing Irish MNC has been bought out (more than 50 per cent) by a foreign company, it is characterised as 'foreign-owned' here.

Given the focus was on researching human resource management, an employee size threshold was also used. Initially considered was the European Works Council (EWC) Directive (94/45/EC) definition of an MNC as 'enterprises employing 1,000 or more employees in the EEA (excluding the UK), with at least two operating sites within Europe, employing 150+ people'. However, we decided to lower the size threshold as we believed that the existing EWC Directive was over-limiting in that it would exclude a number of moderately sized MNCs (Edwards et al., 2008). However, the thresholds were not dropped to a level where organisations might not have management structures in place[ii]. Additionally, there was another pragmatic reason in that it was felt databases would be even more unreliable when it came to smaller sizes. Hence the following two MNC definitions were adopted:

1. Foreign-owned: All wholly or majority foreign owned organisations operating in Ireland, with 500 or more employees worldwide and 100 or more employed in their Irish operations.
2. Irish-owned[iii]: All wholly or majority Irish owned organisations with 500 or more employees worldwide and at least 100 employed abroad.

Phase 2 – Developing the master list

Having clearly defined an MNC, the next step was to identify the total population. To carry this out, all available company listings in Ireland were sourced. The main criteria in determining the suitability of each source were that:

1. They needed to provide both Irish and worldwide employment figures for each company.
2. They should allow you to distinguish whether the enterprise was foreign or Irish owned and, if foreign owned, what its country of origin was.

These issues proved particularly problematic, resulting in many challenges needing to be overcome. A number of recurring themes arose when examining the various databases including, their lack of comprehensiveness, duplication of companies and the inaccuracy of company details. It is clear that, taken in isolation, none of the sources could be relied upon to provide a comprehensive and accurate list of MNCs. Williams (1997) suggested that good practice in situations where no comprehensive list exists or where there are weaknesses in existing listings is to collate the population list from a number of different sources. Taking this as the point of departure it was decided to firstly collate a list from the most commonly utilised sources. Table 2.2 summarises the sources used and main advantages and limitations of each source used.

The first step was to contact the state agencies responsible for providing financial assistance and advice to both foreign owned and indigenous companies. *IDA Ireland* provided a list of foreign owned and *Enterprise Ireland* provided a list of Irish owned companies. Both lists contained country of origin details and contact information, and whilst neither was able to provide specific employment figures, they were able to filter their databases to provide us with lists of MNCs with more than 100 employees in Ireland. The IDA Ireland list contained 284 companies in total but this involved a relatively large amount of double counting, while the Enterprise Ireland list contained 27 Irish-owned MNCs[iv].

Table 2.2: Strengths and weaknesses of sources used for building population of MNCs

Database	State agencies (e.g. IDA Ireland Enterprise Ireland)	Bill Moss Partnership Limited	Irish Times list of Companies	Kompass	Major Companies of Europe	Membership lists provided by 2 Irish bodies[v]
Strengths	• Provides contact details: address, telephone/fax number; website & contact person • Provides country of origin detail • Can filter database to provide MNCs with 100+ employees in Ireland • Gives main activities of MNC	• Provides contact details: address, telephone/fax number; email, website & contact person • Provides employment figures for Irish operations • Gives main activities of MNC	• Provides contact details: telephone, number; website & contact person • Provides employment figures for Irish operations • Gives main activities of MNC	• Provides contact details: address, telephone/fax number; website & contact person(s) • Provides employment figures for Irish operations • Gives main activities of MNC	• Provides contact details: company address; telephone/fax number; email, website, contact person(s) • Can distinguish between whether a company is indigenous or a MNC • Gives main activities of MNC • Lists parent company and subsidiary companies	• Provides contact details: address, & contact person
Weaknesses	• Excludes non-grant aided/assisted MNCs • Weak in listing MNCs in the Services Sector e.g. LIDL, McDonalds, AIB • Does not provide employment figures (either Irish or worldwide) but the IDA can filter database (see strengths) • Duplication	• Unable to provide listing of Irish-owned MNCs • Unable to provide country of origin details for all MNCs on the list • Does not provide worldwide employment figures • Duplication	• Fails to distinguish between foreign-owned and Irish-owned firms • Not all encompassing companies included based on total turnover • Does not provide worldwide employment figures • Limited contact details provided (telephone number only) • Duplication	• Fails to distinguish between foreign-owned and Irish-owned firms • Does not provide worldwide employment figures • Duplication	• Not all encompassing companies included based on sales, premium income or total assets • Does not provide employment figures for worldwide and Irish operations, only one or the other • Duplication	• Does not provide employment figures (either Irish or worldwide) • Fails to distinguish between foreign-owned and Irish-owned firms • No details on MNCs main activities • Limited contact details i.e. no telephone number provided for some contacts • Duplication

Table 2.2: Strengths and weaknesses of sources used for building population of MNCs (continued)

Database	Who owns Whom?	International Financial Services Centre	Business and Finance Top 5000 Companies	Irish manufacturing companies	Irish companies listed on UK Stock Exchange	Irish Stock Exchange
Strengths	• Provides contact details: address, • Can distinguish between whether a company is indigenous or a MNC (i.e. has subsidiaries or not outside of Ireland	• Provides list of all companies operating in the IFSC	• Provides contact details: address, telephone/fax, number, website & contact person • Employment figures for Irish operations • Gives main activities of MNC	• Provides contact details: address, telephone/fax number, email, website & contact person • Gives main activities of MNC	• List of all Irish companies trading on the UK Stock Exchange	• List of all companies trading on the Irish, Stock Exchange
Weaknesses	• Does not provide employment figures (either Irish or worldwide • Fails to distinguish between foreign-owned and Irish-owned firms • No details on MNCs main activities • Limited contact details i.e. no contact person, no telephone number provided	• No other details provided other than a list of all company names operating in the IFSC i.e. no contact details, no employment figures. etc.	• Does not provide worldwide employment figures • Fails to distinguish between foreign -owned and Irish -owned firms • Duplication	• Does not provide employment figures (either Irish or worldwide) • Fails to distinguish between foreign -owned and Irish -owned firms • Duplication	• No other details provided other than a list of all company names listed on the Uk Stock Exchange i.e. no contact details, no employment figures etc	• No other details provided other than a list of all company names listed on the Irish Stock Exchange i.e. no contact details, no employment figures etc

Source: McDonnell et al., 2007: 245-247.

Whilst both lists were strong on providing information for particular populations of MNCs, they suffered from a number of weaknesses when looking to develop a comprehensive list of MNCs operating in Ireland. First, by definition the lists contained only grant-aided or assisted companies and thus excluded companies which did not receive any assistance from the relevant agency. Second, while the list was strong on MNCs in the manufacturing and internationally traded services sectors, it was weaker regarding other areas of the services sector. For example, the listing did not contain foreign-owned organisations such as *Tesco, LIDL, McDonald's*, or many of the major hotel chains, suggesting that MNCs operating in sectors such as retail, catering and hospitality may not make many of the common listings of MNCs in Ireland and thus were not represented in the extant research. Notable exclusions from the list of Irish-owned MNCs were the major Irish banks such as *Allied Irish Bank* and *Bank of Ireland,* both of which boast substantial foreign operations.

Next, *Bill Moss Partnership Limited*, a well-established private consultancy specialising in sourcing company information, was contacted to purchase their database of MNCs. By providing them with the strict employment size criteria, they were able to provide us with a list of foreign-owned MNCs in Ireland but not of Irish-owned MNCs. Again this is an illustration of the difficulty in identifying Irish MNCs. This list contained a total of 406 foreign owned enterprises but again this suffered from a problem of duplication/double-counting. The grant-aided listings and the purchased list were then amalgamated.

The above sources were further explored in greater detail due to the discrepancy in numbers of MNCs. In the case of foreign owned MNCs, the list provided by Bill Moss Partnership Limited had an additional 118 companies to that provided by the state agencies. In addition, whilst *IDA Ireland* listed fewer MNCs, their list included some 84 firms which were not on the list provided by Bill Moss Partnership Limited. Further, there is also a major discrepancy in the case of Irish-owned MNCs with our final population list of 72 MNCs being considerably higher than the list of 27 provided by Enterprise Ireland. These statistics make it starkly apparent that research drawing solely from the one source would have serious methodological concerns in terms of being able to comprehensively define the MNC population. This is not just a criticism of databases in the Irish context but one that pertains in many other countries. For example Alfaro and Charlton (2006: 9-10) note that "the sample of firms entering the database from different countries is...not random, but is determined by the local institutional environment".

Phase 3 – Checking and cross-checking

Due to the discrepancies just outlined, we felt the advice put forward by

Murphy (1997) and Williams (1997) would be well heeded. They called for researchers to be cognisant of the limitations of each of the databases and to carry out spot checks using a number of different sources. Consequently, a number of secondary sources were used to check the accuracy of the master list. Unsurprisingly, these sources suffered from similar limitations.

For example, while the publication 'Major Companies of Europe 2005' (Crawford et al., 2005) satisfied the study's key criteria, the list was not all encompassing because companies were included based on their sales, premium income or total assets. Furthermore, all of the other sources used did not meet at least one of the criteria set out (i.e., the need to provide employment figures for both Irish and worldwide operations, as well as country of origin details). For example, the Irish Times list of Top Companies, whilst providing up-to-date Irish employment figures, did not include worldwide employment figures or differentiate between foreign or Irish-owned firms.

Where it was unknown if the criteria were satisfied, each company was examined individually to establish if it should be included in the population of MNCs. Initially, the Internet was used to check each company's website to establish if they satisfied the criteria. In carrying out this task, the problem of duplication in the listings became more apparent. As an illustration, the listing of foreign-owned MNCs included Johnson & Johnson, Vistakon, Janssen Pharmaceutical and DePuy. On checking websites it was established that Johnson & Johnson owns the other three, thereby giving this MNC a much stronger chance of being selected.

However, checking websites also had limitations: some companies did not have a website, while others did not provide details on either employee numbers or country of origin. To overcome this, all other available sources were used and if there was still uncertainty the companies in question were contacted to try and clarify the situation. Where doubt still remained, it was decided to include the company on the list, thus erring on the side of caution.

A number of other sources were identified but were not used for one reason or another. One such electronic source examined was the Dun and Bradstreet (eWow) database. This business information source is derived from the Companies Registration Office (CRO), the statutory authority for registering new companies in the Republic of Ireland. It provides some difficult to find information on companies such as contact details, employment figures and country of origin, as well as allowing researchers to trace a company's 'family tree'. However, while it is quite a detailed database, the private consulting firm did not recommend purchase due to a number of inaccuracies in the details provided. Given this recommendation, together with the prohibitive cost, the decision was taken against purchasing it. The CRO was also contacted directly. However, they were unable to filter their database to show the particular information that we required. Similarly the Central Statistics Office (CSO) was contacted but to no avail. They could not provide the information in relation to identifiable companies or organisations.

Although there was initially considerable overlap between the lists used, extensive crosschecking helped ensure that the final lists were as comprehensive and accurate as possible. After applying the criteria and having cross-checked a set of 491 foreign-owned MNCs and 72 Irish-owned MNCs was finalised – 563 in total.

Highlighting the representative gap

The database shows 563 MNCs in Ireland according to the definitional criteria stipulated earlier. Table 2.3 illustrates the ownership of these MNCs. As expected US-owned MNCs are the predominant form found. 42 per cent of all MNCs in Ireland are US-owned, followed by the UK at 19 per cent, European (excluding Ireland and the UK) at 18 per cent, Irish-owned at 13 per cent, and the rest of the world at 8 per cent.

When compared with the listings provided by the state agencies there are some interesting points to note. First, there is a significant difference in the total number of MNCs found in each of the listings. Second, there are some interesting variances to note regarding breakdown by nationality of ownership. For example, US-owned MNCs make up 59 per cent of the state agencies list but only 42 per cent in this list, UK-owned make up 19 per cent of all MNCs here compared to 7 per cent in the state agencies listing, whilst Irish-owned MNCs make up 13 per cent of the total population here but only 8 per cent of the total population provided by the state agencies[vi]. From these findings one can see that, for example, UK-owned MNCs have a much stronger presence in Ireland than is evident in the established listings. We suggest that this is probably due to the presence of many UK-owned MNCs in the non-grant aided services sectors, especially retail (e.g. B&Q, Boots and Marks & Spencer) and financial and business services (e.g. Capita Life & Pensions, HSBC and Coyle Hamilton Willis). The difference in the numbers of Irish-owned MNCs is particularly noteworthy. One might expect Irish firms to have been in receipt of funding and/or assistance from the relevant agencies prior to internationalisation. However, the findings here suggest that a substantial number of such firms do not seek such assistance or advice prior to or during internationalisation.

Table 2.3: Population of MNCs in Ireland by country of ownership

Country of origin	Developed list (Number of MNCs)	State agency list (Number of MNCs)
Ireland	72 (13%)	27 (8%)
United States	239 (42%)	193 (59%)
United Kingdom	108 (19%)	24 (7%)
Europe (EU member states)	100 (18%)	61 (20%)
Rest of world (ROW)	44 (8%)	21 (6%)
Total	**563**	**326**

The size profiles, in terms of employment in Ireland, are illustrated in table 2.4. It is quite apparent that MNCs in Ireland tend to be relatively small with only 172 of the 563 MNCs identified in the population employing 500 or more. There were also 47 MNCs where the employment data was particularly sketchy in that it was believed they may employ 100 or more in Ireland but we were unable to establish more accurate employment figures. This once again reinforces the argument about the incomplete nature of existing company databases used for research purposes. Further, we urge caution in taking these figures as concrete and reliable as the same company often had different employment figures provided by the various lists.

Turning to country-specific detail, we found that Irish-owned MNCs represented the largest group of MNCs employing greater than 500 people in Ireland, followed by the US and UK, respectively. Although one cannot dispute the importance of US-owned MNCs as employers, it is interesting to note that in excess of 75 per cent of all US MNCs operating in Ireland are believed to be operating in the small to medium size bracket (less than 499 employees).

Table 2.4: Size of MNCs in Ireland by country of ownership (n)

Employees in Irish operations	Irish	US	UK	EU	ROW	Total
100-199 employees	6	90	36	42	18	192
200-499 employees	6	65	34	35	12	152
> 500 employees	55	59	32	15	11	172
Other	5	25	6	8	3	47
Total	**72**	**239**	**108**	**100**	**44**	**563**

Not surprisingly, MNCs in Ireland are principally located in the services and manufacturing sectors, with a non-existent primary sector. It is interesting to note that there are now more MNCs in services than in manufacturing. 291 of the total population operate in the services sector and 272 in manufacturing.

This suggests Irish industry is following the global shift towards services.

Table 2.5: Industrial sector of MNCs in Ireland by country of ownership (n)

Sector	Irish	US	UK	EU	ROW	Total
Manufacturing	31	143	27	48	23	272
Services	41	96	81	52	21	291
Total	72	239	108	100	44	563

Variation by country of origin is relatively minimal. There are substantial numbers of US-owned manufacturing MNCs particularly in the more 'high value' segments of this industry. UK firms account for the majority of retail firms whilst there are also large numbers of UK and Irish owned MNCs operating in more 'traditional' manufacturing (e.g. food and beverages).

Exploring sectoral breakdown by more specific categories, it was found that the 'engineering, computer, electrical and medical equipment manufacturing' is the largest single sector, followed closely by the 'financial and business services sector'. A particularly interesting finding was the less than one percentage point difference in the number of 'chemical and pharmaceutical manufacturing' MNCs and 'retail and wholesale' MNCs operating here. Despite the largely similar numbers of MNCs between these two sectors little or nothing is known about management practice in the retail/wholesale sector relative to the chemical/pharmaceutical sector.

Selecting the sample

One of the main advantages of undertaking large-scale survey research is the ability to generalise the findings to the greater population. Sampling is the most common method employed in survey research, as often surveying all cases in the population (i.e. a census) is unfeasible due to both time and cost constraints. The underlying principle of sampling is that a subset of the cases in a population can provide useful information that describes the entire population (Williams, 1997).

One of the first stages of sampling, and one of critical importance, is identifying a population and developing a comprehensive sample frame from which to take the sample (Pinsonneault and Kraemer, 1993). This sampling frame or population list is fundamental to the sampling process (Williams, 1997). Identifying the population is of critical importance because the sample will be a microcosm of the population that it is intended to represent (Murphy, 1997), hence the reasoning behind the extensive efforts taken to develop an accurate population.

After generating an accurate and comprehensive sampling frame one must then decide on the sampling method to be used. In selecting this method the aim is to ensure that the sample taken is a representative subset of the total target population and thus the findings can be generalised to the greater population (cf. Gill and Johnson, 2002). Therefore it is clear that the essence of good, reliable and accurate survey research is premised on the comprehensiveness and accuracy of the population list as well as the selection of an appropriate sampling method.

The sampling method employed was that of stratified sampling whereby we stratified the MNC population by five country of origin categories (Irish, UK, rest of Europe, and rest of world), two sector categories (services, manufacturing) and three employment size (in Ireland) categories (100-199 employees, 200-499 employees, greater than 500 employees). This led to the selection of a total of 423 MNCs. Of this sample, 46 companies were subsequently removed due to a) ceasing operations, b) not meeting the selection criteria or c) double-counting. This reflects the difficulty in accurately defining the population of MNCs and also the decision taken to include firms where there remained some doubt as to whether they met the criteria for inclusion. Consequently, an additional 37 companies were added from the residual population to compensate for these losses, bringing the total valid sample of organisations to 414.

Administration of questionnaire

There are five different means of administering a questionnaire; internet, postal, delivery and collection and telephone and structured interviews. It was the latter that was utilised in this case (i.e., the structured interview). The reasoning behind this choice was it gives greater control in ensuring the relevant person completes the questionnaire. It was also felt that the 'personal touch' might have a positive impact on the response rate compared to postal, online or telephone methods. In addition, the questionnaire is quite a detailed and comprehensive instrument and it was felt that the personal interview method would be more appropriate (Murphy, 1997). Further the personal interview is notable for its reduction in the amount of missing data.

Due to level of detail and information required, it was deemed that the most senior HR practitioner able to answer for all of the firm's Irish operations was the most suitable participant.

Due to numbers of interviews required, it was decided that some of the interviews could be outsourced. The survey unit of the *Economic and Social Research Institute* (ESRI), Ireland's leading independent research body on matters relating to Ireland's economic and social development, were the organisation identified and chosen as the most suitable for this work. In addition to undertaking a number of interviews, the support and advice both before and during the process was invaluable. It was also felt that the use of such a reputable and independent research body might make some organisations more inclined to participate.

In order to ensure consistency of administration amongst interviewers, thus enhancing the study's reliability, the authors produced a book of interviewer instructions which detailed the aims and objectives of the study and how the questionnaire should be administered. Further, a comprehensive list of key terms and explanations of same were provided. We travelled to Dublin to conduct a half-day training course of the ESRI interviewers. This took place at the ESRI offices on the 26th April 2006.

Negotiating access

A crucial aspect of the success of any research is gaining a good response rate. Considering the overall aim of this study, this was particularly crucial. It was decided before making contact by telephone looking for the participation of the most senior HR practitioner that it may be beneficial to first send a pre-notification letter. Previous research has indicated that this can have positive effects on response rates (Kerin and Peterson, 1977; Yu and Cooper, 1983) although others have suggested it can actually result in lower organisational level response rates (Schlegelmilch and Diamantopoulos, 1991). On discussion with the director of the survey unit at the ESRI, it was felt that the potential benefits may outweigh the negatives. Furthermore, the Chartered Institute of Personnel and Development (CIPD), the professional membership body for HR practitioners, were asked if they would support the study. They were more than happy to do so and offered to send a letter stating their approval and asking the HR community to participate. Thus, two letters were sent to the sample companies.

A week after the letter was sent to an organisation, telephone contact was made to establish if the identified company was interested in partaking in the study. Both the ESRI interviewers and University of Limerick interviewers undertook these calls. Although contact persons had been identified in a large percentage of firms, it often took a number of weeks to establish direct contact with the most senior HR person.

Main fieldwork phase

The main fieldwork stage began in May 2006 and finished in February 2007. Interviews were conducted with the most senior HR practitioner so as to provide a means to make a 'logical and useful contribution to research and theory building' (Dowling et al., 1999: 286). Once the appropriate participant had been contacted, securing a suitable date and time for the interview was not straightforward. It often took a number of weeks before a definite time slot was found. Interviews took between 40 to 60 minutes on average to complete. Some interviews took longer due to the participant providing additional information outside of the structured questionnaire.

Response rate

414 MNCs were contacted asking them to participate in this study. From this, interviews took place with 260 organisations leaving a final response rate of 63 per cent. This equates to 213 foreign and 47 indigenous-owned MNCs equating to a 60 per cent and 78 per cent response rate respectively. These response rates compare most favourably with organisational level surveys which according to Baruch and Holtom (2008) tend to be around 35 per cent. Particularly positive was that the survey responses were broadly representative of the total population and consequently, re-weighting of the data were not necessary.

Some potential reasons for this high response rate include:

1. The time spent on developing the study population was time well spent. This process involved collating up-to-date contact details for each MNC ensuring high levels of personalisation in requesting interviews. Personalisation is believed to generally improve response rates (Yu and Cooper, 1983; Baruch and Holtom, 2008).
2. Face-to-face interviews are associated with higher response rates (Baruch and Holtom, 2008). Credence was provided to this as some participants indicated that they had recently refused to complete a postal questionnaire from a different research project.
3. We used personal contacts and contacts from colleagues at the University of Limerick to gain access to potential participants. A relatively large number of the targeted participants were also past University of Limerick graduates which further helped. Recently, Cycyota and Harrison (2006) have noted the important role social networks can play in achieving high response rates.
4. The inclusion of previously under-explored categories of MNCs was also a contributory factor to the high positive response to the study. One retail sector HR manager noted that they were more than happy to participate because they had "never been asked before to participate in a study on HRM".

5. Following-up non response has also been put forward as being successful in boosting response rates (Yu and Cooper, 1983). A number of follow-ups were used when non-response had been received on the first attempt. Further telephone calls and emails were utilised which turned out to be successful as the perseverance led to a number of initial non-responses being converted into an interview.

6. The incentive of a copy of the main results may also have been an incentive for participants. The results allowed organisations to benchmark their own organisation's HRM practices with other organisations in their sector and beyond. Participants may have felt the study was worthwhile participating in for this reason. It has been suggested that organisations are tending to ignore research projects by academics due to feelings of irrelevance (Huff, 2000), which may not have been the case here due to the highly practical aspect of the study.

Data analysis

Preparation and data quality checks

Statistical Package for the Social Sciences (SPSS) version 15 was the statistical software used for the data analysis. One of the key reasons for using this statistical package was due to its popularity within the management research field. After entering data into the statistical package is entered it is imperative to undertake a number of checks in preparation for the main statistical analysis. With all due care taken in coding and entering data there will be some level of errors (Saunders et al., 2007). A number of specific checks were undertaken to ensure the accuracy of the data. First, a search for illegitimate codes was carried out. As the majority of the data are categorical, there can only be certain numbers allocated in any coding scheme. Numbers outside of these are therefore errors. Second, each of the filter questions was examined to ensure the rules were correct. Depending on the response provided in a certain question other variables should be coded as missing values. If this does not take place, it represents a further error. The final check was to investigate any illogical relationships. For example, there were questions asking for employment in the main organisational functions/divisions in the Irish operations (e.g. numbers employed in production, marketing etc.). Clearly if the figures provided here were higher than the total employment provided for the Irish operations there was an error. These checks brought a relatively small number of errors and consequently we felt very happy with the integrity and accuracy of the data entry.

Univariate and bivariate analysis

For the purposes of this book the data analysis can be broken down into two types of analysis. Firstly, univariate analysis which refers to the analysis of one variable at a time (Bryman and Bell, 2003). Here we present descriptive findings through the use of frequency tables, bar charts and pie charts, e.g. the incidence of performance appraisal systems, etc. Given that this research representatively captures the MNC population in Ireland this type of analysis provides a representative picture of what all MNCs operating in Ireland are like structurally and what kind of employment policies and practices they engage in. The second type of analysis is bivariate analysis, the analysis of two variables at a time, which helps to uncover whether the two variables are related (Bryman and Bell, 2003). For the purposes of this book, the analysis we used was contingency tables. Bryman and Bell (2003: 245) note that 'a contingency table is like a frequency table but it allows two variables to be simultaneously analysed so that relationships between two variables can be examined'. Such an analysis includes the testing of an independent variable and a dependent variable for a relationship. Independent variables are those that are presumed to impact upon a dependent variable. For example a MNCs country of origin (independent variable) is likely to impact on its industrial relations policies and practices (dependent variables). Throughout each of the chapters we investigate the impact of two particular independent variables:

- Country of origin – either foreign or Irish-owned or five country of origin categories – namely the UK, US, rest of Europe, Ireland, rest of world.
- Sector – manufacturing, services and multi-sector.

Conclusion

This chapter has outlined the research methodology employed to address this study's research aim and questions. It has detailed the research approach taken, the research instrument, the development of the MNC population, sampling, administration of the questionnaire and data analysis. Extensive detail was provided under each of these headings, clearly outlining how the research was conducted. This comprehensive review of the methodology of the research should be of great interest to academics wishing to carry out similar type research projects. The chapter also detailed the main methodological contribution of the overall research project, namely the representativeness of the research. Here we reviewed the extant literature and noted many of the weaknesses that are inherent in existing MNC research. We then followed this critique by providing detail on how we addressed these weaknesses and carried out the first representative survey of MNCs in Ireland. Indeed a number of learning outcomes can be identified:

- the challenges faced and needing to be overcome in order to conduct a representative study of MNCs.
- the length of time and difficulty in designing a reliable and valid research instrument as well as the importance of piloting the interview.
- the length of time it takes to arrange interviews with organisations and some of the more beneficial techniques in boosting response rates.

ENDNOTES

i   Parts of this chapter is drawn from an earlier publication by the authors on the methodological process of the research - Mc Donnell, A., Lavelle, J., Gunnigle, P., and Collings, D.G. (2007) 'Management research on multinational corporations: A methodological critique', *Economic and Social Review*, 38(2), 235-258.

ii There is currently a debate taking place on revising the EWCs directive which has included calls to lower the total employment threshold to 500 (from 1000) and the operation in each country threshold to 100 (from 150).

iii Irish-owned refers to the Republic of Ireland and foreign-owned refers to non-Republic of Ireland.

iv Other state agencies that provided lists included, Shannon Development Company, Údarás na Gaeltachta and Forfás

v   Both of these institutions provided us with copies of their listings on a confidential basis and asked to remain anonymous.

vi These variances are in fact greater than shown above due to the problem of duplication in the state agency listings.

CHAPTER 3
Profiling Multinational
Companies in Ireland

Jonathan Lavelle, Anthony McDonnell, & Patrick Gunnigle

Introduction

This chapter provides a context for our subsequent discussion and analysis of the substantive areas of employment practice examined in this volume. Specifically it provides detailed information on:

- The core characteristics of multinational companies (MNCs) in Ireland. This includes detail such as the nationality of ownership, size and sector, time as a MNC, and the method of internationalisation.
- The make-up of the workforce in these MNCs. For example, detail is provided on the extent of the use of contingent labour such as temporary and part-time employees.
- The position of Irish subsidiaries in the value chain. In recent years a key economic policy goal has been to move MNC subsidiaries up their respective corporation's value chain.
- Respondents' levels of satisfaction with various aspects of the Irish labour force, such as the availability and quality of university graduates, and the workforce's ability to learn new skills.
- The most important factors influencing whether the Irish operations receive new investments or new mandates from their parent company.

Country of origin

The country in which a MNC originates is believed to exert a distinctive effect on the way labour is managed in its international subsidiaries (Ferner, 1997). As a result, the country of origin of the multinational represents an important contextual factor. Chapter 1 notes in detail that the US is the largest source of FDI in Ireland, and as a result we find that the vast bulk of MNCs operating in Ireland are US-owned. In fact 40 per cent of all firms were of US origin, see figure 3.1. This pattern is reflected in the parallel Canadian and UK studies, where US MNCs comprise 50 per cent and 40 per cent of the respondent populations respectively (Bélanger et al., 2006; Edwards et al., 2007) demonstrating the number and scale of US MNCs globally. The next largest ownership group is the rest of Europe (continental European countries excluding Ireland and the UK), accounting for 24 per cent of all respondents, followed closely by indigenous firms (18 per cent). As noted in the previous chapter, research on Irish-owned MNCs is under-developed to say the least despite the clearly significant numbers of such organisations, a finding which may be surprising to many given the little attention paid to them. However the relatively large number of Irish-owned MNCs corroborate FDI statistics which clearly demonstrate a surge in outward FDI from Ireland (UNCTAD, 2006, 2007, 2008). Indeed, some Irish-owned MNCs such as CRH, Kerry Group, and Ryanair represent three examples of Ireland's home grown multinational success stories and are significant players in the global market. However, there are a number of others which are less known. The final population of indigenous owned MNCs was 60, 47 of whom participated in this study. These are far greater numbers than the 20 firms identified in the doctoral research of Noelle Donnelly (1999) or the 11 involved in the work of Monks and colleagues (2001). Thus the findings starkly illustrate the recent phenomenon that is the Irish-owned MNC. UK-owned firms at 13 per cent were the next largest group, with the numbers in the 'rest of the world'[i] category low at 5 per cent. This is quite unlike the parallel UK study, where MNCs from Japan particularly, and certain other Asian countries, had a significant presence (7 percent was accounted for by other non-European MNCs (Edwards et al., 2007)). Clearly, Ireland attracts few Japanese or indeed Asian firms despite the fact that FDI from China and Japan has grown rapidly over the past decade (cf. Wong and Chan, 2003; Rios-Morales and Brennan, 2007). Rather, it appears that Japanese FDI into Europe gravitates towards larger European economies, particularly Germany, France and the UK. We offer a number of reasons for this. First, it may be related to the premise that Japanese firms favour countries with a large domestic market. Clearly the small scale of Ireland's domestic market cannot match those of its larger European counterparts (cf. Rios-Morales and Brennan, 2007). Second, as noted earlier, much of Ireland's success in attracting FDI has been based on attractive financial packages which may not be best suited to "win" Asian FDI. For example Chung et al. (2006) suggest Japanese firms place less emphasis on financial measures relative to Anglo-Saxon countries. Third, Mayuya and Jacobson (1991) posited that Japanese MNCs in the electronics and automobile sectors have had difficulties with establishing in Ireland due to the lack of established infrastructure for these industries, particularly in the 1970s and 1980s.

We now turn to the question of whether these MNCs are privately owned, publicly traded or have they some degree of state ownership? Not surprisingly, the majority (71 per cent) of MNCs in Ireland are publicly quoted companies, while the remaining 29 per cent are privately owned. There are a higher number of privately owned Irish MNCs compared to foreign MNCs (44 per cent versus 25 per cent). This difference may in part be explained by the lateness of industrial development in Ireland with the effect that many of these indigenous firms still remain in family ownership. Just 5 per cent of MNCs reported some level of state ownership with the highest reported among Irish-owned MNCs (11 per cent versus 3 per cent in foreign owned MNCs). One reason for this difference is the critical role that state-owned enterprises played in the early industrialisation and development of modern management in Irish society (Leavy, 1993). In more recent times, some have been privatised and become MNCs (e.g. Aer Lingus).

Figure 3.1 MNC respondents by country of origin

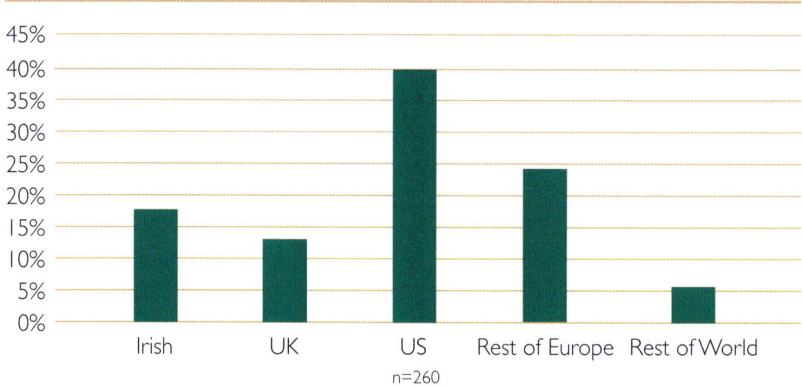

n=260

Size

Table 3.1 Employment in foreign-owned MNCs

Employment worldwide	% of firms	Employment in Ireland	% of firms
500 – 999	4	100 – 499	61
1,000 - 4,999	18	500 – 999	16
5,000 - 29,999	35	1,000 – 4,999	21
30,000 - 59,999	16	5000 +	2
60,000 +	27		

The size profiles of respondent MNCs are outlined in tables 3.1 and 3.2. Employment size may exert an influence on the organisation's approach to how it manages its workforce as well as on the human resource practices deployed (cf. Buckley and Enderwick, 1985). Looking at the employment figures of foreign-owned MNCs (table 2.1) operating in Ireland, it is clear that these firms are significant employers in the global business world. Close to half (43 per cent) of these firms employ 30,000 or more employees worldwide. However, whilst they may be large employers worldwide, this is not necessarily replicated in Ireland with just 23 per cent of foreign firms employing in excess of 1,000 in their Irish operations. Indeed only 2 per cent of foreign firms employ greater than 5,000 employees in Ireland.

Human Resource Practices in Multinational Companies in Ireland: A Contemporary Analysis

Irish-owned MNCs are clearly very large employers by national standards (see table 2.2). Almost two-thirds (57 per cent) employ more than 1,000 workers in Ireland, substantially higher than that of foreign-owned MNCs (23 per cent). The findings highlight that less-acknowledged and known MNCs (i.e., indigenous firms) provide considerably more employment in relative terms nationally. Outward direct investment by domestic firms affords them access to lower cost production and skills or technology that may not be available locally. Positively, the indications are that the higher value-added activities, and consequently jobs, are kept in the home country (Everett, 2006). In terms of worldwide employment, less than a third (30 per cent) employ more than 5,000 people, confirming that there are now a significant number of Irish firms with substantial foreign employment. Notwithstanding this however, clearly Irish-owned MNCs are not yet near the scale of many of their much larger foreign-owned counterparts and remain relatively small by international standards (Scullion and Donnelly, 1998; Donnelly, 1999; Scullion, 1999; Monks et al., 2001).

Table 3.2 Employment in Irish-owned MNCs

Employment worldwide	% of firms	Employment in Ireland	% of firms
500-4999	19	100-499	26
1000-4999	51	500-999	17
5000-29999	28	1000-4999	48
30000-59999	0	5000+	9
60000+	2		

Sector

The sector or range of sectors in which a MNC operates represents a further important influence on the firm's approach to workforce management and on the employment practices deployed. Previous Irish research has, for example, pointed to union avoidance approaches being significantly more prevalent in the electronics and software sectors than in pharmaceuticals and healthcare (Gunnigle et al., 2005). The distribution of respondent firms by sector is outlined in figure 3.2. It should be noted we use the category 'multi-sector' to capture those firms whose activities in Ireland straddle more than one sector. For example, a MNC engaged in manufacturing may also engage in discrete service operations, such as call centres. Our findings indicate that just twenty-four firms (under 10 per cent of the total) were 'multi-sector'. Given such small numbers, we advise particular caution when interpreting subsequent results for the 'multi-sector' category.

Figure 3.2 MNCs in Ireland by broad industrial sector

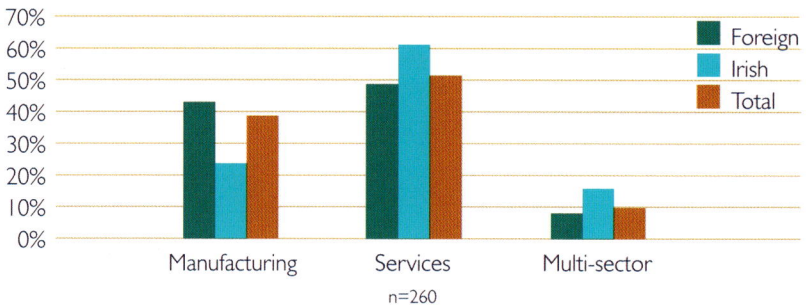

n=260

Despite the fact that manufacturing has long been a key focus of Ireland's industrial policy, it now ranks second (39 per cent) to the services sector (52 per cent) in absolute numbers of foreign-owned MNCs. These findings resonate with international data which for some time has reported the global economy is shifting towards services (cf. UNCTAD, 2004) and developments in Ireland are no different. As demonstrated above in figure 3.2, a larger proportion of foreign firms (43 per cent) are involved in manufacturing than Irish-owned MNCs (23 per cent). Correspondingly, there are more indigenous-owned MNCs (62 per cent) than foreign firms (49 per cent) in the services sector. A likely explanation for this finding is that much of the large influx of foreign firms in the 1970s and 1980s into Ireland were predominantly manufacturing due to a low corporate taxation rate and attractive tax relief on company profits on export sales. Irish-owned MNCs tend to be a more recent phenomenon and thus are more aligned to the services sector 'boom'.

The makeup of the workforce

This section details some of the primary characteristics of the MNC workforce. More specifically, we provide detail on the percentage of male and female employees, as well as the percentage of temporary and part-time staff employed. We also provide detail on the presence of a 'key group' of employees, a major innovation in this study.

Recent decades have witnessed a marked increase in the numbers of women in the Irish labour force. However while this may be the case, it is clear that male employees make up an overwhelming majority of the multinational workforce in Ireland. For example 18 per cent of MNCs answered that more than 76 per cent of their workforce is male, with a further 40 per cent of MNCs reporting that between 51 and 75 per cent of their workforce is male.

Figure 3.3 Percentage of male employees in the workforce

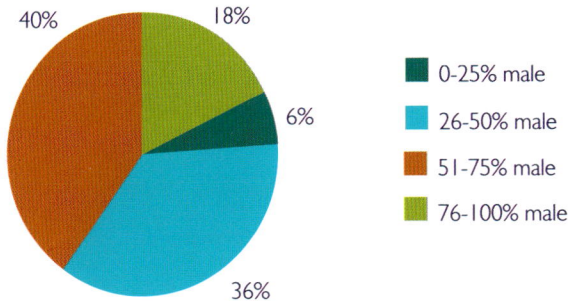

40%   18%

6%

- 0-25% male
- 26-50% male
- 51-75% male
- 76-100% male

36%

It is widely argued that the use of contingent labour has risen in recent times (Forfás, 2007; Garavan et al., 2008). Table 3.3 illustrates the percentage of the workforce in MNCs classified as temporary. In total, just over 18 per cent of all MNCs indicate that greater than 10 per cent of their employees are temporary, with a further 18 per cent reporting between 5 and 10 per cent of their staff are temporary. Looking at the utilisation of temporary staff by country of origin, we find that 86 per cent of Irish-owned MNCs and 73 per cent of foreign-owned MNCs use temporary staff. However the percentage of the workforce that is temporary is lower than in foreign-owned firms. Two in ten foreign MNCs indicated that temporary employees make up more than 10 per cent of their Irish workforce, with the corresponding figure for Irish-owned MNCs at 12 per cent.

Table 3.3 Percentage of employees which are temporary

Temporary Employees	Foreign MNCs	Irish MNCs	All MNCs
0%	27%	14%	25%
0.1 - 5%	35%	57%	39%
5.1 - 10%	18%	17%	18%
> 10%	20%	12%	18%

A slightly different story is found with respect to part-time workers. Table 3.4 once more shows Irish-owned MNCs are more likely to utilise part-time staff relative to their foreign-owned counterparts (88 per cent versus 81 per cent). However, this time around it is indigenous MNCs which are making the greatest use of this type of contingent labour, with 21 per cent of respondent organisations indicating that their workforce is made up of more than 10 per cent part-timers.

Table 3.4 Percentage of employees which are part-time

Part-time employees	Foreign MNCs	Irish MNCs	All MNCs
0%	19%	12%	18%
0.1 - 5%	47%	56%	48%
5.1 - 10%	19%	11%	18%
> 10%	15%	21%	16%

These results suggest that although there is some use of contingent labour it may not be as high as what may have been expected (Garavan et al., 2008). It is unmistakable that there remains an obvious preference or bias towards the use of full-time employees.

Presence of a 'key group'

A major innovation of this study was to examine whether MNCs in Ireland recognised a 'key group' of employees. The idea of the key group originates from the resource-based view of the firm (cf. Barney, 1991). This argues that competitive advantage increasingly stems from a firm's internal resources, particularly employee knowledge/skills. This view underpins recent debates on the importance of knowledge workers and the aspiration of economies to move up the 'value chain' through attracting and developing firms that engage in high value-added (and high margin) activities. An important manifestation of the resource-based view is the presence in firms of a specific category or group of employees who are critical to their firm's competitive strategy by virtue of the particular knowledge and skills they possess.

We defined the key group as "those employees whom you might identify as critical to your firm's organisational learning and core competence. These might be research staff, product designers, major account handlers, developers of new markets, etc". Evidence is provided here on the extent by which MNCs are strategically identifying a key group. These key groups are likely to be specific to the organisational context, in that they will be core to helping that organisation achieve its corporate objectives. Consequently, a variety of key groups is likely.

Just over half of the foreign MNCs (52 per cent) indicated they identify a key group of employees. 17 per cent of MNCs stated they identified more than one group. Hence, some organisations recognise more than one group as critical to the firm's organisational learning and core competence. Where more than one group was reported respondents were asked to focus on the one they viewed as most unique with respect to the skills and capabilities they possess which are difficult to obtain on the labour market. Where they were unable to differentiate on this basis they were asked to think about the largest group. The results showed 81.6 per cent differentiated between groups in terms of their unique skills and capabilities, 5.3 per cent chose the largest group with the remaining 13.2 per cent reporting the group they picked as 'key' were the largest and most unique.

Invariably these groups tended to be small, with the majority (67 per cent) employing less than 49 employees. Almost identical figures were found with respect to the Irish-owned MNCs. A total of 53 per cent recognised a group and once again the majority (67 per cent) employ less than 49 employees. Although the presence of a key group appears comparatively widespread, its incidence was much lower than found in the parallel study of MNCs in the UK, where 80 per cent of firms identified a key group (Edwards et al., 2007). This is worthy of future investigation in order to establish reasons behind the Irish and UK findings. One plausible explanation is that it may, in part, be explained by MNCs in the UK having greater mandates and responsibilities within the parent company than Irish subsidiaries. This view is given some support through the analysis of Edwards and colleagues (2007) which found, of those firms with a key group, four in ten agreed or strongly agreed that the UK operations generated significant expertise in research and development (R&D). Only two in ten MNCs agreed or strongly agreed the UK operations generated significant R&D expertise where firms did not recognise a key group. Thus, it seems firms conducting value added activities (e.g. R&D) were more likely to have a key group.

In terms of the nature of the key group, there was a wide variety of roles selected, ranging from analysts to client executives to chemists to research and development (R&D) staff. Throughout our survey, we investigated the extent to which firms adopted similar or different employment practices for their 'key group', as compared to two other categories of employees, namely the largest occupational group (LOG) and 'managers'. Responses on these issues are addressed in subsequent chapters of this report.

Other key MNC characteristics

Next, we individually examine Irish-owned and foreign-owned MNCs in greater detail. Regarding the foreign MNCs, we look at how long the present worldwide company has been in Ireland and the method by which they first established. In the case of the indigenous MNCs, we look at factors such as the period and method of internationalisation.

Foreign-owned MNCs

The date a firm establishes is often used in explaining variation in HRM practices. However, particularly within the MNC literature, we argue that much ambiguity exists around the use of this variable "date of establishment". This ambiguity relates to firms that have been acquired or merged with another firm. Specifically, there is a lack of clarity on the actual date of establishment that is used. Does the date of establishment refer to when the firm originally set up in the particular host country? Or does the date of establishment refer to when the firm was acquired or merged? For example, a firm may be in existence since the early 1900s in Ireland but subsequently may have been acquired in the late 2000s, so which date do you choose? This choice is an important consideration, as depending on the particular issue under investigation it may distort the findings. For instance, it is widely acknowledged within the industrial relations literature that trade union recognition levels tend to be much higher in older organisations (Turner et al., 2002). Cognisant of this, we present the date of establishment when the MNC first established in Ireland (i.e., for an acquired or merged firm we take the date of the acquisition or merger). Our findings indicate that the majority of foreign MNCs in Ireland are of comparatively recent vintage. Figure 3.4 shows that three-quarters of foreign-owned MNCs (75 per cent) have established here since 1980.

Figure 3.4 Year the worldwide company first established in Ireland

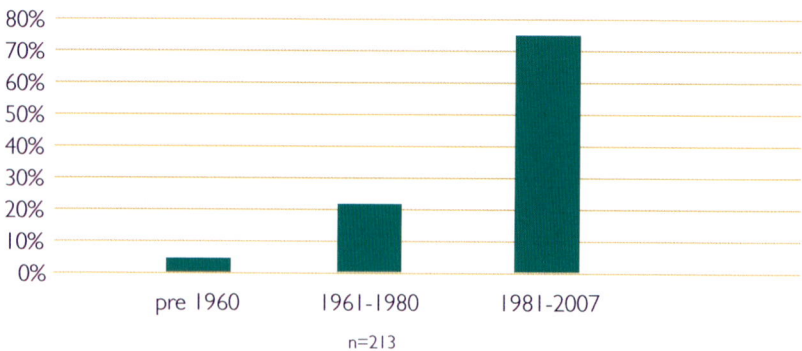

n=213

These periods can be classified as important in terms of changes in economic policy. For example, the 1960s was where public policy changed to an outward looking strategy, often referred to as the export-led growth phase (Ruane and Uğur, 2005) or the liberalisation of the Irish economy (Kirby, 2002), striving to attract foreign firms to accelerate Irish industrial development. Unsurprisingly considering the economic policies, a mere 4 per cent of firms have operated in Ireland pre-1960s with significant growth in the preceding years.

The method by which a MNC locates in a particular host environment can be a significant explanatory variable. For example, MNCs that enter by way of a new facility, or 'greenfield site', are much better placed to follow their home country policies and practices than if they were to acquire an existing operation (Gamble, 2003). The primary method by which foreign MNCs established in Ireland was through opening a greenfield site. Considering the fact that industrial development was somewhat later in Ireland than other European countries, the acquisition of existing Irish firms was possibly not a viable alternative for many inward-investing MNCs. As indicated in figure 3.5, just over half of foreign-owned MNCs (53 per cent) entered Ireland by establishing a greenfield site. Of the remainder, most (47 per cent) entered by way of acquisition or a merger.

Figure 3.5 Method of worldwide company's first establishment in Ireland

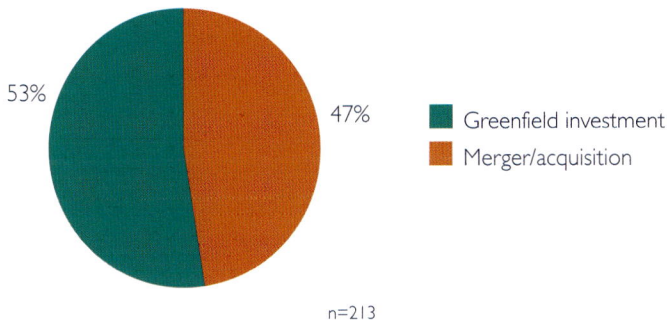

n=213

This supports previous research which suggested Ireland as being a unique case in terms of developed economies in that FDI inflows have tended to be dominated by greenfield establishments rather than mergers and acquisitions (Forfás, 2003; Thompson and Keating, 2004).

Turning now to the nature of MNC operations in Ireland, we first examined whether MNC operations here focused on a single site or were spread over a number of sites. As figure 3.6 illustrates, the overwhelming majority of MNCs (65 per cent) operated at two or more sites in Ireland, while the remainder (35 per cent) were single site operations.

As outlined in chapter 1, the economic climate has changed quite dramatically over the recent past, particularly during the latter half of 2008. A recurring theme in the popular media during this period has been the withdrawal of foreign-owned MNCs and attendant job losses among this cohort. Particular attention has focused on large, predominantly manufacturing, MNCs cutting jobs or relocating their plants to cheaper destinations to 'escape' the high cost of doing business in Ireland. Table 3.5 presents a snapshot of the newspaper coverage of MNC closures over a six week period in 2008.

Figure 3.6 How many sites do MNCs have in Ireland?

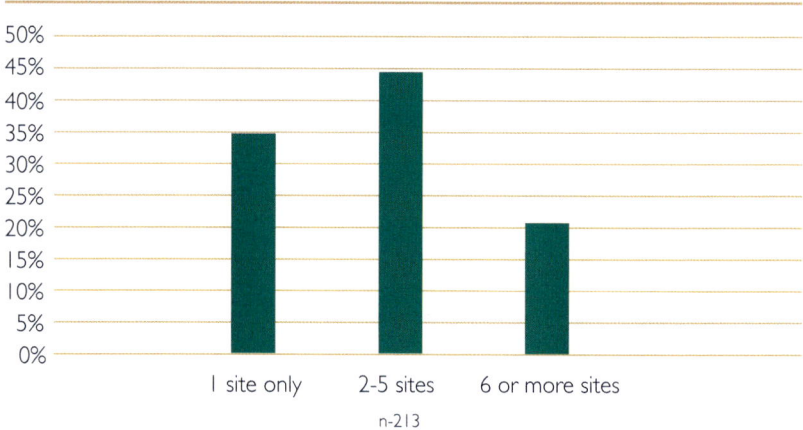

n-213

Table 3.5 Recent MNC job losses

Headline	Date	Source	Impact
US multinational to seek a further 50 redundancies in Waterford	16 Sept 2008	Irish Times	Job losses
Electronics company to cut 200 jobs in Cork	24 Sept 2008	Irish Times	Job losses
Manufacturing sector reeling as Tyco lays off 320 workers	26 Sept 2008	Irish Independent	Job losses
Shock over 380 job cuts in Kildare, Waterford	15 Oct 2008	Irish Times	Job losses
Axing of 250 pharmaceutical jobs 'a knee-jerk' reaction	16 Oct 2008	Irish Independent	Job losses
Waterford Crystal seeks 280 job losses	17 Oct 2008	Irish Times	Job losses

Concurrently however, there have also been quite a number of job and expansion announcements, as outlined in Table 3.6. These appear to have slipped under the radar so to speak, with considerably less attention paid to job creation than to MNC closures and job losses. In effect what we see is the simultaneous reporting of MNC closures and expansions but somewhat greater media focus on the closures aspect of FDI. The following example of a news report during 2007 is illustrative. This relates to the headline news item of the impending closure of a German automotive components manufacturer *Iralco*, which had just gone into liquidation with the seemingly imminent loss of 420 jobs. However, the contemporaneous announcement by UK retailer Tesco of plans to investment €150m in Ireland and create 1,225 new jobs in 16 new stores country went virtually unnoticed, as did its reporting of increased sales of 10% to almost €3 billion and an estimated profit of €156 million. We make this point to demonstrate that MNC investment and disinvestment takes place in parallel. While economic recession is likely to detrimentally impact on levels of FDI, Ireland continues to attract substantial inward investment as outlined in the following table.

Table 3.6 Recent MNC expansions

Headline	Date	Source	Impact
US insurer to create 70 jobs	19 Sept 2008	Irish Times	Expansion
US firm says graduate pool a factor in Dundalk decision	24 Sept 2008	Irish Times	New site
Cook Medical to create 200 jobs	1 Oct 2008	Irish Times	Expansion
Firms to create over 220 jobs in Midwest	22 Oct 2008	Irish Times	Expansion and new sites
Pharmaceutical and hotel firms to create 390 jobs	3 Nov 2008	Irish Times	Expansion

We addressed the issue of MNC investment and closure within Ireland by asking whether MNCs had been involved in a significant investment in a new site or expansion of existing sites. We also asked respondents if they had closed any sites over the previous 5 years. Looking at investments in new sites or existing sites, we find that approximately half of our respondent firms had established a new site or expanded an existing site over the previous five years. This presents quite a positive picture from an FDI perspective. Irish-owned MNCs were more likely to establish a new site or expand an existing site than their foreign-owned counterparts, though the differences were very small. In terms of sector, MNCs operating in the services and multiple sectors were more likely to have invested in a new site or expanded an existing site (54 per cent) compared with manufacturing MNCs (49 per cent).

On the other hand, just over a quarter (27 per cent) indicated that they have closed one or more sites during the same period (14 per cent closed one site and 13 per cent closed more than one site). US owned (17 per cent) and 'rest of Europe' MNCs (19 per cent) were least likely to report having closed a site, with Irish-owned MNCs by far the most likely to have closed a site (51 per cent). MNCs operating in multiple sectors reported a higher incidence of site closures (42 per cent) compared with services MNCs (27 per cent) and manufacturing MNCs (23 per cent).

By and large, our findings indicate a more positive picture of MNC activity than might have been expected, with levels of MNC expansion exceeding contraction. Of course, caution must be exercised insofar as these data were collected in 2007 and the dramatically changed business environment is like to have impacted greatly on many of the MNCs studied in the interim.

Figure 3.7 Expansion and closure of sites, by sector

n=259

We also sought to investigate a trend in employment among MNCs operating in Ireland. We asked respondents whether the number of employees had increased or decreased over the last three years. As presented in table 3.7, the majority of MNCs (44 per cent) reported significant increases, with 27 per cent reporting a slight or significant decrease. Sectoral effects are discernible. For example, services sector MNCs are much more likely to report significant increases in employment (54 per cent) compared to MNCs operating in multiple sectors (38 per cent) and manufacturing (32 per cent). We also find that manufacturing MNCs are more likely to report a decrease in employment, with 38 per cent reporting a slight or significant decrease in employment as compared to 21 per cent and 20 per cent in MNCs operating in multiple sectors and the services sector respectively.

Table 3.7 Changes in employment over the previous 3 years

Employment	Manufacturing	Services	Multi-sector	Total
Increased significantly	32%	54%	38%	44%
Increased slightly	13%	19%	33%	18%
No change	18%	8%	8%	11%
Decreased slightly	21%	10%	4%	14%
Decreased significantly	17%	10%	17%	13%

Whilst again caution must be exercised in analysing these data, our results indicate a reasonably positive picture in terms of employment in the MNC sector. While a number of MNCs have withdrawn investment from the country, a greater number have been expanding their Irish operations. In essence, we are witnessing a high level of 'job churn', i.e. concurrent job loss and job creation, especially in the manufacturing sector. As indicated above, some MNCs, particularly in the manufacturing sector, have moved to lower cost locations while numerous others are likely to follow suit. However, Ireland continues to attract new FDI while some MNCs continue to operate very successfully. A recent survey by the American Chamber of Commerce of US companies in Ireland identified some 1500 current job vacancies in their organisations, many of which are considered high-value jobs (Irish Independent, 2008). The most recent Irish Management Institute report (Irish Management Institute, 2008) on the multinational sector , found just 36 per cent of MNCs expected employment to decrease, compared with 38 per cent who expected no change and 25 per cent expected an increase. This raises a number of important questions in regard to HRM and employment relations, such as the extent to which lower quality jobs are being replaced by higher quality jobs, unionised labour by non-union labour, permanent jobs by less permanent jobs, etc. Whilst there is little doubt that Ireland's competitive position has worsened in recent times, it continues to attract FDI. Indeed, Ireland is now clustered in the group of countries with the second largest level of inflows and outflows (UNCTAD, 2008). This is an expected development with Ireland 'adopting the profile of a more typical developed economy' (Forfás, 2006: 39) as it moves up the 'value chain' and becomes more important as a source rather than destination of FDI.

Ireland's position in the value chain

As noted above, a key policy goal of 'Ireland Inc' is that MNC operations move up their respective corporation's value chain. The value chain refers to the range of value-adding activities involved in bringing a product or service from conception to end use, such as research and development, design, production, marketing, distribution and customer support (cf. Porter, 1985; Sturgeon, 2001). A defining characteristic of modern globalisation is the growing geographical dispersion of value chains, a trend facilitated by advances in technology, improved transportation and greater trade liberalisation. This results in the physical fragmentation of production, whereby firms seek to optimally situate different value chain activities in different locations to gain cost or other advantages. This may often embrace some form of outsourcing. The trend of MNCs seeking to organise production through a linked network of operations in different countries requires decisions on where to locate high and low value-added activities and whether these should be undertaken by the firm itself or outsourced. One immediate consequence is the difficulty of establishing the national origin of products since, for example, customer service may be delivered from Ireland for products designed in the US and produced in India (Bélanger et al., 2006). The position of the Irish operations of foreign-owned MNCs in this emerging global network of production poses key questions and challenges. Are Irish operations moving up or down their firm's value chain? How are the mandates of Irish operations developing? It may not simply be a question of Ballina or Bangalore, but rather what is the scale and quality of a particular firm's investment in Ballina and Bangalore, and what are the related inter-dependencies.

To help address this issue, we examined the perceived importance of the Irish operations to the global performance of the parent company. The findings are summarised in figure 3.8. Our analysis indicates that the majority of respondents (71 per cent) believe that the Irish operations are either 'important' or 'very important' to the parent company's global performance. The remaining 29 per cent indicated that the Irish operations ranged from being 'not at all important 'to somewhat important' in terms of their contribution to the performance of the parent company. These findings are further corroborated by a recent report on MNCs in Ireland which found that 66 per cent of MNCs reported their Irish operations to be either very important or important, with just 6 per cent reporting that their Irish operations were very unimportant (Irish Management Institute, 2008). These findings present MNCs operating in Ireland in a positive light in relation to their place in their overall corporate value chain.

Figure 3.8 How important are the Irish operations to the global performance of the parent company?

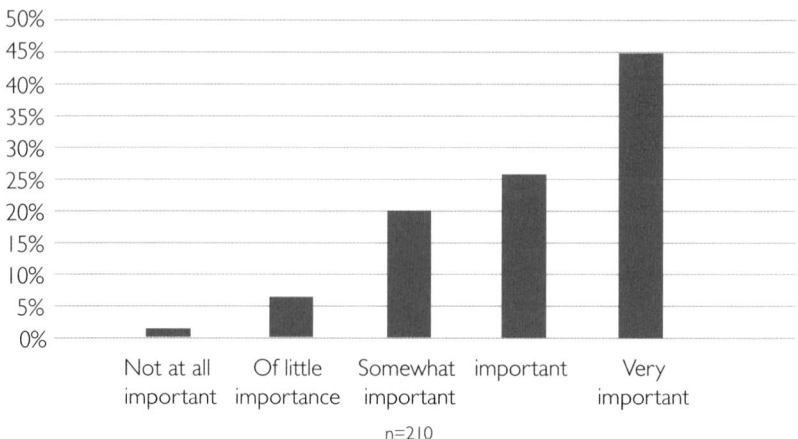

n=210

Arguably of greater interest and more noteworthy was the question asking respondents whether "this importance has changed over the past five years". In spite of the rising economic costs and the closures of MNCs in recent years, respondents were quite positive in their answers. Whilst 15 per cent indicated the importance of the Irish operations had slightly or significantly decreased and a further 29 per cent believe there had been no change, over half of our respondents (56 per cent) believed the importance of the Irish operations to the performance of the parent company had increased over recent years. Again a similar issue was addressed in the Irish Management Institute report which found that 60 per cent of respondents felt that their importance had stayed the same (an increase of 24 per cent in 2005), with 22 per cent reporting an increase and 18 per cent reporting a decrease. These findings are a source of positive news for the strategy pursued by IDA Ireland which aims to move existing MNCs up their respective corporate value chains.

Figure 3.9 Has this level of importance of the Irish operations to the global performance of the parent company change in the past five years?

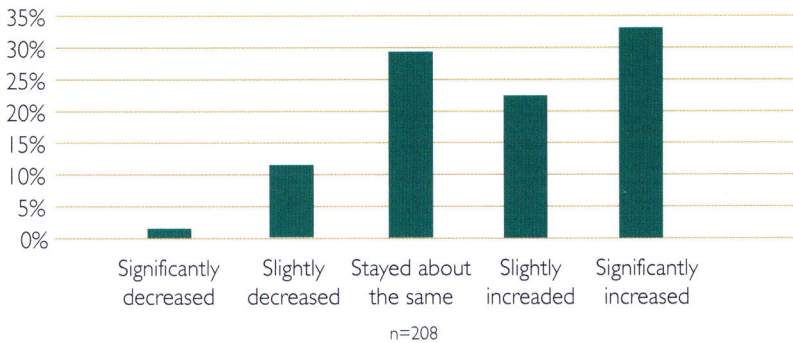

n=208

Another measure of the position of the Irish operations of foreign-owned MNCs in their respective corporate value chains is the extent to which Ireland is a regional or divisional headquarters (HQ). Respondents were first asked what levels or divisions of business organisation existed in their worldwide company (international product, service or brand based division, regions and global business functions) and then asked whether any of these levels or divisions had their HQ in Ireland. Overall we find quite a positive picture in terms of foreign-owned MNCs choosing Ireland as a location for their business divisions HQs (see table 3.8). Similar figures are reported across the three different types of HQ with 12 per cent of all MNCs that have global business functions report their HQ is located in Ireland, followed by 11 per cent of MNCs with an international, product, service or brand based divisional HQ and 10 per cent of MNCs having a regional HQ. These figures suggest that Ireland is a reasonably popular location for MNCs to locate their divisional, regional and global business functions HQs. Some recent examples in 2008 of MNCs that have announced Ireland as their preferred location for their regional HQ's, include *DTS Licensing Limited, Freightquote, Solaris, SATIR, and Eyewonder*. There are very little differences according to country of origin or sector across all three types of HQ's.

Table 3.8 Headquarters (HQ) in Ireland

Business division	%
International product, service or brand based division HQ	11%
Regional HQ	10%
Global business functions HQ	12%

Irish-owned MNCs

We now turn to the often forgotten MNCs, namely those that are Irish-owned. As might be expected, the majority (69 per cent) internationalised since 1980, with the remaining 31 per cent having internationalised prior to this. Thus, indigenous-owned MNCs are relatively 'new' MNCs (i.e., they have internationalised quite recently), confirming the small scale studies that have taken place (Scullion and Donnelly, 1998; Donnelly, 1999; Scullion, 1999; Monks et al., 2001), which is not unsurprising given the fact that industrial development was late-starting in Ireland (O'Malley, 1985, 1992). The early internationalisers tended to be old state-owned companies, the oldest Irish banks and also those operating in the agriculture/food sphere. Of interest is that 82 per cent indicated the Irish company was formed post 1980, suggesting that the great majority of Irish MNCs operated in the domestic market for some time prior to establishing international operations. Furthermore, it lends support to the view that Irish owned MNCs are long established national success stories rather than new start-up firms employing substantial numbers in foreign sites (O'Malley, 1998).

A surprising result was the finding that most Irish MNCs internationalised through the establishment of a greenfield site (51 per cent). Considering their comparative lateness in internationalising and the competitive markets they would have been entering, one might have expected a greater proportion to have internationalised by merger or acquisition. This was an unexpected finding and in contrast to the findings of Donnelly (1999), which found twelve of the fifteen respondent Irish firms had internationalised through acquiring a foreign company. Due to the competitive pressures which characterise today's global business environment, firms need to gain a stronghold quickly so as to make up ground on long-established firms. It may have been expected that mergers or acquisitions would have been used to greater effect considering the lateness by which these firms undertook internationalisation. Internationalisation by acquisition helps 'shorten the evolutionary process as the company leapfrogs over one or more stages [of the international development process]' (Welch, 1994: 151). Whilst the larger sample size here may be one reason for accounting for the difference, the other possibility is that firms subsequently used the mergers and acquisitions (M&A) method to increase their international standing. When one considers that anecdotal evidence suggests the UK and US tended to be the first foreign location (Scullion and Donnelly, 1998; Scullion, 1999), firms may have felt greenfield establishment did not pose a major risk. This survey only explored the initial entry method; thus, it is unable to inform on subsequent international development. In the past few years, the M&A activity of Irish firms has been extraordinary. For instance, in 2002 there were 25 disclosed and 22 undisclosed acquisitions by Irish companies of foreign firms, totaling €2.4 billion (Ion Equity, 2003). The most recent annual M&A survey based on the year 2007 found a clear move towards foreign transactions by Irish firms borne out by the finding that 68 per cent of the 228 acquisitions were of non-Irish companies worth approximately €10.65 billion (CFM Capital, 2008). Analysis of outward FDI flows by Everett (2006) found most of the recent surge was by means of mergers and acquisitions.

Figure 3.10 Method of internationalisation

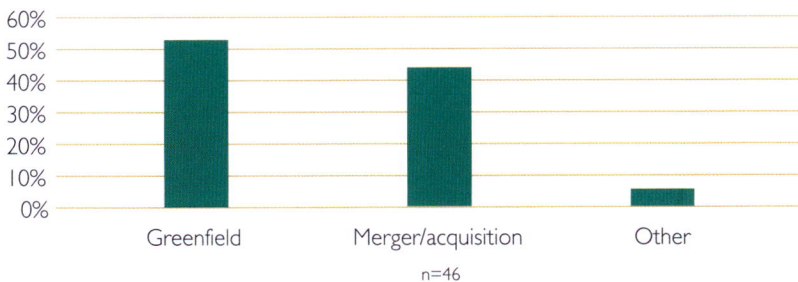

n=46

It was also revealing to find that Irish-owned MNCs are quite 'international' in that they have operations in a number of different countries. In fact, 83 per cent have operations in two or more countries, 38 per cent of which are in more than six nation states. Just under a fifth (17 per cent) operate in only one country other than Ireland, most commonly the UK. Such 'single country MNCs' represent some of the most recently internationalised Irish firms. In fact, all but one internationalised post-1988. These findings suggest that Irish-owned MNCs have now moved beyond just the UK or US as outward FDI locations. Indeed, analysis of merger and acquisition data and firms' annual reports indicate that Irish firms are now operating in excess of 25 different countries. These results suggest that Irish firms are now establishing in more atypical markets going against the grain of the commonly held idea that 'direct investment has a strong affinity to neighbouring countries' (OECD, 2005: 27).

Figure 3.11 Number of foreign countries where Irish MNCs have operating sites

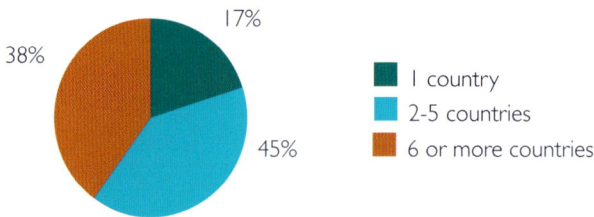

An argument against the increased internationalisation of indigenous firms is the potential loss of employment in the home country due to the transfer and outsourcing of activities to foreign locations. For example, the loss of American jobs to foreign subsidiaries of US firms has been a particular concern highlighted by the former Bush and current Obama administration in the US. In our study, we asked respondents in Irish-owned MNCs if they had established new sites or expanded existing sites in Ireland and also whether any Irish operations have been closed. The findings are quite mixed. Most positively is the finding that 61 per cent have been involved in a significant investment in a new Irish site or expansion of an existing site over the previous five years. However, we also find that just over half (51 per cent) closed one or more sites during the same period.

As in the case of the foreign-owned MNCs above, we examined the perceived importance of the foreign operations to the overall global performance of the parent Irish MNC. The findings are summarised in figure 3.12. These indicate that the great majority of Irish MNCs (87 per cent) believed their foreign operations were either 'important' or 'very important' to the company's global performance. In addition, 43 per cent indicated that this importance of their foreign operations had 'increased significantly' over the past five years. Given the rapid internationalisation of Irish firms in recent years, one might have expected a somewhat higher figure. However, it possibly indicates that whilst domestic firms are looking internationally for growth, the Irish operations remain an important part of their global business.

Figure 3.12 How important are the foreign operations to the global performance of the parent company?

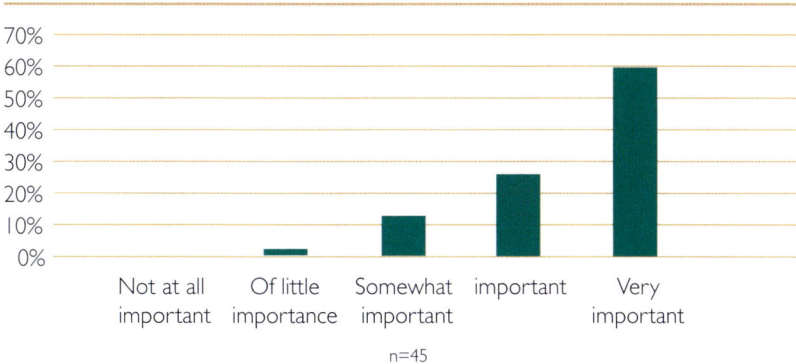

n=45

Satisfaction with the Irish labour force

In addition to financial incentives, particularly low corporation taxes, something which is advanced as a critical aspect of Ireland's attraction to inward investing MNCs, is the availability and quality of labour (cf. Arrow, 1997; Wrynn, 1997; Tansey, 1998). Our study addressed this issue by seeking the opinion of respondents in MNCs, both foreign- and Irish-owned, on various aspects of their own workforce, as well as their opinions on the Irish labour force more generally. More specifically we asked respondents to rate the following:

- Availability of university graduates
- Quality of university graduates in their employment
- Quality of professional school and technical graduates in their employment
- Workforce's ability to learn new skills
- Workforce's ability to work with IT
- Workforce's ability to work in teams
- Work ethic of the workforce

The findings are summarised in table 3.9.

Table 3.9 Satisfaction with the Irish labour force

Rating	Availability of university graduates	Quality of university graduates in employment	Quality of technical graduates in employment	Ability to learn new skills	Ability to work with IT	Ability to work in teams	Work ethic
Very poor	2%	0%	0%	0%	0%	0%	0%
Poor	10%	1%	2%	0%	1%	0%	2%
Fair	22%	9%	9%	10%	11%	10%	16%
Good	43%	49%	61%	48%	46%	51%	54%
Very good	22%	40%	28%	41%	43%	38%	28%

Clearly most respondents were very satisfied with the various aspects examined. However, the most pressing and noticeable concern was in relation to the availability of university graduates. Some 12 per cent stated they thought availability to be 'very poor' or 'poor' while a further 22 per cent reported it as 'fair'. Many of the respondents commented on the availability with a selection of these presented below:

> "The quality of university graduates is very disappointing particularly in relation to their basic skills in laboratory techniques and even more starkly their health and safety skills...It really is a seriously scary issue that graduates coming from these universities have little knowledge of what is taking place in the workplace".
> **Irish Manufacturing MNC**

> "We are looking for more and more graduates and availability of them to us is becoming a bigger issue all the time. It is difficult for us to source them due to the food industry not being viewed as glamorous and as a result we are finding it very difficult to attract the calibre of candidates we want".
> **UK Manufacturing MNC**

> "We are finding it very difficult to get science and engineering graduates at the moment. I think it is a cyclical thing whereas a few years ago it was difficult to get IT people but now there are loads of them but it is the sciences that we are struggling to get graduates of sufficient quality".
> **US Manufacturing MNC**

This should clearly be of concern to policy-makers and MNCs. It places a question mark over the government's strategy of moving Irish industry 'up the value chain', given that successful implementation would require a strong supply of suitably qualified graduates. Shortages of suitable graduates may not only be problematic for firms already established in Ireland, but it may also be a major negative factor in trying to attract new industry there. In most of the other aspects investigated, respondents were very positive, with an average of more than eight in ten reporting satisfaction levels of either 'good' or 'very good' in relation to the different measures of their workforce characteristics which we examined. However, some MNCs also noted some issues around work ethic, which may be of concern in the future:

> *"The quality of graduates is generally only fair. I think that is due to a number of things such as their personality and also their work ethic, that leaves a lot be desired in a number of cases".*
> **US Manufacturing MNC**

> *"Work ethic among the workforce has definitely fallen over the last couple of years".*
> **European Multi-Sector MNC**

> *"The work ethic of new employees which often tend to be graduates is a lot worse than the older employees. I feel there is the attitude that there are loads of jobs out there and that they really seem only interested in taking their salary and that's it – they do the minimum".*
> **Irish Services MNC**

Indeed these quotes above regarding work ethic and attitudes of workers are similar to comments made by MNC respondents in a survey of employers' perceptions of graduates in the workplace (Expert Group on Future Skills Needs and Higher Education Authority, 2008). Whilst this survey specifically compared Irish versus non-Irish graduates over a range of different skills, issues such as work ethic and attitudes of workers were singled out for comment by employers, with many noting that Irish graduates have got "lazy".

Influencing factors on new investment decisions for the Irish operations

We have already noted the evolution of Ireland's industrial development strategy and its contemporary focus on attracting higher 'value-added' activities. However, beyond some anecdotal evidence, we have limited knowledge of how the mandates of subsidiaries of foreign MNCs in Ireland are developing. This section explores the opinions of subsidiary level managers on what they see as the most important factors influencing whether the Irish operations receive new investments or new mandates from their parent company. Thus, respondents were asked to rank from 1 to 7 the most important factor, with 1 being the most important factor and 7 the least important factor. Table 3.10 illustrates the findings.

Table 3.10 Rankings of importance of factors in influencing decisions on new investments or new mandates for the Irish operations

Ranking	Labour availability	Labour costs	IR climate	General infrastructure	Overall operating costs	Capacity of operations to innovate	Financial incentivs
1	19%	24%	2%	2%	31%	10%	16%
2	12%	25%	5%	5%	29%	13%	14%
3	12%	20%	9%	15%	20%	9%	15%
4	26%	13%	11%	11%	10%	11%	17%
5	13%	11%	23%	16%	5%	18%	11%
6	7%	4%	23%	28%	3%	18%	13%
7	10%	2%	27%	22%	2%	21%	13%

Perhaps not surprisingly, cost concerns emerge as clearly the most important area of distress among foreign MNCs in Ireland. As is illustrated in Table 3.10 overall operating costs were cited as the most important influencing factor (i.e., a ranking of 1), followed by labour costs. Similar results were found in the Irish Management Institute report which investigated issues around the competitiveness of the Irish economy and the number one ranked issue was that of labour costs (Irish Management Institute, 2008). Correspondingly, they were the least likely to receive the lowest ranking (i.e., 7). This is perhaps expected as the corporate sector and employers' bodies have been vocal for a number of years in relation to the deteriorating cost environment in which Irish companies operate. This has also been cited as the primary reason behind the relatively large number of foreign MNCs closing their Irish operations and transferring their business abroad, often to lower- cost locations (cf. Gunnigle et al., 2003). Indeed, the following quotes garnered during the fieldwork phase of the research provide a qualitative example of the most important factors in winning new investments:

> "Labour costs and labour availability are the worrying things going forward".

US Manufacturing MNC

> "In terms of the factors influencing decisions on new investments, labour

costs, overall operating costs and financial incentives are important… "
European Manufacturing MNC

Labour availability and financial incentives also received relatively high rankings, coming in after the cost issues. This follows a similar trend in previous literature, where availability of workers and corporation tax were ranked relatively high (Irish Management Institute, 2008). Issues such as the industrial relations climate and general infrastructure did not emerge as areas of concern: indeed a mere 7 per cent of respondents gave these two factors a ranking of either 1 or 2 (i.e., the most important and second most important factor). Of possible concern though is the finding that the 'capacity of the Irish operations to innovate in the development of goods, services and processes' is not ranked very high in terms of its importance in influencing investment decisions. Indeed, after the industrial relations climate and general infrastructure, it is most likely to receive the least important ranking (i.e., 7). As mentioned above, government policy in recent years has shifted to the attraction of value-added jobs. However, this finding suggests that MNCs are not placing great importance on the capacity of the Irish operations to innovate. Rather, cost issues and labour availability are more pressing concerns. Thus, the focus on attracting more value-added type investments may not itself be sufficient; instead, the issues of cost and labour deficits need to be addressed concurrently.

Conclusion

Our findings indicate that MNCs in Ireland are a relatively heterogeneous group, originating from the US, UK, and Europe, as well as a small number of other countries. In addition, there are a large number of indigenous MNCs. Most MNCs tend to be located in the services sector, followed by manufacturing. There are also a number of MNCs classified as multi-sector. Firms vary greatly in terms of their Irish and worldwide employment figures. Indigenous MNCs tend to be the largest domestic employers, whilst foreign firms have the largest worldwide employment

Just over half of the MNCs recognise a 'key group' of employees, which range from analysts, to client executives, to chemists, to research and development staff. Seven in every ten MNCs indicate that male employees make up in excess of half of the workforce. In spite of anecdotal evidence to the contrary, the use of 'atypical' forms of employment (i.e., part-time and temporary workers) is relatively low.

Foreign-owned MNCs tend to be relatively new to the country, with two thirds establishing post 1980, with 'greenfield' establishment the predominant form of entry. An overwhelming majority of foreign MNCs have two or more sites in Ireland. Irish-owned MNCs were late to internationalisation, with almost seven in ten companies internationalising post-1980. Somewhat surprisingly, just over half internationalised through the establishment of 'greenfield' sites rather than through merger/acquisition. They also tend to be quite international in that 83 per cent have operations in more than two countries.

Whilst much has been made over the last couple of months of 2008 regarding MNCs pulling out of Ireland or announcing job losses, our findings present quite a positive picture on the scale of job losses and site closures and also new expansions. We acknowledge that the research took place in a different economic climate to the one pertaining in the latter half of 2008 so some caution must be exercised in interpreting the results. Nonetheless we find that over half of the respondents said they had received new investment over the previous five years with a little over a quarter reporting they had closed a site. Similarly, we pointed to quite a positive picture in terms of employment growth also. Indeed these findings are mirrored in a more recent survey by the Irish Management Institute on MNCs, where an in-depth review of MNCs expansions and closures reveal similar findings to ours. Thus, whilst the situation may not be as optimistic as it was a year ago, our findings nonetheless are quite positive regarding the future of MNCs in Ireland.

There are also positive indications regarding Ireland's position in the corporate 'value chain'. Respondents predominantly believed the Irish operations were of great importance to the overall performance of the parent company and that this importance had increased over the past five years. Allowing for the fact that these data are quite subjective, and one may expect MNCs to err on the side of the positive, we would argue that the respondents were quite aware of their position in the corporate value chain and presented an accurate picture of that position. This finding bodes well for the future of MNCs operating in Ireland.

An overwhelming majority of respondents are extremely satisfied with various measures of the Irish labour force, such as quality of graduates, and the workforce's ability to learn new skills. One noticeable concern is in relation to the availability of university graduates. Perhaps not surprisingly, cost issues are clearly the most important area of anxiety among foreign MNCs. Operating costs and labour costs are the most important influencing factor in whether the Irish operations receive new investment or new mandates from the parent company.

ENDNOTE

[i] It should be noted that the number of MNCs in the 'rest of the world' category is quite small at fourteen. Furthermore, this is quite a disparate group in terms of country of ownership, encompassing firms from southern and central Asia, the Americas (excluding the US) and the Antipodes. We therefore advise caution in interpreting subsequent results for this ownership category.

CHAPTER 4
The HR Function

Patrick Gunnigle, David G. Collings, Anthony McDonnell & Jonathan Lavelle

Introduction

"Determining the anatomy and impact of the human resource management function and its associated activities remains an important, if sometimes uncertain, line of inquiry in organisation science" (Morley et al., 2006: 609). In this regard, authors such as Sparrow and Hiltrop (1994) identified several key transitions in the role of the HR function in the closing part of the twentieth century, most especially a detectable shift from traditional and specialist areas of HRM towards a broader concern with the strategic nature and impact of the HR role. A wider body of evidence emphasizes a changing landscape of the HR function and its associated terrain, including a greater emphasis on the integration of the HR function into strategic decision-making, the greater decentralisation of HR activity to line managers, and a shift away from a preoccupation with industrial relations and collective bargaining to other areas of HR activity such as communications, training and development, workplace learning, career management and human capital accumulation (Morley et al, 2006). However, the contemporary nature of the HR function is not especially well documented, particularly in the context of the MNC.

Given the critical role played by foreign-owned MNCs in Ireland, it is hardly surprising that commentators have noted their influence on management practice. In particular, we find broad consensus that inward FDI has generally acted as a source of innovation, particularly in the diffusion of new HR approaches and in promoting the role of the specialist HR function (cf. Murray, 1984; Gunnigle, 1998; Gunnigle et al., 2003). More specifically, MNCs have been associated with the diffusion of high performance work systems (HPWS) (cf. Mooney, 1989; Flood et al., 2005) and performance management/ performance-related pay systems (cf. Gunnigle et al., 1998). Comparisons between foreign-owned and indigenous firms point to a significantly greater uptake of 'sophisticated' HR practices among foreign-owned companies (cf. Roche and Geary, 1996; Geary and Roche, 2001; Flood et al., 2005).

However, as indicated earlier, important shortcomings characterising much of this research are the small sample sizes used and an over-reliance on data garnered from grant-aided MNCs in the manufacturing sector. Our more extensive and representative database allows us to more comprehensively review the role and structure of the HRM function in MNCs in Ireland, both foreign-owned and indigenous.

A key stream of literature on the management of MNCs seeks to achieve a better understanding of the links between strategy and international HRM (De Cieri and Dowling, 1999; Schuler et al., 1993; Scullion and Starkey, 2000). In this regard, the key strategic challenge for top managers in MNCs is balancing the need for integration with pressures for local responsiveness (Rosenzweig and Nohria, 1994). More recent research suggests that at the international level the firm's strategic choices impose constraints or limits on the range of international HRM options available to them (De Cieri and Dowling, 1999). Previous research on MNC subsidiaries has distinguished between those that are autonomous, those that are controlled from higher levels, and those that are the source of information and resources for other sites (cf. Gupta and Govindarajan, 2000). A key contribution on the role of the HR function in the MNC is Scullion and Starkey's (2000) empirical study. They explored the role of the corporate HR function in the context of the internationalised firm and identified three distinctive orientations with regard to the role of the corporate HR function: *centralised companies*, where large corporate HR staffs exercised control over the careers and mobility of senior management and high potentials worldwide; *decentralised companies*, with a smaller corporate HR function with a more limited role in managing the careers and mobility of senior management and high potentials worldwide and; *transition companies* that were in the process of moving from a decentralised approach to a more centralised approach. In a similar vein, the parallel study on HR in MNCs in the UK (Edwards et al., 2007: 17) identifies three potential scenarios regarding the role of the HR function:

- *An autonomous HR function*: where the national operations are 'left to their own devices', reporting to senior management in the host country but with limited reporting beyond the national level.
- *A controlled HR function*: where national level HR is tightly controlled and monitored by higher levels of management outside the host country (at regional, divisional or corporate level).
- *A limited autonomy HR function*: a variant of the 'controlled HR function' where host country operations have some influence on the crafting of international HR policies and are not simply implementers of polices developed outside the host country.

In this chapter, we consider evidence on the nature and role of the HR function in MNCs. We address the means through which MNCs seek to coordinate and control HR policy and practice across borders. We particularly focus on the role of the HR function in this regard, including the role of information technology and the use of shared services provision to aid the delivery of HR services at the national and international level.

IT-based networks and services

A key development in HR service provision over the past two decades has been the increased use of information technology (IT). This is all the more relevant in MNCs, where IT systems may be used to monitor policy implementation and performance, and also to facilitate communications and networking, across borders. It thus provides an insight on the extent to which corporate management has access to HR data on its international operations and can compare performance on HR metrics across sites and countries. We specifically examined the usage of IT-based HR information systems (HRIS) and 'shared services' provision on an international level.

In regard to the diffusion of HRIS, respondents were asked whether the worldwide company had an "HR Information System (such as PeopleSoft or SAP HR) that holds data relating to the firms international workforce". The responses for both foreign and Irish-owned MNCs are outlined in figure 4.1. Just over half (54 per cent) of all MNCs in Ireland reported the use of HRIS that operate on an international basis. This is a similar figure to that found in the parallel UK study, where some 52 per cent used such a system (Edwards et al., 2007). However, among MNCs in Ireland, a greater proportion of foreign-owned MNCs (56 per cent) than Irish-owned MNCs (43 per cent) reported the use of HRIS on an international basis.

Figure 4.1 Use of HRIS System on an international basis: Foreign v Irish MNCs

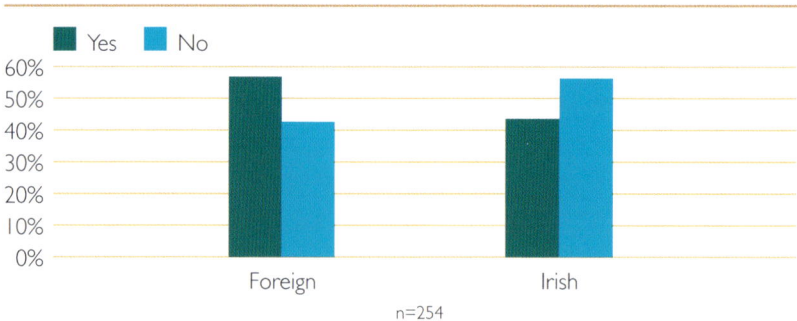

n=254

There were some discernable differences in regard to ownership. As indicated in figure 4.2, American firms were the highest users of HRIS (70 per cent), while 'rest of the world' MNCs were the least likely. This again resonates with the UK findings where US MNCs were among the greatest users of HRIS and Japanese MNCs the least (Edwards et al., 2007). Arguably this trend could be traced to the nature of control systems in MNCs of different nationalities.

Specifically, US MNCs tend to rely to a greater degree on formalised, centralised control through standardised policies rather than expatriates from the head quarters (see Ferner et al., 2004). Conversely, it is argued that Japanese firms rely to a far greater degree on personal control through expatriates from the HQ (Harzing, 2001). Clearly, HRIS would have a much greater role to play with regard to formalised and standardised control systems as they would facilitate head-office in monitoring subsidiary performance across a number of performance metrics and the like. Conversely, HRIS may play a lesser role in the latter situation in Japanese firms where personal relationships play a far greater role in this regard. Because of the small number of Japanese MNC subsidiaries in Ireland, and hence in our sample, this finding should be considered tentatively. However, the consistency with the parallel UK study does provide a degree of confidence in the finding and interpretation.

Figure 4.2 Use of HRIS by country of origin

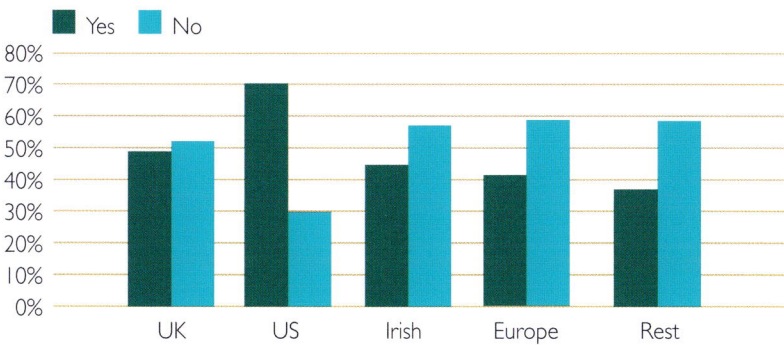

Figure 4.3 Use of HRIS by sector

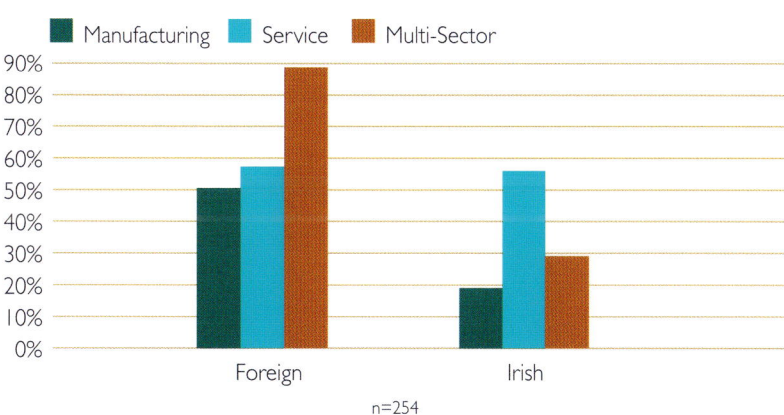

n=254

Human Resource Practices in Multinational Companies in Ireland: A Contemporary Analysis

The impact of sector on the take-up of HRIS is outlined in figure 4.3. Among Irish MNCs, the service sector accounted for the greatest number of firms with HRIS. However, among foreign-owned MNCs, multi-sector firms were by far the largest users, followed by those in the service sector.

HR shared services provision

Shared services provision on an international level has clearly increased over recent years. Such provision incorporates an 'economy of scale' approach whereby particular HR services are provided from one facility to service company operations, either solely in the country of operation, or across operations in different countries. The provision of shared services across countries provides another important indicator of the extent to which the HR function's operations are integrated on an international basis (cf. Edwards et al., 2007). In our study, respondents were first asked whether their firm made "use of shared services centres" which catered for "a range of operating units or divisions". Those who used such centres were then asked whether these centres were local (i.e., just serviced Irish operations) or international (i.e., catered for operations in other countries) in character.

The findings on the overall use of shared services centres are outlined in figure 4.4. These indicate that shared services centres are used in four out of every ten (39 per cent) MNCs in Ireland. Interestingly, the deployment of shared services centres was higher among Irish-owned MNCs (48 per cent) than in foreign-owned MNCs (37 per cent). There are several factors that might help account for the significant use of shared services centres among Irish-owned MNCs. Firstly, there may be a 'size effect'. Irish-owned MNCs tend to be larger employers in Ireland, relative to foreign-owned MNCs (see chapter 2) and consequently may have a greater need for shared services facilities to cater for their workforce. Arguably they gain greater economies of scale in doing so. Secondly, there is also the issue of where these firms are establishing new foreign subsidiaries. Irish MNCs have operations in a relatively large number of countries, with a significant number operating in developing regions. Shared services centres may therefore aid coordination of activities and aid decision-making across these operations. It may provide specific HR expertise to managers in subsidiaries, particularly those in developing countries, when such expertise may otherwise be unavailable.

Focusing on ownership specifically, we find that after Irish-owned MNCs, UK- (46 per cent) and US- (45 per cent) owned MNCs were the highest users of shared services centres, while those from the rest of Europe (22 per cent) and the rest of the World (29 per cent) were the lowest: see figure 4.5. The parallel study of MNCs in the UK found American firms to be the most likely to have shared services centres (Edwards et al., 2007).

Figure 4.4 Use of shared services centres

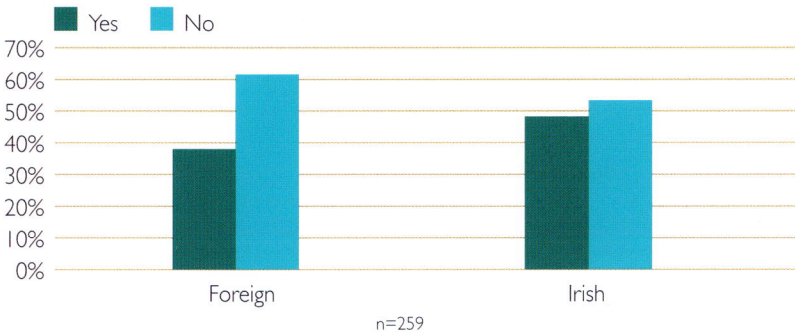

n=259

Figure 4.5 Use of shared services centres by country of origin

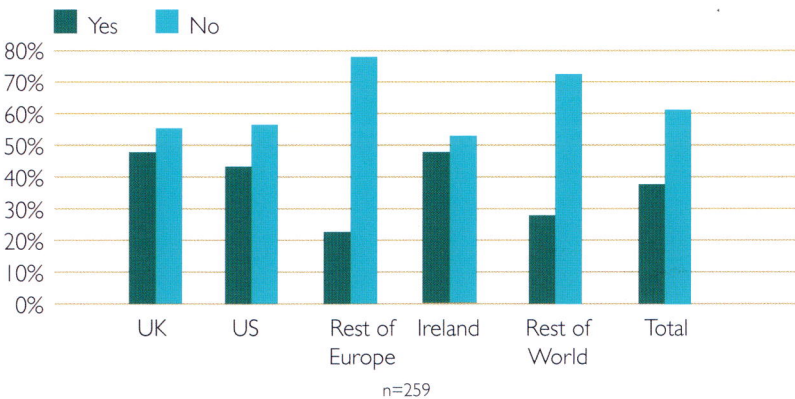

n=259

The impact of sector on the deployment of shared services centres is outlined in figure 4.6. These findings indicate that seven in ten (71 per cent) foreign 'multi-sector' MNCs use a shared services centres but less than a sixth (14 per cent) of Irish 'multi-sector' MNCs do so.

As mentioned above, we further investigated those firms that reported the use of shared services centres to establish whether such centres serviced the Irish operations only or whether they catered for operations in other countries. Among this smaller cohort of MNCs, a slight majority (55 per cent) of their shared services centres catered for operations in more than one country (see figure 4.7). The use of shared services centres on an international basis was more common among Irish-owned MNCs (62 per cent) than in foreign-owned MNCs (54 per cent). This again appears to indicate that Irish-owned MNCs are by no means 'behind the curve' in deploying new and innovative employment practices.

Figure 4.6 Use of shared services centres by sector

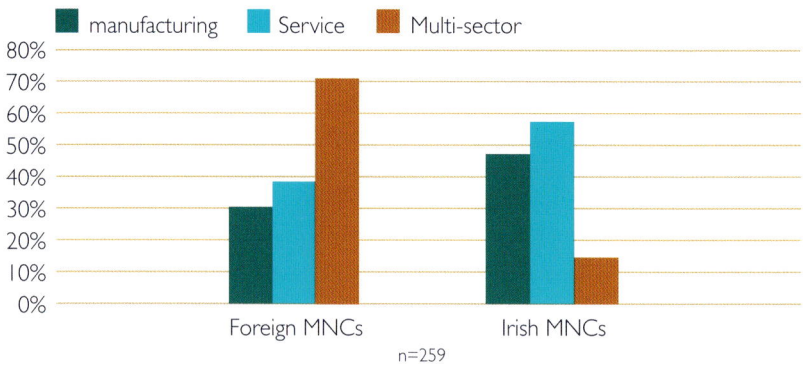

Figure 4.7 Shared services provision on an international basis

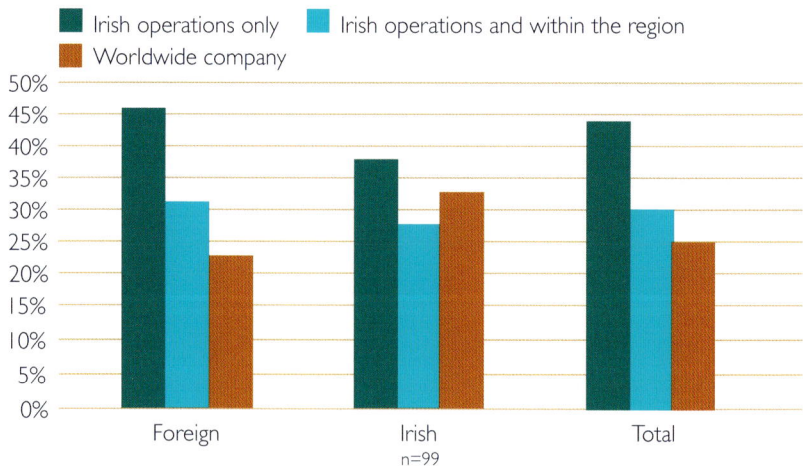

International HR policy development & coordination

The development and coordination of HR policy across different countries is clearly a key concern for MNCs. In particular, commentators have pointed to the potential importance of policy-making bodies that operate at an international level (cf. Scullion and Starkey, 2000; Tregaskis et al., 2005). However, we have very limited knowledge of how such policies are developed and diffused internationally and the institutional arrangements used by MNCs in this regard (cf. Scullion and Collings, 2006). We specifically look at international HR networks. In this regard we adopt Tregaskis et al.'s (2005: ix) definition of international HR networks as "the range of opportunities that exist for national and international HR managers of multinational companies (MNCs) to discuss their organizations' human resource policies and practices". Tregaskis and colleagues note that the, albeit limited, extant evidence on cross-national HR teams indicates that these are important mechanisms for MNCs operating in internationally competitive markets.

This study investigated the incidence of such international bodies and their role in policy development and coordination. Here respondents were asked whether there was a 'body within the worldwide company, such as a committee of senior managers that develops HR policies that apply across countries'. The findings are summarised in figure 4.8. These indicate that the majority of MNCs (58 per cent) in Ireland have a body whose responsibility it is to develop HR policies on an international basis. This figure is somewhat higher than the equivalent figure of 53 per cent found in the parallel study of MNCs in the UK (Edwards et al., 2007). The presence of such bodies was slightly higher among foreign-owned (59 per cent) than among Irish-owned (53 per cent) MNCs.

Figure 4.8 International HR policy formation body

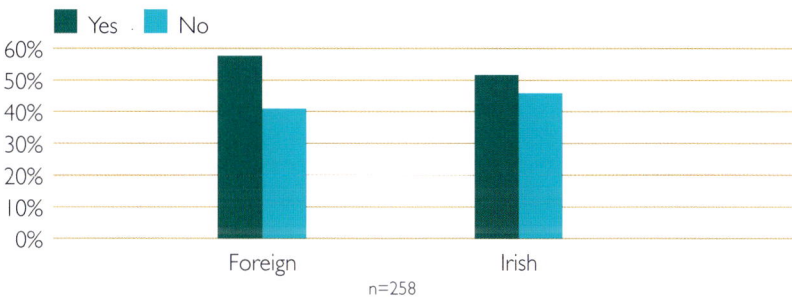

n=258

As indicated in figure 4.9, international HR policy making bodies are most prevalent in US firms, where over seven in ten reported the presence of a body with responsibility to develop HR policies on an international basis. With regard to size, larger firms, both Irish and foreign, were more likely to have such bodies.

Figure 4.9 International HR policy formation body by country of origin

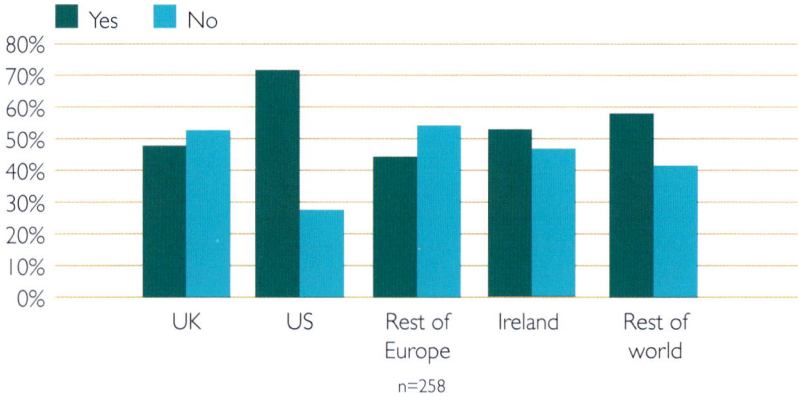

n=258

Sector was also found to be influential. Foreign-owned firms engaged in operations spanning multiple sectors in Ireland were more likely to have such a body/committee, with almost eight in ten (76 per cent) of all foreign-owned MNCs having one (see figure 4.10). Among Irish-owned MNCs, those in the manufacturing sector were most likely to have an international HR policy-making body (73 per cent). This may well stem from that fact that those in the manufacturing sector may be older than many of their service sector counterparts, and thus have had more time to build up HR policy development and coordination across their international operations. It may also be that this is a cheaper alternative than international assignments, one of the conventional, if expensive, means of sharing best practice. Such a shift may be representative of a wider shift away from a sole reliance on traditional long term (3 to 5 year) international assignments and the emergence of a portfolio approach to international staffing, including short-term assignments, global virtual teams, frequent business travel (see Collings et al., 2007) and arguably international HR policy bodies. However, we cannot be definitive on this and the factors explaining differences in international HR policy development merit further empirical investigation.

Looking specifically at foreign-owned MNCs, the study investigated whether such international bodies contained a representative from the Irish operations. The extent of such national representation is identified by Edwards et al. (2007) as a useful means of distinguishing between a 'controlled HR function', whose primary role is to implement policies developed outside of Ireland, from a 'limited autonomy HR function' whereby the Irish operations have an input into policy formulation. This was found to be the case in some 51 per cent of foreign MNCs, a little below the figure of 55 per cent found in the parallel study of MNCs in the UK.

Figure 4.10 International HR policy formation body by sector

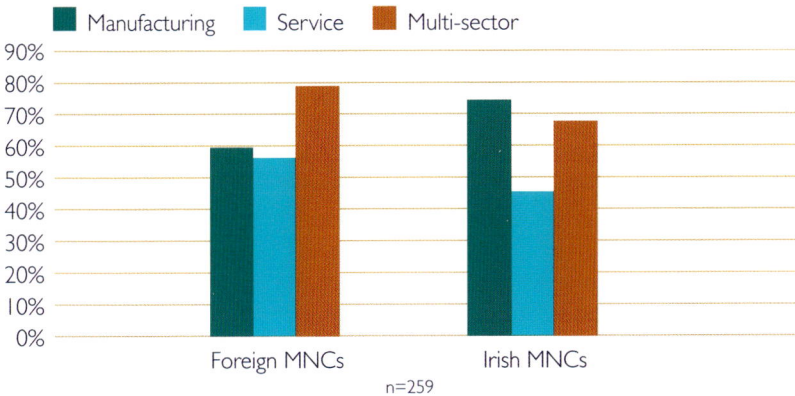

n=259

Edwards et al. (2007: 19) further note that the extent to which the HR function makes a 'systematic attempt to bring managers together across sites' is a useful indicator of inter-country integration in HR policy formulation, as opposed to a more centrally driven corporate control approach. Our study examined that nature and frequency of contact between HR managers in different countries, and the results are outlined in Figure 4.11 and 4.12.

Figure 4.11 International networking (foreign MNCs only)

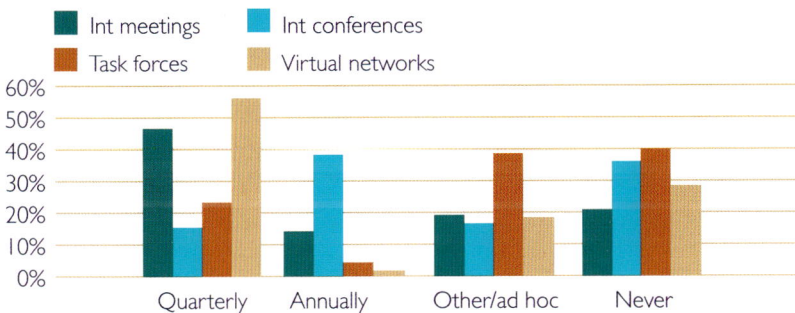

These findings point to a reasonably high level of international interaction between HR practitioners in MNCs. Eight out of every ten MNC in Ireland reported holding regular meetings between HR practitioners from operations in different countries. The incidence of such meetings was slightly higher among foreign-owned MNCs (79 per cent) than Irish-owned MNCs (74 per cent). Just under half (48 per cent) claimed to hold such meetings at least once every quarter. This is in line with the parallel study of MNCs in the UK that found 54 per cent had regular meetings at least quarterly. There was also a high utilisation of networking via international conferences, task forces, and virtual means among foreign-owned MNCs in Ireland. However, the incidence of international working using these mechanisms was decidedly lower among Irish-owned MNCs. Just over six in ten (64 per cent) foreign-owned MNCs and just less than four in ten (37 per cent) Irish MNCs reported holding international conferences involving HR practitioners from different countries. In terms of frequency, these conferences were at least annual events in half of all foreign MNCs but in just a quarter of Irish MNCs. This is significantly lower than found in the UK study where nearly seven out of ten (69 per cent) MNCs there reported holding conferences for HR practitioners annually or more frequently.

Figure 4.12 International networking (Irish MNCs only)

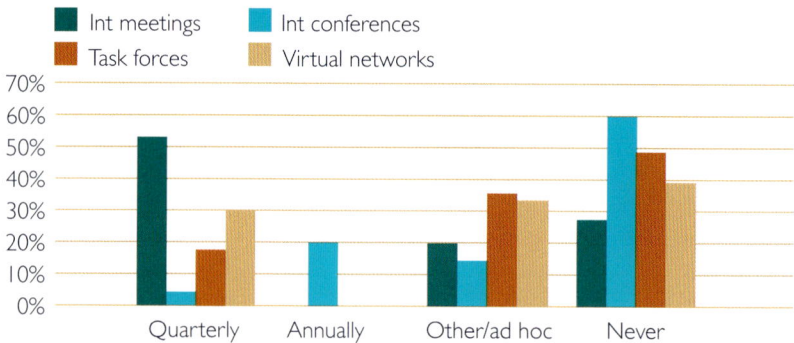

Approximately two-thirds of foreign-owned MNCs and just under half the Irish-owned MNCs (49 per cent) used international task forces, mostly on an ad hoc basis. This is slightly lower than that found in the UK study where task forces were used by three-quarters of MNCs there. Virtual networking was used by almost three quarters (72 per cent) of foreign-owned MNCs and 62 per cent of Irish MNCs. Overall, the extent of international networking was lower in Irish MNCs than among their foreign-owned counterparts.

American MNCs report the highest incidence of international networking (across all four networking mechanisms on which we collected data). With regard to the impact of sector, our findings indicate that MNCs engaged in multiple sectors report the highest levels of international networking. Again as expected, larger MNCs were most likely to bring HR practitioners together on an international basis.

Monitoring by higher level international management

Figure 4.13 Monitoring by higher-level management (foreign MNCs only)

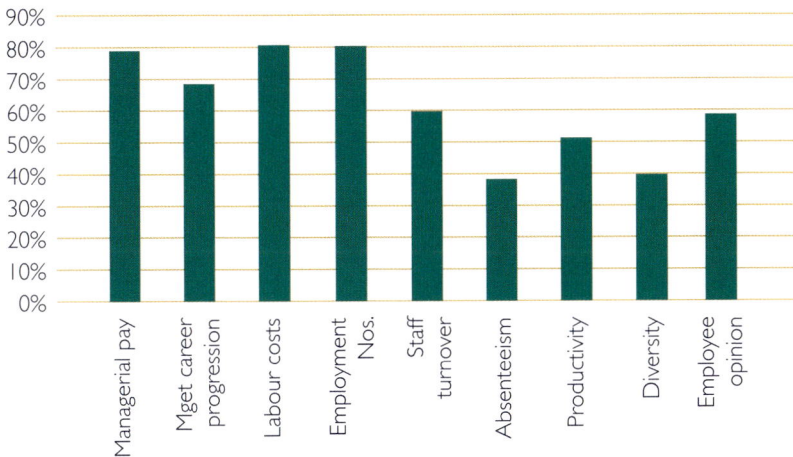

An additional indicator of the degree of autonomy accorded to the subsidiary level HR function is the extent to which higher managerial levels from outside the country of operation monitor HR policy and performance. To this end, we asked respondents in foreign-owned MNCs whether management outside of Ireland monitored information on some nine areas of HR. The results are outlined in Figure 4.13. These indicate a high level of monitoring by senior management at an international level. The most highly monitored areas were employment numbers (81 per cent) and labour costs (80 per cent), followed by issues relating to managerial grades (pay and career progression, 78 per cent and 67 per cent, respectively). The other areas of HR examined were subject to lower levels of monitoring by senior level management outside of Ireland. Labour turnover was monitored by six in every ten MNCs, while a similar proportion (58 per cent) gathered information on employee opinion. The level of monitoring on other issues was lower, particularly with regard to absenteeism.

Interestingly, the four most highly monitored areas (employment numbers, labour costs, managerial pay and career progression) were the same as in the parallel study of MNCs in the UK (Edwards et al., 2007).

A slightly different research focus was adopted with regard to Irish MNCs. Here respondents were asked whether senior management in the MNCs headquarters in Ireland monitored information on these similar nine items in their foreign operations. These findings are outlined in figure 4.14. Given that the data from Irish MNCs reflects a headquarters perspective, in contrast to the data from the foreign-owned MNCs in our study which depict a subsidiary perspective, the pattern of responses are remarkably similar. In particular, the most highly monitored items among both foreign and Irish MNCs are managerial pay, labour costs and employment numbers, while diversity and absenteeism are subject decidedly lower levels of monitoring by senior management.

Figure 4.14 Monitoring by higher level management (Irish MNCs only)

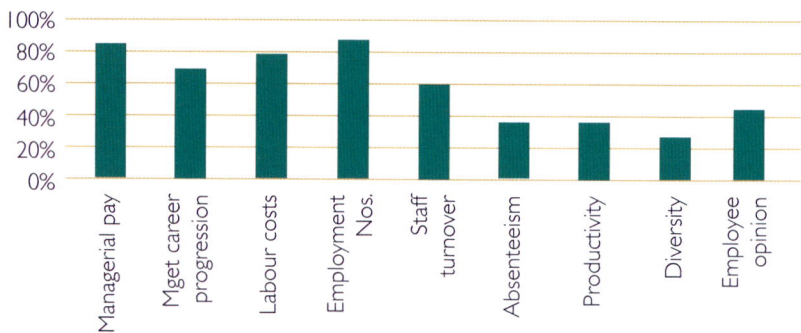

In attempting to explain these trends, we find that among foreign-owned MNCs in Ireland, American subsidiaries reported the highest level of monitoring by international management outside of Ireland. In regard to sector, firms in both the manufacturing and service sector reported high levels of monitoring. However, the level of monitoring was markedly lower among multi-sector firms. The may be due to the greater diversity of activities of multi-sector MNCs, with the consequence that it is more difficult for international level management to monitor HR performance across diverse establishments and operations. The level of monitoring was higher among larger MNCs.

Overall approach to workforce management

Recent decades have witnessed a greater organisational focus on aligning business strategy with HRM policy and practice, with the goal of improving firm performance (cf. Boxall, 1992; Purcell et al., 2003). Indeed the very concept of 'strategic HRM' implies the development of a strategic corporate approach to workforce management, whereby firms seek to formulate an overall corporate HR philosophy and strategy that complements their business strategy and enhances the 'bottom line' (cf. Boxall, 1992; Purcell, 2004).

One of the seminal contributions on multinational strategy in this regard was Perlmutter's (1969: 11) paper which explored the multi-nationality of firms, through developing a typology of multi-nationality based on their orientation towards "foreign people, ideas and resources" in the headquarters and foreign operations. Initially, Perlmutter identified three approaches among MNCs: *ethnocentric, polycentric* and *geocentric*, while in later work (Heenan and Perlmutter, 1979) a fourth approach, namely *regiocentric*, was added. We outline these approaches below and point to some linkages with Bartlett and Ghoshal's (1989) more recent contribution to the MNC strategy literature (for a more thorough discussion see Collings and Scullion, 2006).

Ethnocentric organisations are primarily home-country orientated. In these organisations home based policy, practice and even employees are viewed as 'superior' and foreigners can be viewed as, and feel like, second class citizens. The ethnocentric orientation resonates with Bartlett and Ghoshal's (1989) classification of 'global companies'. Bartlett and Ghoshal characterise global companies by standardisation and the promotion of organisational efficiency. They are focused on the integration of production of standardised products in a cost-effective manner. Therein most key functions tend to be centralised and the role of subsidiaries is limited

Polycentric organisations are primarily staffed by host country nationals (HCNs) or managers from the subsidiary location and foreign subsidiaries are generally afforded a large degree of autonomy. Perlmutter (1969: 11) has compared these organisations to "loosely connected group[s] with quasi-independent subsidiaries as centres". The polycentric orientation is consistent with Bartlett and Ghoshal's (1989) 'multi-domestic approach'. In this regard, multi-domestic companies are characterised by a decentralisation of decision making and manufacturing driven by a desire for local responsiveness. The differentiation of management practices to accommodate local requirements is more important than the standardisation, which is characteristic of global firms

Geocentric organisations view nationality and superiority as unrelated concepts and in these firms individual competence is more significant that nationality. From a staffing perspective, positions at both HQ and subsidiary level are filled with the 'best person for the job' regardless of nationality. Generally these firms display quite complex organisational structures and require high levels of communication and integration across borders. Bartlett and Ghoshal's (1989) 'transnational model' of organisation resonates with Perlmutter's geocentric orientation. The MNC is conceptualised as an integrated network of sub-units within which expertise and resources are neither centralised nor completely de-centralised.

Regiocentric organisations are conceptualised and structured on a regional basis and managers are generally selected on the basis of "the best in the region", with international transfers generally being restricted to within the region. Under this structure, subsidiaries may have a relatively large degree of autonomy from the corporate HQ (Heenan and Perlmutter, 1979).

Clearly these typologies represent a number of ideal types of multinational organisation. Consequently, it unlikely that many MNCs will exactly fit any of the 'ideal' types and, indeed, it is probable that most organisations will display elements of more than one type (cf. Bonache and Fernandez, 1999). However, they do offer a useful frame for our evaluation of how MNCs approach the whole realm of workforce management. Specifically, our survey focused on the extent to which MNCs adopted a uniform management approach in their international operations and explored the origins of such approaches, if any (cf. Sparrow et al., 2004; Edwards et al., 2007). Respondents were presented with a series of statements relating to their company's approach concerning the management of its workforce and asked the extent to which they agreed or disagreed with each using a 1 to 5 scale. The findings are summarised in table 4.1.

Table 4.1 Approach to workforce management (Agree/Strongly agree)[ii]

Agree/Strongly Agree	Foreign MNCs	Irish MNCs	Total
Worldwide approach covering all global operations	53%	50%	53%
Regional approach (for Europe)	57%	68%	59%
Development of approach left to divisional level	43%	56%	45%
Development of approach left to national level	69%	65%	68%
Mix of traditions	47%	35%	45%
Country of origin has overriding influence	55%	64%	57%

The data show that a worldwide approach or philosophy HRM is present in just over half (53 per cent) of the firms surveyed. This was somewhat lower than found in the parallel UK study, where some 61 per cent agreed or strongly agreed that there was a worldwide approach. Among MNCs in Ireland, a worldwide approach was more prevalent among foreign-owned than Irish-owned MNCs. A regional approach was also present but less common.

The next two statements addressed the level at which an organisation's approach to HRM originates. These explore whether the development of a specific HR approach is left to international divisions or to national operating companies. Here the majority of firms, both foreign-owned (69 per cent) and Irish-owned (65 per cent), felt this lay with national level operations, a figure significantly higher than that found in the UK study (45 per cent). A lower proportion (45 per cent) of MNCs felt HR policy was developed at the level of international divisions. The equivalent figure in the UK study was 34 per cent. A number of firms reported the presence of strong worldwide and regional philosophies, similar to the parallel study of MNCs in the UK where it was surmised that one possible explanation is that MNCs deploy "a broad worldwide philosophy and a more specific regional one within this" (Edwards et al., 2007: 22).

We further investigated the importance of 'country of origin' in shaping the overall approach to workforce management. This is seen as a useful indicator of the extent to which the company's approach is dominated by home country traditions and norms in line with Perlmutter's 'ethnocentric' approach. The findings indicate that almost six in ten (57 per cent) MNCs report that the traditions in the country of origin have an 'overriding influence' on the approach to HR management in their foreign subsidiaries, i.e. are characterised by a high level ethnocentrism. As indicated in Figure 4.15, American-owned MNCs (67 per cent) are most likely to report the presence of a global HR approach and that the traditions of the parent company have an overriding impact on this approach. A similar patter was found in the parallel study of MNCs in the UK. This is also consistent with the wider literature on the nature of HRM in US multinationals (see Almond and Ferner, 2006; Ferner et al., 2004) which suggests that firms of US origin display standardised and formalised approaches to management of their subsidiaries. We did not find any significant differences according to sector. However, larger firms were more likely to have a global HR approach and to report that parent country traditions exerted the major influence on this approach.

Figure 4.15 Presence of worldwide HR approach by country of origin

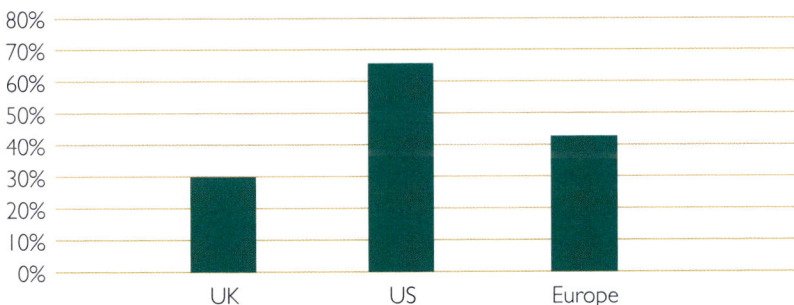

Conclusion

In this chapter, we have reviewed evidence on the nature and role of the HR function in MNCs in Ireland. We concentrated, in particular, on the extent and means through which MNCs seek to coordinate and control HR policy and practice at an international level. One key dimension in this regard concerns the deployment of information technology in HR service provision. This role incorporates the potential deployment of IT in the international delivery of HR services and in senior level monitoring of HR performance among subsidiary operations. Our findings suggest that just over half of all MNCs in Ireland make use of a HRIS on an international basis, with foreign-owned MNCs more likely to use such systems than Irish MNCs. Among the cohort of foreign-owned MNCs, American companies reported the highest level of IT use in delivering HR services across borders. The findings further indicate that 'shared services' usage occurs in four in every ten MNCs in Ireland. Shared services centres were more common in Irish-owned MNCs than among their foreign-owned counterparts. The use of shared services centres on an international basis was also more common among Irish-owned MNCs.

As noted earlier, we have limited knowledge of how HR policies are developed and diffused at international level. Our findings shed some light on this deficit, highlighting that almost six in every ten MNCs in Ireland report the presence of a body with a mandate to develop HR policies on an international basis. International HR policy-making bodies were most prevalent in US firms. We also found a high level of international networking between HR managers. Eight in every ten MNCs in Ireland reported regular meetings between HR practitioners from operations in different countries. We also find a high level of networking via other means, namely international conferences, task forces, and virtual means among foreign-owned MNCs in Ireland. However, the extent of such international HR networking was much lower in Irish-owned MNCs.

An important aspect of international management is the extent of monitoring by senior level management of HR performance and practice in subsidiary operations. Our data point to a high level of monitoring. However, most of the monitoring effort focuses on specific aspects of HRM, namely employment numbers, labour costs and managerial pay and development. American firms reported the highest level of monitoring.

Furthermore, we explored the extent to which MNCs in Ireland were characterised by a uniform global HR approach or philosophy. We found the presence of a global HR approach in just over half of all MNCs in Ireland. Such an approach was more common in foreign-owned than in Irish-owned MNCs. We also considered the extent to which country of origin influences the overall

HR approach. Here we found that a small majority of MNCs report that parent country traditions have an 'overriding influence' on the approach to HR management in foreign subsidiaries. American MNCs were by far the most likely to report the presence of a worldwide HR approach covering all their global operations.

Finally, our findings provide more general insight into the role of the HR function in MNCs. Specifically, in the introduction we alluded to the changing role of the HR function as evidenced through, inter alia, the integration of the HR function into strategic decision making. While our data do not allow us to comment specifically on this shift, they do allow us to make some more general observations. In this regard we argue that innovations such as shared service centres, and the development of HRIS represent potential means through which HR resources can be more effectively utilised and through which HR can contribute to the organisational bottom line. As Wood *et al.* (2008) note, HRIS can create added value for managers and employees through more effective and efficient information flows. Such technology may also allow HR to stake a claim in helping to create competitive advantage and align the function more closely with business/corporate strategy. It can do so in at least three ways: first, by reducing HR transaction costs and headcount (e.g. supplying HR information to large numbers of people on a virtual rather than physical basis); second, substituting physical capability by leveraging the 'law of digital assets' to re-use information flexibly an infinite number of times at little or no marginal cost (e.g. in delivering e-training and e-learning to large numbers of people); and, third, by enabling more effective virtual 'customer relationships' and internal labour markets by increasing the reach and richness of two-way information (e.g. enabling internal/external recruitment and search, career development and performance management, employee engagement surveys to tailor specific 'employee value propositions' to small groups of employees, more flexible working to attract people from non-traditional recruitment pools, outsourcing of key HR services, etc) (Wood et al., 2008).

Overall, our findings point to a considerable degree of variety in the HR approaches and practices of MNCs. In particular, we highlight certain patterns of MNC behaviour that are driven by characteristics such as ownership, scale, structure, and areas of business activity, many of which merit further in-depth empirical investigation.

ENDNOTES

i   It should be noted that only a minority of MNCs operated across multiple sectors (18 foreign-owned MNCs and 7 Irish-owned MNCs).

ii Totals come to more than 100% reflecting fact that the HR approach of MNCs may be influenced from multiple sources/levels

CHAPTER 5
Pay and Performance Management

Thomas Turner, Jonathan Lavelle, Anthony McDonnell
& Patrick Gunnigle

Introduction

The idea that pay policies have strategic impact has become a major theme within the compensation literature since the 1980s. This strategic perspective on compensation is based on the fact that organizations differ in pay policies and the belief that matching pay policies to business strategy results in higher organizational performance (Milkovich, 1988). A strategic approach to managing human resources is often associated with the development of high work performance systems (Becker and Gerhart, 1996). An important element of such systems is the way rewards are structured (Roche and Turner, 1994; Huselid, 1995). The commitment model, integral to many versions of the high performance work system, emphasizes linking rewards to performance (Pfeffer, 1994; MacDuffie, 1995; Hueslid, 1995). In return, high wages and benefits including employment security are offered to employees along with stock ownership and profit sharing schemes. The fundamental premise is that matching pay policy and business strategy impacts firm performance (Milkovich, 1988). Key aspects of pay policy frequently mentioned in strategic compensation theory are external competitiveness and financial reward mechanisms inside the organisation. External competitiveness refers to the level of pay an organization offers relative to that of its competitors. It has a critical impact on attraction/retention and labor cost objectives. The higher the pay level, the better the organization's ability to acquire a competent workforce. Pay determination has traditionally been a critical focus of industrial relations interactions. At enterprise level the debate on the nature of pay systems has tended to focus on two aspects: the ability of organizations to ensure that basic pay levels reflect market conditions (particularly the external labour market) and the introduction of merit/performance-related payment systems.

The importance of pay and other reward mechanisms in foreign MNCs is substantial as these companies tend to be wage leaders for domestic Irish firms and now employ more workers in the manufacturing sector than Irish firms. While the number employed in domestic Irish firms in manufacturing increased by 3 per cent from 105884 in 1990 to 108743 in 2005, the number employed in foreign firms increased by 54 per cent from 88293 to 136280 (Turner et al., 1997; CSO, 2007). Workers employed in foreign firms on average received 20 per cent more than those employed in domestic firms in 1990 (calculated by dividing labour costs by total number of employees) and 36 per cent more in 2005 (CSO, 2007). This chapter explores the policies that MNCs adopt in the area of pay systems and performance management. This is one of the key issues for HRM, and often an indicator of a firm's wider management style. It may be seen as reflecting the firm's strategic approach to the management of employees, its approach to individual employees, and the principal messages of its corporate culture. It is also a core element in the management of those managerial and professional categories often regarded as key to international competitive advantage.

Nationality of ownership has been seen as a major factor influencing the kinds of pay and performance policies that MNCs adopt. American companies, for example, have long been regarded as HR 'innovators' in such aspects as individual performance appraisal, performance-related pay, and employee share ownership (Gunnigle et al., 1997; Dunning, 1998). National influences stem from the characteristics of the parent-country business system: the US, for instance, has had a long history of pay innovation. This can be traced to the attempts of firms to deter unionisation by providing innovative terms and conditions to employees, and by linking pay to individual performance (Foulkes, 1980; Jacoby, 1997; Gunnigle et al., 1998; Roche and Turner, 1998). By contrast, in many European countries, such as Germany and the Netherlands, sectoral pay bargaining and company-level employee representation through works councils have traditionally limited the scope for individually-focused forms of pay and appraisal systems. Pay systems typically have a sectoral dimension too. Payment by results and group-based performance-related pay schemes tend to be more widespread in manufacturing, whereas individual performance-related pay is generally more widely diffused in services.

A number of specific pay and performance practices in foreign and Irish MNCs are examined here. First, the overall strategy on pay levels with regard to whether companies' aim to pay employees above, below, or at the market average for their sector are measured. Second, the use of various systems of reward such as profit-related pay and share ownership are reported. Third, methods of performance appraisal are given: whether companies use formal systems for different groups of staff, the way that appraisal is implemented, the uses to which it is put, and so on.

Pay policy in MNCs

Companies were asked to assess where the company aimed to be as a whole on pay levels in relation to comparators in the same sector or industry. Responses were categorised into targeting pay in the top quartile, second quartile, above the median/mid-point, and below the median/mid-point, for three specific groups of employees: the largest non-managerial occupational group (LOG), key group and managers. As depicted by figure 5.1 managers and the key group were more likely to be paid above the median than the LOG, which is consistent with the findings of a parallel survey in the UK (Edwards et al., 2007).

Indeed, 31 per cent of MNCs that recognised a key group aimed to be in the top quartile, which would appear to suggest they regarded the key group as being critical to the company's success and were willing to pay superior rates of remuneration for their services. There were also some differences between foreign and Irish-owned MNCs. First, 59 per cent of foreign-owned MNCs aimed to pay their key employees in the top or 2nd quartile compared with 65 per cent of Irish-owned MNCs. Second, 50 per cent of foreign-owned MNCs aimed to have pay for managers at the top or second quartile compared to 53 per cent of Irish-owned MNCs. Third, 32 per cent of Irish MNCs, compared to 41 per cent of foreign-owned MNCs, aimed to pay the LOG in the top or 2nd quartile. Overall, few companies aimed to have pay levels below the median/midpoint in comparison to others in any of the three groups of employees. Indeed, a substantial proportion of companies tended to aim to have pay levels at the midpoint for each group of employees: 60 per cent for the LOG, 40 per cent for the key group and 48 per cent for managers.

Figure 5.1 Pay policy of MNCs

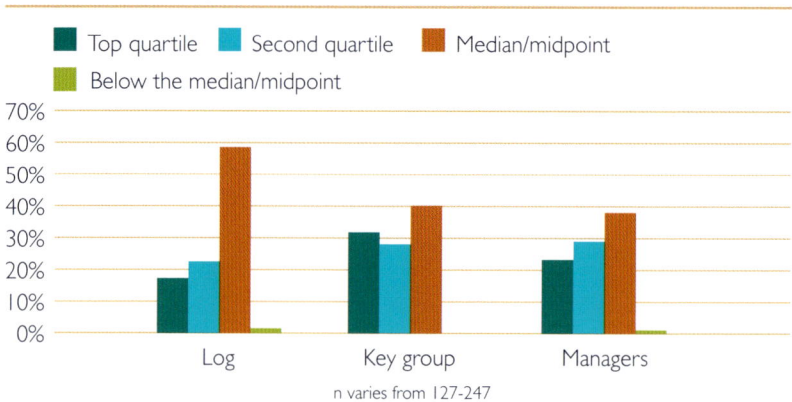

n varies from 127-247

Figure 5.2 indicates pay levels by country of origin. Again there is a pattern consistent across all MNCs of aiming to pay key employees in the top or 2nd quartile. This is particularly the case for UK MNCs. Indeed, UK firms consistently aimed to pay a greater proportion of employees in the three categories in the top or 2nd quartile compared to other MNCs: 56 per cent of the LOG, 75 per cent of the key group and 65 per cent of managers. European-owned MNCs were next, followed by Irish (except for pay levels for the LOG) and lastly US MNCs.

Figure 5.2 Pay policy by country of origin

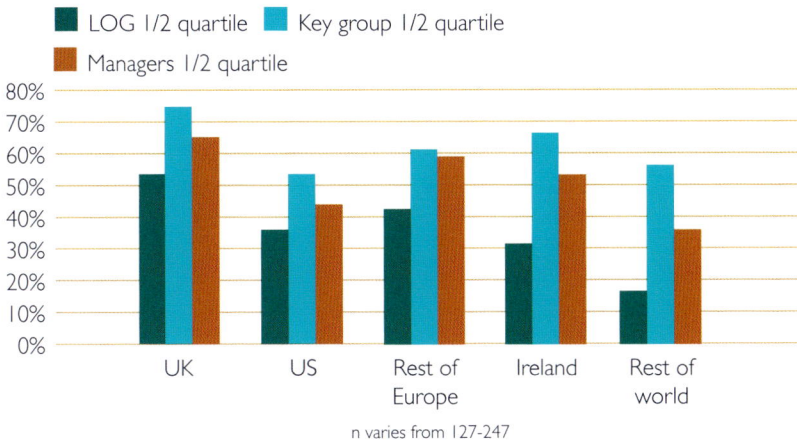

n varies from 127-247

A greater proportion of MNCs consistently aimed to be in the first or second quartile regarding pay for all three groups of employees in the service sector of the economy compared to MNCs in the manufacturing sector or multi-sector (see figure 5.3). In particular, there was a substantial difference between companies in the service sector and those classified as multi-sector.

Figure 5.3 Pay policy by sector

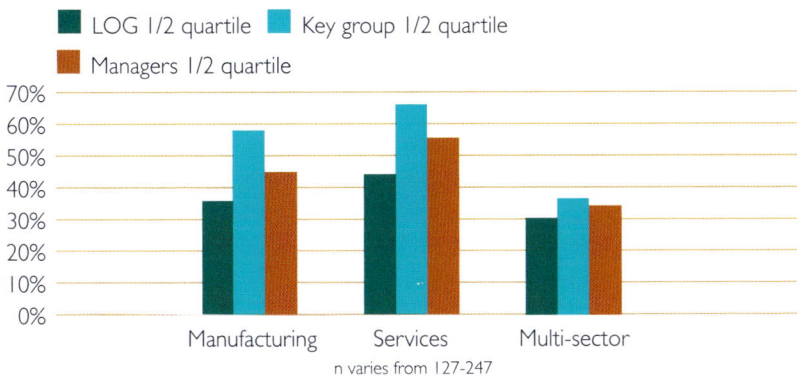

n varies from 127-247

Profit sharing and employee share options

Although profit sharing and employee shareholding has received little attention in Ireland it has been strongly promoted by employers, the government and successive national wage agreements (D'Art and Turner, 2004 and 2006). During the 1990s, profit sharing and employee shareholding schemes entered the biggest growth period in their history (D'Art and Turner, 2006). Prior to 1982, employee share ownership or cash-based profit sharing schemes were a rarity in Ireland. The Finance Act of 1982 and subsequent amendments were designed to encourage the voluntary and widespread adoption of share-based profit sharing through taxation incentives for companies and individual employees. Initially, there was a guarded response from unions and employers to the government initiative (D'Art, 1992). In response, the government introduced a series of amendments in the Finance Acts of 1984 and 1986 designed to make the schemes more attractive to companies and participants. These changes provided a renewed stimulus to the growth of approved schemes. Yet, probably, a critical factor accounting for the favourable attitude shift of the social partners towards financial participation was the presence of corporatist type agreements since 1987. In a total reversal of its previous position, the Irish Congress of Trade Unions switched to promoting profit sharing at the level of the individual firm as a way of securing a more equitable outcome to wage restraint (MSF, 1998; ICTU, 1999). Likewise, IBEC encouraged its member firms to consider schemes for the financial involvement of their employees. In the period 1983 to 2005, a total of 443 approved profit sharing/employee share ownership schemes were established. From 1983, there was a steady annual growth in the number of schemes established and employees covered. A total of 482,774 of employees were recorded as being covered by profit sharing/employee share ownership schemes from 1983 to 2003. However, this is very likely an overestimate because it counts employees who participated more than once in a profit sharing scheme. Revenue estimates that the true or actual number of employees involved in approved profit sharing schemes between 1983 and 2003 was 236,559. Using this adjusted method, the percentage of private sector employees covered by a profit sharing scheme in any one year has ranged from 2 percent to 12 percent. The percentage of private sector employees participating in these schemes peaked in 1999 and then subsequently declined.

At the enterprise level, share ownership is used to provide employees with a financial stake in the company and so dissolve conflicts of interest between capital and labour. Moreover, schemes of profit sharing or employee shareholding are most frequently used to enhance organisational outcomes such as productivity and profitability. More than a century of profit sharing practice has produced numerous studies attempting to evaluate the outcomes of these schemes. Some studies compare profitability levels in profit and non profit sharing companies as a measure of a schemes success (Conte and Tannenbaum, 1978; Livingston and Henry, 1980). Other studies focus on the effect of profit sharing on employee behaviour and attitudes (Metzger, 1975; D'Art, 1992). Yet, evidence for the success of these schemes regarding employee motivation, attitudinal change and improved company profitability is at best uneven, at worst inconclusive (see Baddon, et al., 1989; Poole and Jenkins, 1990; Ramsay, 1991).

In practice, the goals, motivations and expectations for profit sharing schemes can vary between organisations and the adoption of a particular perspective or approach is to some extent determined by the type, size and market situation of the firm. A number of reasons for establishing schemes of employee financial participation can be identified. In some cases, the primary motivation of management in establishing a profit sharing scheme is the attraction and retention of staff through encouraging employee attachment to the firm. This approach to profit sharing is most commonly found in large, capital-intensive multinational corporations. Cash or shares are distributed to all permanent employees, the amount usually varying according to the individual's salary or length of service. In the wider society, the sharing of profits with employees helps to project an image of the caring, socially responsible corporation and good employer. It has a practical benefit in that it is likely to widen the pool of potential recruits, thus facilitating management selection of the most talented. From a strictly economic viewpoint, the apparent intangibility of these benefits to the corporation is offset by tax concessions granted by many governments to companies operating such schemes. In some instances, the profit or share scheme is only one element in a package of fringe benefits, additional to standard wage or salary (D'Art, 1992).

A second reason for the introduction of financial participation is the expectation that it will result in some concrete economic benefit or competitive advantage for the company. Such a cost-benefit approach is more likely to be adopted in small firms operating in a competitive market. In these circumstances, profit sharing or employee shareholding, it is hoped, will enhance labour-management co-operation, increase the quality and quantity of employee output and reduce absenteeism. For some managers with a cost-benefit perspective on financial participation, this may not be the only or principal expectation of profit sharing. In the US, for instance, many profit sharing schemes appear to primarily function as cheap pension substitutes (see Latta, 1979). Lastly, profit sharing or employee shareholding can be used as a defence or deterrent against union organising drives (Roche and Turner, 1998). For instance, management may threaten to abandon the scheme if workers opt for union membership. This strategy has met with some success in North America (Czarnecki, 1970). Where employee shareholding features among the bundle of Human Resource practices it may have the potential to weaken union influence partly through establishing an individual relationship between the company and its employees. Effective application of this strategy may weaken the appeal of collectivism and even in the organised enterprise its tendency may be to marginalise the union (see Poole, 1989; Flood and Toner, 1997).

Financial schemes in MNCs

MNCs, particularly US firms, have traditionally sought to bind their employees into 'shareholder capitalism' through the use of employee share ownership schemes. Moreover, the deregulation of financial markets from the 1980s, and the rise of the concept of 'shareholder value' have further enhanced the use of employee stock options as a device to link the remuneration of managers (O'Sullivan, 2000). Here, the use of three financial schemes (employee share ownership, profit sharing and share options) is examined. Results indicate a relatively even spread with approximately one third of MNCs indicating the use of the three incentives for each category of employees (see figure 5.4). There are some notable differences between foreign and Irish-owned MNCs regarding share options which are used to a greater extent by foreign than Irish MNCs, 14 per cent compared to 26 per cent for the LOG, 35 per cent compared to 41 per cent for the key group and 44 per cent compared to 50 per cent for managers.

Figure 5.4 Financial schemes for employees

n varies from 130-254

As table 5.1 depicts, US MNCs are more likely to use the three forms of financial incentives than others. This is particularly pronounced in the use of employee share ownership for the three groups of employees. This confirms previous research in Ireland and internationally on the use of such schemes in foreign and domestic firms (see Morley and Gunnigle, 1997; Björkman and Furu, 2000). Conversely, with the exception of share options, both rest of world and European MNCs are less likely to use employee share ownership and profit sharing schemes than US, UK and Irish MNCs.

Table 5.1: Financial schemes for employees by country of origin

		UK	US	Rest of Europe	Ireland	Rest of World
LOG	Employee share ownership scheme	29%	40%	17%	30%	7%
	Profit sharing	33%	31%	21%	26%	8%
	Share options	25%	27%	23%	14%	33%
Key group	Employee share ownership scheme	25%	50%	22%	33%	17%
	Profit sharing	31%	42%	26%	41%	14%
	Share options	31%	45%	35%	35%	67%
Managers	Employee share ownership scheme	32%	44%	16%	35%	8%
	Profit sharing	50%	34%	28%	34%	25%
	Share options	36%	66%	29%	44%	64%

MNCs operating in more than one sector use the three financial incentive schemes for all employees to a greater extent than MNCs in manufacturing and services. In particular, the use of profit sharing schemes is significantly more prominent in multi-sector companies, at 43 per cent compared to 20 per cent in the manufacturing sector for the LOG and 29 per cent in the service sector. The pattern is similar for the key group and managers. The use of share options, although still greater in multi-sector companies, tends to be more evenly spread across the three sectors.

Using the Cranfield survey from 1995, it is possible to get some idea of the trends in profit sharing and employee share ownership schemes over a ten-year period. As table 5.2 indicates, the coverage for share ownership and profit sharing for the LOG group shows a consistent increase across all MNCs between the two surveys. The increased use of both schemes is relatively similar for European MNCs. However, the largest increase for the LOG group in US MNCs is in share ownership schemes, whereas in UK MNCs it is in the proportion covered by profit sharing schemes. The use of both schemes has changed little for the key group in UK MNCs but has increased substantially for this group in US and European MNCs. There appears to be some evidence of a trend away from share ownership for managers in MNCs towards profit sharing, particularly in UK and to a lesser extent in US MNCs. The use of both schemes increased for managers in European MNCs, but this was from a relatively low base. Overall, these trends show a greater use of incentive schemes by foreign MNCs since 1995. This may be interpreted as part of a process signalling the individualisation of the employment relationship in these firms. However, it is also likely that such incentive schemes exist in parallel with established standard pay systems, at least for routine employees.

Table 5.2: Profit and share owner schemes 1995 to 2007

	UK			US			Europe		
	Cran survey 1995 %	MNC survey 2007 %	Change 1995 - 2007	Cran survey 1995 %	MNC survey 2007 %	Change 1995 - 2007	Cran survey 1995 %	MNC survey 2007 %	Change 1995 - 2007
LOG*									
Share owners	21	29	**+8**	22	40	**+18**	4	17	**+13**
Profit sharing	16	33	**+17**	23	31	**+8**	7	21	**+14**
Key group**									
Share owners	26	25	**-1**	33	50	**+17**	4	22	**+18**
Profit sharing	26	31	**+5**	30	42	**+12**	11	26	**+15**
Managers									
Share owners	42	32	**-10**	47	44	**-3**	7	16	**+9**
Profit sharing	37	50	**+13**	33	34	**+1**	18	28	**+10**

Source: Morley and Gunnigle, 1997.
* For this group we use the manual employees from the Cranfield survey as the comparator. In the 1995 survey employees were divided into four groups: Managers, Professionals, Clerical, Manual. It is interesting to note that the results for clerical and manual were broadly similar.
** For the key group we use professional employees from the Cranfield survey as the comparator.
*** The Cranfield data used in the above table is not directly comparable to this study as it did not purposely set out to examine the pactices of MNCs. Nonetheless it provides a benchmark which to compare our findings against.

Merit pay and Performance Related Pay (PRP)

The use of merit pay systems has always formed a part of the traditional remuneration package in many organisations. However, such schemes, based largely on the notion that money is a prime motivator, have not always proved affective. Indeed, some have argued that merit based pay systems rarely fulfill their potential and can even act to de-motivate employees (Pearce, 1987; Sargent, 1990). Nevertheless companies frequently introduce individual PRP to increase employee commitment and foster culture change (Kessler, 1995). Some writers question whether individual PRP is compatible with the general logic of the commitment model (cf. Beer et al., 1984:139-51). Less controversial is the principle that organisations require scope to tailor their payment systems and packages to their competitive situation and the flexibility to permit pay to drive performance. This implies policies of pay determination which assign a major role to pay-fixing at the level of the firm and/or at various levels within the firm.

Performance related pay has been defined as 'an intention to pay distinctly more to reward highly effective job performance' beyond what the firm is willing to pay for 'good solid performance' (McBeath and Rands, 1989: 133). PRP is an attempt to establish an explicit link between financial reward and individual/group performance. Support for such systems is based on the concept that it is fair and logical to reward individual employees differentially based on some measure of performance. However, problems may arise in attempting to develop reliable and acceptable mechanisms for evaluating employee performance. These include the limited criteria used (e.g. work study), inconsistency of application (e.g. performance appraisal) or bias and inequity in employee evaluations. A more fundamental issue may be resentment towards the exercise of managerial control via performance measurement and reward distribution inherent in many reward-for-performance approaches.

There is some evidence of increased utilization of performance related pay systems in Ireland (Gunnigle et al., 1998). Gunnigle and Morley (1997) noted an increased use of merit/PRP methods during the 1990s. Merit and performance related pay represented the most commonly used incentive amongst organizations in Ireland. This trend was more pronounced in US-owned companies than Irish-owned companies. Traditionally, merit or performance-related pay has tended to be largely confined to managerial and professional categories. Thus, a significant indicator of the development of a more individualist approach to pay rewards reward systems is the degree to which companies utilize individual performance related systems for non-managerial and non-professional grades. Organizations differ in policies concerning the size of merit raises and the extent to which employees in a firm are covered by performance related pay. Typically, most professional and managerial employees participate in merit pay plans while lower routine and manual employees have lower coverage (administrative support and operations).

Performance related pay in MNCs

PRP is extensively used for all employees, particularly for the key group and managers. US MNCs tend to be more likely to use PRP for the LOG and the key group. However, the differences are not significant. In the UK Edwards *et al.* (2007) found nationality to be a factor, with US MNCs more likely to have variable pay for all three groups and more likely to use variable pay for the LOG. There are no substantial differences in the use of PRP across the different sectors in our data.

Figure 5.5 Performance related pay by country of origin

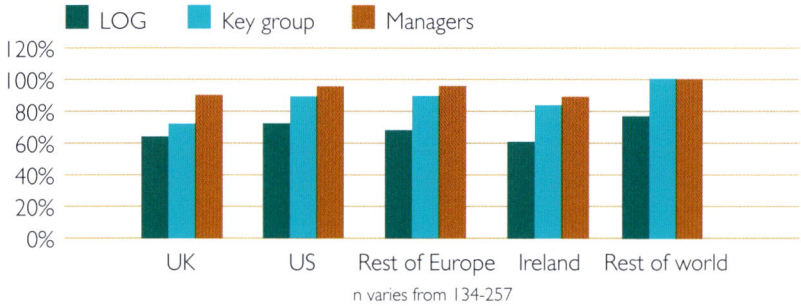

n varies from 134-257

Performance appraisal

Performance appraisal systems are generally developed to measure job performance and are concerned with how well an employee performs in his/her job. McMahon and Gunnigle (1994) identify a range of objectives associated with performance appraisal from a survey in Ireland. The most frequently cited objectives were to:

• Improve future performance
• Provide feedback on performance
• Agree key objectives
• Identify training needs
• Improve communication
• Assess promotion potential

Overall, a central purpose of appraisal for companies is to provide a means of assessing the employee's performance for appropriate rewards. Performance appraisal is considered one of the practices essential to high performance work systems (Huselid, 1995). For example, such systems advocate the abandonment of narrow routine and repetitive jobs associated with mass production for new work arrangements which stress team-working, autonomy, judgment and skill;

systematic training and the monitoring and appraisal of employee performance (Lawler and Mohrman, 1987). However, as Roche and Geary (1996) argue, the increased use and sophistication of these high performance practices, including performance appraisal, can act both to exclude or marginalise trade unions and to bind the employee more closely to the firm. In particular, the adoption of performance related pay systems linked to formal appraisals of individual performance is likely to accentuate individualism and weaken a collectivist orientation to standard rates of pay (Rollinson, 1993; Roche and Turner, 1994). The incidence of performance-related pay based on formal performance appraisals for all employee grades, particularly non-managerial/professional categories, is seen as a strong indicator of an individualist (as opposed to collectivist) approach to industrial relations (Blyton and Turnbull, 1992). Traditionally, most bonus systems (e.g. measured day work) were based on quantitative evaluations of employee performance and were normally the subject of collective bargaining. As such, standardised bonus or performance related payments were very much integral to the collectivist industrial relations tradition (Mooney, 1980). In contrast, performance appraisal, it can be argued, is essentially an individualist management tool (Beer et al., 1984) and may be used to either replace collective bargaining or reduce its significance in pay determination.

Performance appraisal systems

Figure 5.6 Systems of regular performance appraisal

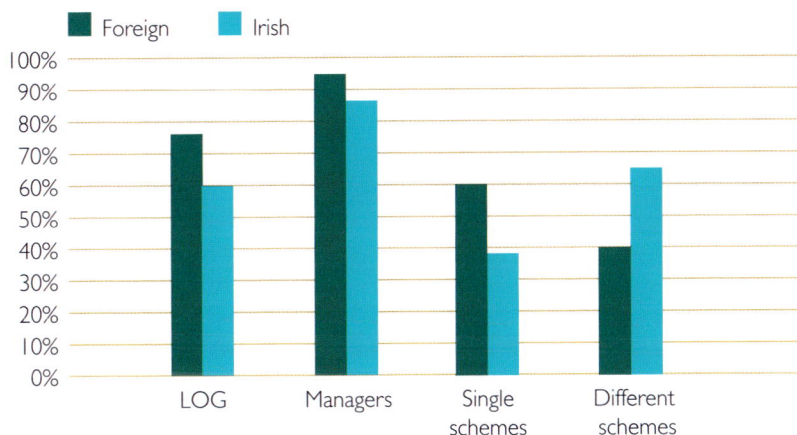

A key finding in relation to the use of performance appraisal schemes is that, for each of the groups, the vast majority of companies have formal schemes: 94

per cent of managers and 75 per cent of the LOG in foreign MNCs have these schemes, compared to 87 per cent of managers and 60 per cent of the LOG in Irish-owned companies. Again there is a difference between Irish and foreign-owned MNCs, suggesting performance appraisal schemes are still not as prevalent in Irish-owned MNCs, particularly for the LOG. One factor that may account for this is the high level of unionisation in Irish MNCs. Irish MNCs are more likely to have different schemes for different groups, at 62 per cent, compared to 40 per cent of foreign MNCs. Conversely, 60 per cent of foreign MNCs report having a single integrated appraisal scheme for all employees compared to 38 per cent of Irish MNCs.

There is a significant nationality effect that is consistent across all three sectors. Regular appraisal for the LOG and managers is highest in US MNCs, followed by rest of world MNCs, UK MNCs, European MNCs and is lowest in Irish MNCs (see figure 5.7). There is a significant difference in the use of a single integrated system of appraisal: 40 per cent or less of Irish and UK MNCs, compared to over 60 per cent of US and European MNCs, have such a scheme in place.

Figure 5.7 Systems of performance appraisal by country of origin

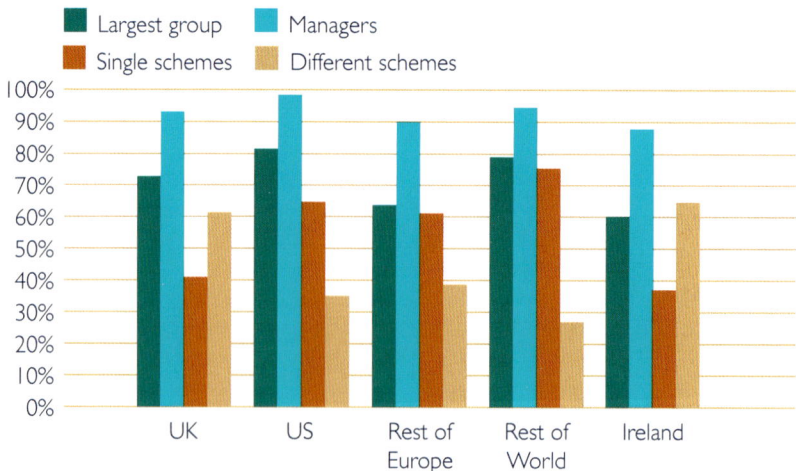

Methods of performance appraisal

Figure 5.8 reports on the use of two particular methods of appraisal: 'forced' distribution (FD) and peer/360 degree feedback. FD systems oblige appraisers to place a certain proportion of appraised staff in different performance categories or grades, normally with the aim of avoiding the 'bunching' of staff in the higher grades. Such systems have become increasingly prominent as companies have sought to gain competitive advantage by using the outcome of appraisal systems as the basis for decisions on pay, promotion, and redundancy. They are particularly important in business systems such as the US, where some labour markets are characterised by 'employment at will', so that companies are easily able to respond to changes in market conditions by adjusting the size of their workforce.

The use of both methods of appraisal is significantly more common in foreign than Irish MNCs. In the foreign-owned MNCs, 28 per cent applied the method of forced distribution to the LOG and 25 per cent used peer/360 degree feedback for this group. Only 8 per cent of Irish MNCs used FD for the LOG and 23 per cent used peer/360 degree feedback. Similarly, foreign MNCs used both methods for the managerial group to a greater extent than Irish MNCs: 30 per cent used forced distribution FD and 53 per cent employed peer/360 degree feedback, compared to 13 per cent and 38 per cent respectively for Irish MNCs.

Figure 5.8 Methods of performance appraisal

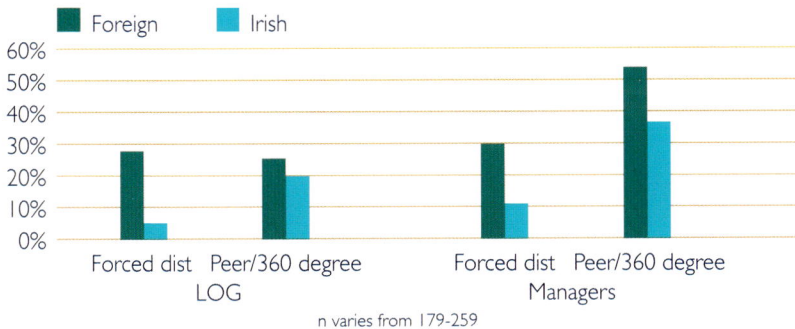

n varies from 179-259

This pattern is confirmed in figure 5.9. However, as expected, there is a significant difference between US MNCs and others, with a greater percentage of US MNCs using forced distribution and peer appraisal for both the LOG and managers. This is different to the UK findings where, surprisingly, no nationality effect on forced distribution or peer appraisals was apparent (Edwards et al., 2007).

Figure 5.9 Methods of performance appraisal by country of origin

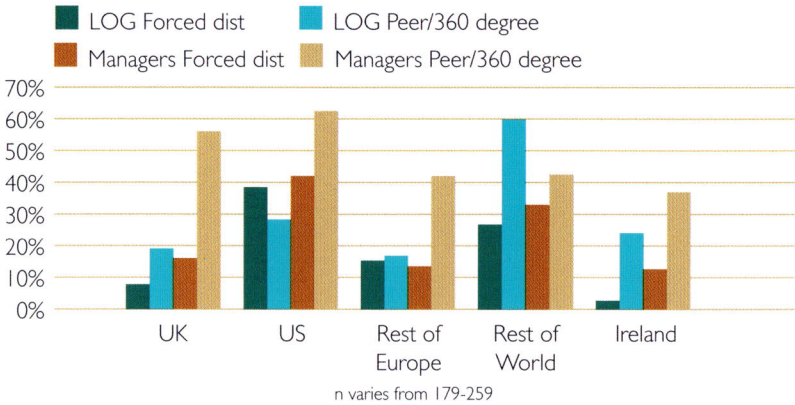

n varies from 179-259

However, similar to the UK findings, the use of forced distribution for the LOG and managers was more likely in the service sector, but the differences were slight.

Again using the Cranfield survey from 1995 it is possible to get some idea of the trends in the coverage of performance appraisal schemes for two employee groups: managers and the largest occupational group. Table 5.3 indicates a substantial increase in the coverage of performance appraisal for the largest occupational group of employees. There was an increase of more than 30 percent in the use of performance appraisal for the LOG group across all foreign MNCs. Aside from European MNCs, there was little change in the coverage of performance appraisal for managers. Taking into consideration the increased trends in the use of incentive schemes for the LOG noted earlier, this would appear to provide some evidence of a growing focus on measuring the performance of individual employees.

Table 5.3: Performance appraisal coverage, 1995-2007

	UK		US		Europe	
	Cranfield survey 1995 %	MNC survey 2007 %	Cranfield survey 1995 %	MNC survey 2007 %	Cranfield survey 1995 %	MNC survey 2007 %
LOG*	42	71	41	82	32	65
Managers	95	91	94	97	75	90

*   For this group we use the manual employees from the Cranfield survey as the comparator.
**   The Cranfield data used in the above table is not directly comparable to this study as it did not purposely set out to examine the pactices of MNCs. Nonetheless it provides a benchmark which to compare our findings against.

Conclusion

The strategic area of pay and performance management of MNCs in Ireland was examined in chapter. As noted earlier, the average wage for workers employed in foreign firms compared to domestic firms has increased substantially in recent years. Not surprisingly then our results indicate that the vast majority of MNCs aim to have pay levels at or above the median/midpoint for all employees. Also MNCs tend to have a policy of ensuring that the pay levels of the key group are in the top or 2nd quartile. Within the general pattern there are important variations related to structural factors of nationality and sector. Nationality is associated with differences across a range of policies. For example, UK firms consistently aim to pay a greater proportion of employees in the top or 2nd quartile compared to other MNCs. Key differences across sectors include the fact that MNCs in the service sector consistently aim to be in the 1st or 2nd pay quartile compared to MNCs in manufacturing or multi-sector.

Given the centrality of MNCs in Irish industry, the use of various reward schemes is likely to have an influence or spill-over effect on domestic Irish firms. Results show that share ownership, profit sharing and share options are used by approximately one third of MNCs for each category of employees. US MNCs are more likely to use the three forms of financial incentives than others. With regard to regular performance appraisal, we found that it is commonly used for the majority of employees in MNCs. Regular appraisal for the LOG and managers is highest in US MNCs, followed by UK firms and is lowest in Irish firms. A greater proportion of US MNCs use forced distribution and peer appraisal for both the LOG and managers. Regular appraisal is significantly more common for the LOG in the service sector.

Overall, the trend in the use of profit sharing and share ownership schemes by foreign MNCs appears to have increased since 1995. This may be interpreted as part of a process signalling the individualisation of the employment relationship in these firms. However, it is also likely that such incentive schemes exist in parallel with established standard pay systems, at least for routine employees. However, a similar trend is evident in the use of regular performance appraisal for the largest group of employees. Finally, while there are some differences due to sectoral location (manufacturing or services), country of ownership has a more substantial impact. US MNCs are more likely to use regular performance appraisal and various reward mechanisms than other MNCs. In contrast, UK MNCs are more likely to aim to pay their LOG in the 1st or 2nd quartile.

CHAPTER 6
Employee Representation
and Consultation

Jonathan Lavelle, Anthony McDonnell, & Patrick Gunnigle

Introduction

Collings (2008) in his review of MNCs and employment relations (ER) notes that whilst international human resource management (IHRM) has received widespread attention in the literature, comparatively, ER issues within MNCs have not received anywhere near the same attention, with some notable exceptions (Gennard and Steuer, 1971; Bomers and Peterson, 1977; Cooke, 2003a; Almond et al., 2005; Ferner et al., 2005). Yet despite this, Collings (2008: 176) postulates that "...[international employment relations] research has the potential to provide insights into aspects of the management of employees in MNCs which are often neglected in the mainstream IHRM literature, including trade union recognition and avoidance, collective bargaining and the like". This chapter sets out to partly redress this imbalance by investigating employee representation and consultation policies and practices within MNCs operating in Ireland. In doing so, the chapter is organised into two broad sections. The first section deals with employee representation, covering issues such as trade union recognition, union density, non-union structures and collective bargaining. A recurring theme within the ER literature is the question of whether significant ER differences exist between foreign and indigenous owned companies. Indeed this debate has been particularly intense in the Irish context with foreign-owned MNCs ER policies and practices receiving some considerable attention (cf. Kelly and Brannick, 1985; Roche and Geary, 1996; Turner et al., 1997a&b; Geary and Roche, 2001; Turner et al., 2001). Yet despite the extant research on MNCs in Ireland, there is no holistic and authoritative picture of the ways in which MNCs manage their employees (Mc Donnell et al., 2007). The literature suggests that MNCs from different countries of origin have distinct preferences with regard to collective employee representation structures. These preferences are said to derive from the existing national models of employee representation which prevail in the particular country of origin. American MNCs, for example, have displayed a distinct tendency not to engage with trade unions and collective bargaining (De Vos, 1981). Patterns of employee representation also tend to vary between industrial sectors (Roche and Turner, 1994; Gunnigle et al., 1997; Roche, 2001). For example, trade unions are more likely to be found in the manufacturing sector than in the services sector. We investigate the impact of both these potential effects on employee representation practices.

The second section of the chapter deals with employee consultation, examining the area of information and consultation and European Works Councils. Both European Union (EU) Directives on European Works Councils (94/45/EC) and Information and Consultation (2002/14/EC) have been transposed into Irish law in recent times and have the potential to shape the ER landscape within Ireland. The Irish ER system has traditionally been characterised as voluntarist (Von Prondzynski, 1998) with very little employment legislation impacting on the management of employees. Thus recent changes introduced by these Directives represent a departure from the existing ER system. However, there has been little attention paid to the impact of both Directives, particularly within the MNC literature. We address this research gap by providing a representative picture of how MNCs in Ireland are adopting to these Directives and employee information and consultation more generally.

Trade union recognition

The issue of trade union recognition among foreign-owned MNCs in Ireland has received widespread attention in the ER literature, particularly over the last 20 years (Kelly and Brannick, 1985; Enderwick, 1986; Gunnigle, 1995; Roche and Geary, 1996, Turner et al., 1997a&b; Geary and Roche, 2001; Turner et al., 2001; Gunnigle et al., 2005; Collings et al., 2008a). Indeed, one might point to two contrasting perspectives which characterise this literature. The first perspective, labelled the 'conformance thesis', points to earlier bodies of work by Kelly and Brannick (1985) and Enderwick (1986). This literature suggested that foreign-owned MNCs largely conformed to the existing ER system in Ireland, i.e. recognising trade unions and engaging in collective bargaining. The second perspective, the 'new orthodoxy', questioned this conformance thesis. Commentators here noted that foreign-owned MNCs were no longer adapting to local ER practice, but rather evidence suggested that they were beginning to introduce policies and practices more reflective of their own home country. This body of literature particularly pointed towards a growing trend of trade union avoidance strategies among foreign-owned MNCs, particularly US-owned MNCs, operating in Ireland (Gunnigle, 1995; Roche and Geary, 1996; Gunnigle et al., 1997; Geary and Roche, 2001; Gunnigle et al., 2005). But as noted in Chapter 2, much of this existing literature fails to capture the MNC population and thus the literature offered no representative picture of MNCs' ER policies and practices in Ireland until now.

In order to address this debate on whether MNCs are engaging with trade unions in Ireland, respondents were asked if they recognised trade unions for the purposes of collective employee representation for all their employees. We found that 61 per cent of all MNCs operating in Ireland recognised trade unions at one or more sites. This figure is much higher than findings in a parallel study in the UK (Edwards, et al., 2007) which found 47 per cent of MNCs recognised a trade union[i]. Breaking this down further, 25 per cent of MNCs recognised trade unions at all of their sites, 15 per cent at their sole Irish site, and 21 per cent at some or most of their sites. The figure of 61 per cent of MNCs engaging with trade unions is quite high given that much of the extant research often depicts MNCs as union-avoiders; for example, Cooke (2001) noted that foreign-owned MNCs have become more and more aggressive in their efforts to avoid union representation. We point towards a number of reasons, mainly related to the parameters of the research, which explain this high figure. The first issue relates to the size thresholds used in our definition of a MNC. Our focus was on the investigation of relatively large firms – large in terms of employment numbers - which is particularly noteworthy in the area of ER, as the literature would suggest that larger firms have a higher propensity to recognise trade unions (Beaumont and Harris, 1989; Roche, 2001). The second reason relates to the level at which the research was conducted. Unlike much of the previous literature, the focus of our investigation was at an organisational level rather than establishment level which characterised the previous literature. As a result, where a multi-site MNC recognised a trade union at just one site, this case was categorised as a unionised MNC. Additionally, the coverage of foreign-owned and Irish-owned MNCs was greater than previous studies, with the result that they have had quite a positive effect on the numbers engaging with trade unions. For example, among foreign-owned MNCs, we covered firms operating in sectors which have often not been captured in the extant literature (i.e., MNCs operating in sectors which have traditionally not been aided by Ireland's industrial promotions agencies). Specifically, we point towards MNCs in the retail and leisure sectors, where many of these MNCs are of UK origin and, as seen below, are characterised by comparatively high levels of union recognition. We also captured a greater number of Irish-owned MNCs and, as seen below, they are much more likely to recognise trade unions.

As depicted by table 6.1, there is a discernible pattern of union recognition, varying according to the country of origin of the MNC. At the broad level, foreign-owned MNCs were much less likely to recognise trade unions (56 per cent) than their Irish counterparts (81 per cent). This contrasts sharply with Geary and Roche (2001) who found that foreign-owned MNCs were much more likely to recognise trade unions than Irish firms. Breaking this down further we find that Irish MNCs were the most likely to recognise trade unions (81 per cent), followed by MNCs from the UK (80 per cent) and the rest of Europe (70 per cent) whereas US MNCs (42 per cent) and MNCs from the rest of the world (43 per cent) were least likely to engage with trade unions. These findings follow a similar pattern to those in the parallel study of MNCs in the UK, which found that US MNCs were also the least likely to recognise trade unions (Edwards et al., 2007). Also, US MNCs preference for not recognising trade unions in Ireland has been acknowledged in the Irish ER literature (Gunnigle,

1995, Turner et al., 1997a&b, Geary and Roche, 2001, Gunnigle et al., 2005) and, as such, it is of no surprise that they are the least likely to engage with unions. In relation to high union engagement figures among Irish and UK-owned MNCs, it appears that "the pluralist traditions of both the Irish and UK ER [employment relations] systems appear to resonate amongst MNCs from these systems" (Lavelle, 2008: 58).

There is some debate over the impact of sector on trade union recognition among firms operating in Ireland. For example, Roche and Turner (1994) pointed towards the important impact sector has on trade union recognition in their analysis, whereas Turner et al. (1997) found no evidence of an impact of sector on union recognition levels among foreign-owned firms in Ireland. We find quite a significant sectoral effect with union recognition highest among MNCs in the manufacturing sector (74 per cent) and also MNCs operating in multiple sectors (79 per cent), compared with 48 per cent of services sector MNCs recognising a trade union. This sectoral effect is consistent with the findings in the parallel UK study, where union recognition was more than twice as common amongst manufacturing MNCs compared with those in services.

Table 6.1 Trade union recognition by country of origin

	UK	US	Rest of Europe	Ireland	Rest of World	Total
No sites	20%	58%	30%	19%	57%	39%
Some sites	14%	12%	11%	9%	7%	11%
Most sites	3%	10%	8%	21%	0%	10%
All sites	51%	6%	25%	47%	7%	25%
Single Irish site	11%	14%	25%	4%	29%	15%

We also investigated Irish-owned policy on union recognition overseas by asking respondents if their foreign operations recognised unions for the purposes of collective employee representation. We found that Irish-owned MNCs were less likely to recognise unions in their foreign operations, compared with their Irish operations, with over four in ten (43 per cent) Irish MNCs not recognising unions in their foreign operations (see figure 6.1). This low level of recognition amongst its foreign operations is in contrast to the high level of recognition in Ireland, as outlined above. One plausible explanation for this is Irish MNCs have a long tradition of dealing with trade unions in Ireland but the same pressures, be they legal or otherwise, may not exist to engage with trade unions in their host environment. A further possible explanation is that Irish MNCs are relatively new in terms of locating overseas, and much of this overseas investment has occurred at a time when trade union density levels have fallen globally (Visser, 2006).

Figure 6.1 Union recognition in foreign operations of Irish MNCs

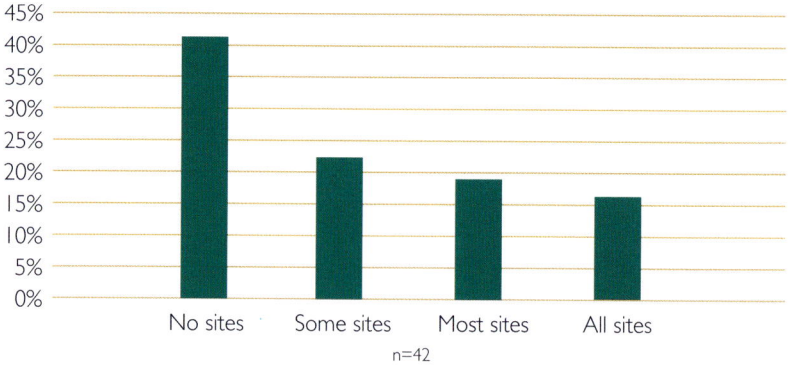

n=42

We also asked Irish MNCs about their policy towards trade union recognition in their foreign operations, see figure 6.2. A large majority (45 per cent) of Irish MNCs reported that they expected their foreign operations to follow local practices, 16 per cent reported that there was a policy not to recognise trade unions in their foreign operations, a further 16 per cent reported there was a policy to recognise trade unions, whilst 23 per cent reported there was no policy. Thus it would appear that there is no strong pressure either to engage or not engage with trade unions in Irish MNCs overseas operations, but rather that is a decision for local management.

Figure 6.2 Irish MNCs foreign policy on trade union recognition

n=44

Where trade unions are recognised, there appears to be a preference for recognising a single union, with 43 per cent of all unionised MNCs recognising one union, compared with 29 per cent recognising two unions and 28 per cent recognising three or more unions. One possible explanation for this 'single union' preference is offered by Murray (1984), cited in Roche and Geary (1996), where he found multiple unionism was associated with higher levels of industrial action, particularly within firms that had two or more unions. There appears to be a country of origin effect, whereby 48 per cent of all foreign-owned MNCs recognise only one union compared with just 28 per cent of Irish MNCs. This is consistent with the literature suggesting foreign-owned companies' preferences for single union deals (Gunnigle, 1993; Geary and Roche, 2001). For example Geary and Roche (2001) found that US firms and other foreign-owned firms were, respectively, five times and two times more likely to have single unions. Fifty six per cent of MNCs operating in multiple sectors recognised one union compared with 44 per cent of services sector MNCs and 40 per cent of manufacturing MNCs.

We also found quite a high level of trade union density[ii] in MNCs, with a majority (53 per cent of all MNCs) reporting that over half of their employees' were members of a trade union, whilst more than a quarter of MNCs reported that 75 per cent or more of their employees' were members of a trade union (see figure 6.3). These figures are similar to those found in the latest Cranfield-University of Limerick (UL) survey (1999) (see Morley et al., 2001), where over half of the respondents said over half of their workforce belonged to a trade union. Slight differences are recorded at the higher end of union density (76-100 per cent) between the Cranfield-UL study and these findings, where 35 per cent of firms reported density levels greater than 76 per cent (Morley et al., 2001). However, these figures are substantially lower than those reported by Geary and Roche (2001) who found high union density levels (over 75 per cent), ranging from 88 per cent to 93 per cent of all firms. Lower union density figures were reported amongst US MNCs, where only 10 per cent of US MNCs had union density above 75 per cent, similar to previous evidence (Gunnigle et al., 1997). As anticipated, union density was much higher amongst MNCs in the manufacturing sector, with almost a third (31 per cent) having 75 per cent or more of their employees in trade union membership, compared with 23 per cent in services sector MNCs and 21 per cent in multi-sector MNCs. This finding is consistent with previous evidence Gunnigle et al., (1997) and is rather unsurprising given that services sector MNCs are much more likely to have part-time employees, and they as a group, are less likely to be union members (Roche, 2001).

Figure 6.3 Trade union density

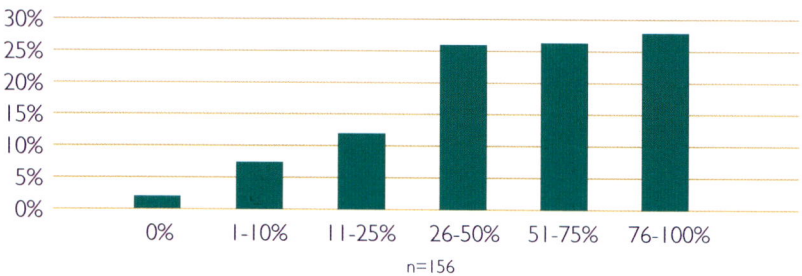

n=156

MNCs that engage with trade unions were asked whether trade union representatives generally adopted a cooperative approach, an adversarial approach or if their approach depended on the issue. Almost half (49 per cent) of the respondents replied that it depended on the issue whilst 46 per cent reported a cooperative approach. Only 5 per cent reported that trade unions adopted an adversarial approach. The following qualitative quote, regarding the relationship between MNCs and trade unions, was gathered during the fieldwork:

> "We have no issues with unions. They have a good shop steward and we work well together…they don't cause too many problems".
> **UK Manufacturing MNC**

These findings are not all that surprising. For instance Geary and Roche (2001) reported a high incidence of respondents saying there were good or very good relations between management and unions. UK MNCs were more likely to report a cooperative approach (67 per cent), whilst only 32 per cent of Irish MNCs reported a similar approach. Geary and Roche (2001) also found that Irish-owned firms were the least likely to report good or very good relations between management and unions. Services sector MNCs were marginally more likely to report a cooperative approach (52 per cent), than manufacturing MNCs (43 per cent) and multi-sector MNCs (39 per cent).

Non-union structures of collective employee representation

Given the quite significant and prominent role played by trade unions in Ireland over the last century, it is unsurprising that very little focus has been paid to non-union structures of employee representation. Geary (2007:98) outlines that employee voice in Ireland has largely been seen as "…synonymous with union voice". However, two important changes have occurred within the Irish ER system in recent times that have brought the attention of non-union structures to academics and practitioners alike. First, there has been a decline in trade union recognition levels and more of a focus on alternative structures to employee representation. One particular high-profile case is that of the Irish MNC *Ryanair*, where their non-union structures of representation have received quite a lot of attention. *Ryanair* challenged an Irish Labour Court ruling in a dispute over union recognition where it successfully argued that its non-union body was an acceptable structure to represent its employees (Fitzgerald, 2007). The second development has been the implementation of the Information and Consultation Directive (2002/14/EC) (see below for further discussion). This Directive provides statutory provision for information and consultation structures within organisations with explicit reference to employee representative structures, be they union or non-union variety.

We sought to investigate the incidence of such structures among MNCs in Ireland and asked if they had any non-union based structure(s) of collective employee representation, such as works committees or company councils. Just under a third (32 per cent) of MNCs indicated that they had some structure in place, with almost six in ten (59 per cent) MNCs indicating these structures had been established in the previous three years. These findings are similar to those pertaining in existing research (Gunnigle et al., 1997; Turner et al., 1997a&b; Geary and Roche, 2001) but contrast with more recent work by Geary (2007), who found that employee consultative committees were quite rare in Ireland (Geary, 2007), with just 14 per cent reporting the existence of employee consultative committees. It is interesting to note that these non-union structures are of recent vintage and one could plausibly explain this by the legitimisation of these non-union structures (e.g. Ryanair) within the Irish ER landscape and also the impact of the EU Information and Consultation Directive. One respondent noted that:

> "Due to the new EU Directive [Information and Consultation Directive] we established a staff forum which consists of employee representatives meeting once a week to discuss issues related to major changes".
> **US Services MNC**

MNCs from the US and also the rest of the world were marginally more likely to have these structures in place, which is in contrast to the UK findings where both these groups were the least likely to have such structures, whilst Irish MNCs were the least likely to report such structures. This contrast between foreign and Irish-owned MNCs is consistent with previous literature on these types of structures with Geary and Roche (2001) and Geary (2007) pointing to similar trends. Services sector MNCs were also marginally more likely to have such structures in place. As expected, non-union structures were most common in MNCs which did not engage in union recognition; however, it is interesting that over a quarter of unionised MNCs (27 per cent) had such structures in place.

Combining both union and non-union structures almost a quarter (23 per cent) of all MNCs had neither union nor non-union structures in their organisation (see table 6.2). 16 per cent had non-union only structures, 16 per cent had a hybrid model which includes both union and non-union structures, whilst 45 per cent of MNCs had union structures only. Similar to the results of the UK study, US MNCs were the least likely to have any form of representative structures. Irish and UK owned MNCs were much more likely to have union forms of collective employee representation. Manufacturing and services sector MNCs were much more likely to have 'union only' representative structures in place, with non-union structures more prevalent in services sector MNCs as compared to manufacturing and multi-sector MNCs.

Table 6.2 Union and non-union structures of representation by country of origin

	UK	US	Rest of Europe	Ireland	Rest of World	Total
Neither union or non-union structures	9%	34%	21%	11%	29%	23%
Union only structures	66%	25%	52%	64%	36%	45%
Non-union only structures	11%	24%	10%	9%	29%	16%
Hybrid: union & non-union structures	14%	17%	17%	17%	7%	16%

Trade union recognition in new sites

The issue of trade union avoidance among firms has a long history with characterisation of such strategies ranging from trade union suppression to trade union substitution. Gunnigle et al. (2009) note that whilst these categorisations, 'suppression versus substitution', provide a useful framework for analysing union avoidance strategies by employers, they suffer from some significant drawbacks. Specifically by focusing on the above direct employer opposition strategies, more subtle and indirect forms union resistance are missed (Gunnigle et al., 2009). A key body of literature in this regard looks at the issue of 'double-breasting', a subtle form of union avoidance (cf. Lipsky and Farber, 1976; Doherty, 1989;

Beaumont and Harris, 1992; Northrup, 1995; Gunnigle et al., 2009). Double-breasting refers to the practice whereby multi-establishment organisations simultaneously operate establishments on both a union and non-union basis in a particular host environment. Beaumont and Harris' (1992) work on double-breasting arrangements in the UK has been particularly useful by outlining the forms that double breasting might take - namely unionised companies (a) opening a new operation on a non-union basis and/or (b) acquiring an existing non-union company and continuing to operate it on a non-union basis. We investigated the incidence of double-breasting, among MNCs in Ireland by asking unionised MNCs if (i) they recognised trade unions in their new sites (greenfield sites) and (ii) if they have acquired union or non-union sites and if they continued to run these sites on that basis.

Looking at double-breasting through the establishment of greenfield sites, we find that 53 unionised MNCs had established a new site, with 51 per cent recognising trade unions in all of these new sites. Just under a quarter (23 per cent) recognised unions at some/most of their new sites with 26 per cent of MNCs not recognising unions at any of their new sites. Thus, while 23 per cent recognised unions at some of their new sites, by default this means they also *do not* recognise unions at some of their other new sites. Coupled with MNCs not recognising unions at any of their new sites, we found that 49 per cent of all MNCs in total were engaging in some form of double-breasting.

Figure 6.4 Engaging in double breasting (greenfield) by country of origin

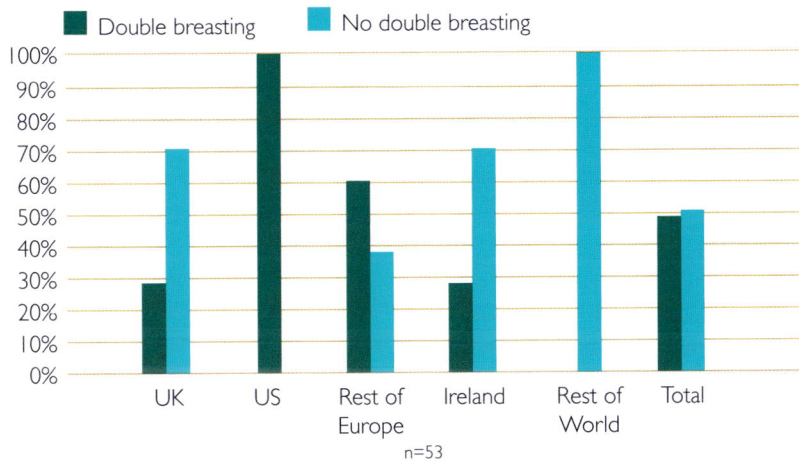

n=53

As illustrated in figure 6.4, there is a strong country of origin effect. Irish (71 per cent) and UK MNCs (71 per cent) establishing operations on new sites were much more likely to recognise unions at each of these new sites. In contrast, US MNCs were least likely to recognise unions in their new sites with 80 per cent not recognising unions at any of their new sites (the remaining 20 per cent only recognised unions in some/most sites). Furthermore MNCs operating in manufacturing (78 per cent) and multiple sectors (71 per cent) were the most likely to engage in double breasting compared to MNCs operating in the services sector (38 per cent).

We now turn to the incidence of double-breasting through the form of merger or acquisition. MNCs were asked if they had acquired any new sites in Ireland over the previous five years and if they had, whether the acquired sites were unionised or not. From this we established whether MNCs were engaging in double-breasting through the form of acquisition or merger. A total of 45 unionised MNCs reported that they had acquired sites over the past five years. Just under half (48 per cent) of MNCs are not engaging in double-breasting, with the remaining 52 per cent engaging in double-breasting. In regard to country of origin effects, we found that US MNCs are more likely to engage in double breasting through acquisition (64 per cent), with Irish MNCs also quite likely to engage in double breasting (56 per cent) -- see figure 6.5. MNCs operating in the services sector were more likely to engage in double breasting (63 per cent) compared to MNCs operating in multiple and manufacturing sectors. Thus the impact of sector appears to be significant in explaining patterns of trade union representation in acquired sites.

Figure 6.5 Engaging in double breasting (acquisition) by country of origin

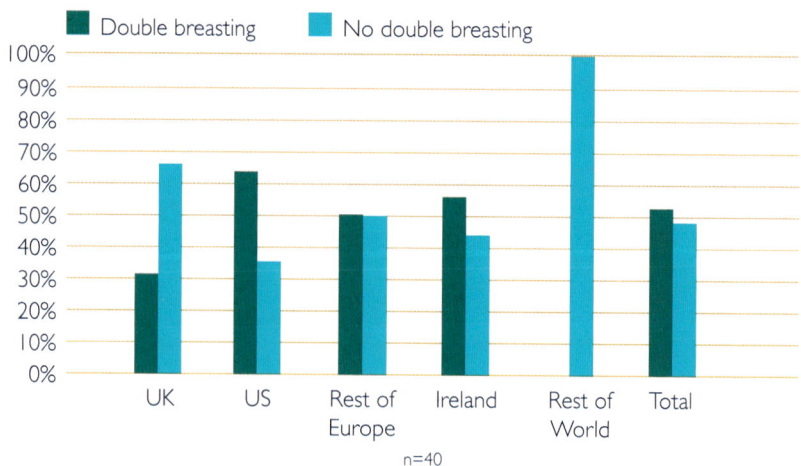

n=40

In summary, we point towards quite a significant number of MNCs engaging in double-breasting, by means of the establishment of the new greenfield sites and/or merger or acquisition. This is consistent with an earlier survey carried out by Industrial Relations News which looked at unionisation and new job announcements among MNCs between 2001 and 2003. They found that just 18 per cent of MNCs that were expanding their operations in Ireland intended on recognising trade unions in these sites (Higgins, 2004). One of the more common themes amongst these findings is that US MNCs are the most likely to engage in double-breasting either through greenfield and/or merger/acquisition. This finding is unexpected given that US MNCs are less likely to engage with trade unions. Furthermore it is consistent with previous case study analysis of US MNCs operating in Ireland, where Gunnigle et al. (2005) first pointed towards this trend of double-breasting in Ireland. Indeed these findings are a worrying concern for trade union penetration among MNCs in Ireland. Whilst unions have struggled to gain a foothold in newer-investing MNCs, they were safe in the knowledge that they had a strong base among traditional existing MNCs. Coupled with the policy of the promotional agencies to expand existing MNCs, the future for unions in MNCs appeared quite bright. However our findings illustrate a much different scenario developing, one which is of major concern for trade unions. As noted by Gunnigle et al. (2005: 251), "Union penetration is being challenged at two critical junctures in the FDI 'life cycle'— among new inward investing MNCs, and now in longer established MNCs which are increasing their foothold in the country". This is quite a significant development in the Irish ER system and it is a trend that is likely to continue.

Collective bargaining

Colling et al. (2006) note that the strongest indicator of trade union influence is that of collective bargaining. Within Ireland, collective bargaining has traditionally been seen as the primary means of managing relations among employees, unions and employers (Gunnigle et al., 2006). MNCs that recognise unions were asked what percentage of their largest occupational group (LOG) were covered by collective bargaining arrangements. Almost seven in ten MNCs (69 per cent) reported that over three-quarters of their LOG were covered by such arrangements. Overall, collective bargaining occurs in over 90 per cent of unionised MNCs, a figure similar to that in the parallel UK survey (Edwards et al., 2007). As illustrated by table 6.3, the coverage of collective bargaining is higher amongst Irish, UK and European MNCs. This is in contrast to Geary and Roche (2001), who found that a greater percentage of US-owned firms engaged in collective bargaining compared against Irish-owned firms. Almost eight in ten manufacturing MNCs (79 per cent) had collective bargaining coverage greater than 75 per cent compared with 57 per cent amongst services sector MNCs and 63 per cent of MNCs operating in multiple sectors. In summary, the high levels of coverage of collective bargaining within unionised MNCs would indicate a strong influence by unions in these organisations.

Table 6.3 Coverage of collective bargaining by country of origin (Union only)

	UK	US	Rest of Europe	Ireland	Rest of World	Total
0%	7%	12%	12%	3%	17%	9%
1-10%	4%	0%	2%	0%	0%	1%
11-25%	4%	7%	5%	9%	17%	7%
26-50%	0%	12%	5%	6%	0%	6%
51-75%	15%	5%	5%	9%	17%	8%
76-100%	70%	63%	71%	73%	50%	69%

The determination of pay increases

Table 6.4 Agreements or procedures used for the determination of pay increases

LOG	Agreements for determination of pay increases	Managers
79%	National Level Collective Bargaining	28%
7%	Industry Level Collective Bargaining	1%
13%	Company/division	15%
6%	Establishment/site	4%
8%	Individual	66%
4%	Other	6%

Since 1987, Ireland has witnessed a return to centralised bargaining where trade unions, employer representatives and the government have negotiated national pay deals which include, among other issues, basic wage increases. However, a range of mechanisms can be used in the determination of pay increases and we investigate the incidence of such mechanisms among MNCs operating in Ireland. This question was asked of respondents in relation to their managerial and LOG staff. As depicted in table 6.4, the most popular method of pay determination for managers was that of "individual", whilst for the LOG it was "national level collective bargaining". These findings are consistent with those of Gunnigle et al. (1997) who found that managerial pay was determined at a company or individual level, whilst for manual employees pay was determined at the national level. However, the use of national level collective bargaining was also quite high for managers. We point to quite a significant sectoral effect. 92 per cent of manufacturing MNCs reported that they used national level collective bargaining for their LOG, against 68 per cent of services sector MNCs and 65 per cent of multi-sector MNCs.

Table 6.5 The use of national level collective bargaining agreements (Union only)

LOG	National wage agreements (unionised MNCs)	Managers
81%	Follow closely the terms of agreement	76%
17%	Paid somewhat above the terms	24%
2%	Paid somewhat below the terms	0%

Where "national level collective bargaining" was used MNCs were asked about their policy towards the national agreements (see table 6.5). There has been a history of many companies, particularly among large MNCs, of agreeing 'above the norm (ATN)' pay deals whereby companies will pay above the terms of these national wage agreements. For example Sheehan (1996), cited in Roche and Geary (1996), identified a small number of companies in the pharmaceutical and chemical sector in the Cork region that paid above the terms of the agreements. Geary and Roche (2001) identified between 30 and 66 per cent (depending on country of origin) of companies gave pay awards which exceeded the national pay agreements. More recently, an Industrial Relations News report in 2005 concluded that number of 'above the norm' pay deals under the national agreement 'Sustaining Progress', although lower than the previous wage agreement (the Programme for Prosperity and Fairness), was higher than under the other national deals (Dobbins, 2005). We found that a high proportion of MNCs reported that they followed closely the terms of the agreement for both managers (76 per cent) and their LOG (81 per cent). Almost a quarter (24 per cent) of MNCs that used "national level collective bargaining" to determine pay increases for managers paid somewhat above the terms of the agreement, compared with 17 per cent for the LOG. Just 2 per cent of MNCs using "national level collective bargaining" for the LOG reported that they paid somewhat below the terms of the agreement. Overall, these findings are somewhat lower than that of Geary and Roche (2001) but consistent with recent work by Gunnigle et al. (2005) who noted a similar trend in their case study analysis of US-owned MNCs, whereby these MNCs had traditionally agreed ATN deals but in more recent times had rowed back on this policy and decided to follow the terms much more closely. Given the worsening economic climate in recent months, one would anticipate a sharp fall in the number of MNCs agreeing these ATN deals.

UK MNCs were more likely to pay somewhat above the terms of the agreements for their managerial staff only. MNCs operating in the services and multi-sectors were also more likely to pay above the norm for its managerial staff only.

We also investigated the impact of national level pay (partnership) agreements on non-union MNCs. Non-union MNCs were first asked if the national agreements influenced decisions regarding pay increases. Six in ten non-union MNCs reported that the national agreements had some influence on pay decisions regarding the LOG and almost half (48 per cent) on pay decisions with regard to managers. These findings are unsurprising given the prominent role these agreements have in the Irish ER system. Further we found that these agreements were much more influential for manual labour:

"The non union plants say that national level agreements have no influence on pay decisions for managers but have a major influence regarding the LOG".

US Manufacturing MNC

Table 6.6 The use of national level collective bargaining agreements (Non-union only)

LOG	National wage agreements (non-union MNCs)	Managers
38%	Follow closely the terms of agreement	34%
56%	Paid somewhat above the terms	61%
5%	Paid somewhat below the terms	5%

As depicted by table 6.6, those MNCs that reported national agreements as having an influence were much more likely to pay somewhat above the terms of the agreement, with 61 per cent of all managers being paid above the norm and 56 per cent of LOG likewise. Thus, what we find is that non-union MNCs are much more likely to pay above the terms of national agreements than unionised MNCs. This trend is consistent with existing case study research which suggested that non-union MNCs used the national agreements as external benchmarks for pay increases and often paid above the average level of increase contained in the agreements (Collings et al., 2008a). One possible reason for this is that non-union MNCs often use a higher level of pay as a union avoidance strategy. This theme was raised in one of the interviews:

"Although we strictly do not look at the national level agreements here in this non-union plant we do take account of them and we ensure we pay above it. It is a type of union avoidance strategy so to speak".
US Manufacturing MNC

UK MNCs were less likely to pay above the norm for their managerial staff (33 per cent) compared with US (69 per cent), European (55 per cent), rest of world (75 per cent) and Irish (71 per cent) and also for their LOG, UK (20 per cent), US (58 per cent), European (55 per cent), rest of world (80 per cent) and Irish (63 per cent).

Employer associations

Marginson and Meardi (2006) suggest that foreign investors have generally avoided joining indigenous employers' organisations; this however is not the case in Ireland. An overwhelmingly majority (92 per cent) of MNCs were members of an employer association, with IBEC (86 per cent of all MNCs) being the preferred choice of the great majority. Manufacturing MNCs were slightly more likely to be a member of IBEC with 94 per cent of MNCs a member compared with 90 per cent of services sector MNCs and 92 per cent of multi-sector. These findings are consistent with much of the previous literature which reports high levels of membership of employer associations (Geary and Roche, 2001; Gunnigle et al., 2001). We also found that 96 per cent of unionised MNCs were a member of an employer association versus 85 per cent of non-union MNCs. Whilst there is some level of difference, it is quite minimal which suggests that non-union MNCs are almost as likely to be a member of an employer association (a trade union for employers) as unionised MNCs. The enthusiasm of non-unionised MNCs to be a member of an employer association is quite surprising given that Wallace *et al.* (2004: 164) note that "membership…suggests an approach to industrial relations which emphasises the role of collectives or combinations as opposed to individuals". Thus, one could expect that joining an employer association would be against the philosophy of these types of non-union MNCs, but the evidence suggests otherwise. One plausible explanation for the high membership levels of employer associations is that there is a political advantage to be gained by being a member. For example, similar to the role of trade unions in Ireland, IBEC plays a significant role in the political, social and economic environment in Ireland and is one of the key social partners involved in the negotiation of national pay agreements. Thus membership of an employer association like IBEC affords MNCs a key role in decision-making on economic and social issues within Ireland which they otherwise would not have access to.

Figure 6.6 Employer Associations

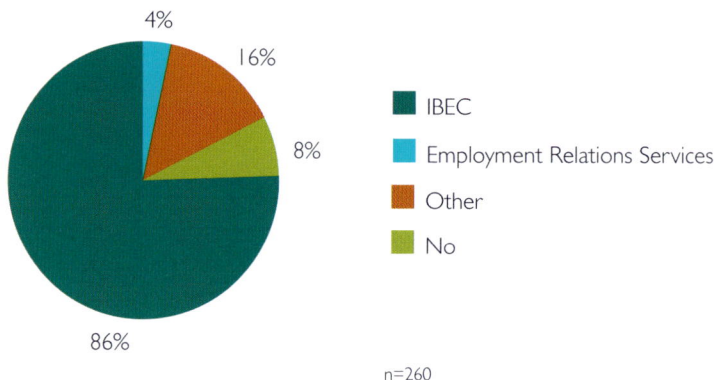

- **IBEC**
- **Employment Relations Services**
- **Other**
- **No**

4%
16%
8%
86%

n=260

Information and consultation

Figure 6.7 Provision of information and consultation

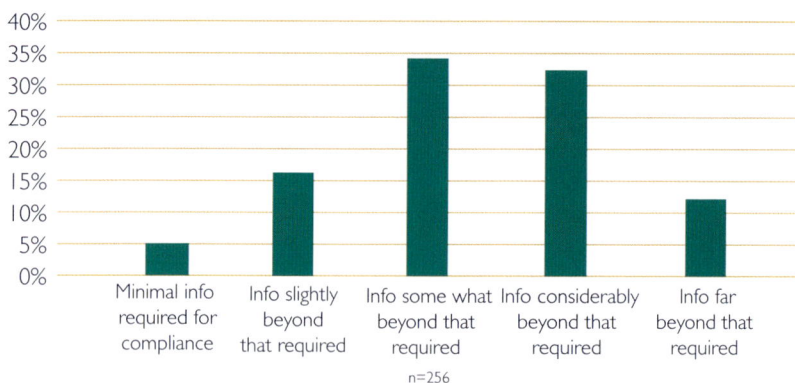

Minimal info required for compliance	Info slightly beyond that required	Info some what beyond that required	Info considerably beyond that required	Info far beyond that required

n=256

The provision of information and consultation to employees has become an area of interest in the last decade, particularly with the implementation of the European Works Council and Information and Consultation Directives. We investigated how much information and consultation is provided to employees by asking respondents about management approach to the area of information and consultation. As depicted by figure 6.7, just over a third of MNCs (34 per cent) claimed to provide "information somewhat beyond that required" with a further 33 per cent providing information considerably beyond that required and 12 per cent providing information far beyond that required. It would appear that MNCs are quite happy to provide a relatively high level of provision of information and consultation to employees.

The Information and Consultation (I&C) Directive (2002/14/EC) was introduced into Irish law on a phased basis by the Employees (Provision of Information and Consultation) Act, 2006. It provides a legislative framework for the provision of I&C structures within organisations, thus providing employees with a legal right to be informed and consulted on a range of issues such as business and employment matters, representing a significant departure from the voluntarist tradition of the Irish ER system (Dundon et al., 2006). Respondents were asked if this Directive had prompted any changes in arrangements for employee consultation. Forty two per cent of all MNCs reported that indeed the Directive had prompted changes in arrangements for employee consultation. This is quite similar to the parallel survey in the UK where 37 per cent of MNCs imitated that the Directive had prompted changes in arrangements. Within Ireland, some initial reports suggested that there was a low uptake of information and consultation arrangements between employers and employees (Industrial Relations News, 2007). More generally, research on the impact of the Directive on national ER systems by the European Foundation for the Improvement of Living and Working Conditions (EFILWC) acknowledged that whilst it is very early to provide an definitive conclusions on the impact of the Directive that early indications were that the Directive has had very little impact on national IR systems (EFILWC, 2008). However, in Ireland we find that Directive has impacted upon MNCs arrangements for information and consultation. Although representing a departure from the traditional ER system it is not all that surprising that MNCs have embraced the Directive given that they had a significant input into the drafting of the transposed legislation in Ireland, predominantly through the lobbying efforts of the American Chamber of Commerce of Ireland (Industrial Relations News, 2005). Quite a strong country of origin effect is noted. Only 18 per cent of Irish MNCs reported changes compared with 30 per cent of UK MNCs, 54 per cent of US MNCs, 43 per cent European MNCs and 57 per cent of rest of world MNCs. Thus where changes have occurred, these have been predominantly being in foreign-owned MNCs.

European Works Councils

The European Works Councils (EWCs) Directive (94/45/EC) sets out the requirements for companies with operations in the EU to establish a European Works Councils which brings worker representatives together to discuss issues affecting the company and its workers. Similar to non-union structures of employee representation very little is known about the incidence of EWCs in

Ireland. Our findings show that four in ten MNCs (40 per cent) had a EWC in place, greater than that reported in the parallel survey in the UK which found a EWC present in 28 per cent of cases. This finding is also considerably more than what the European Trade Union Institute for Research, Education and Health and Safety (ETUI-REHS) found, where they noted only 14 per cent of eligible companies in Ireland had a EWC, compared with an overall EU average of 35 per cent (Industrial Relations News, 2006). As depicted by figure 6.8, European MNCs were more likely to have a EWC (53 per cent) with Irish MNCs the least likely to have a EWC (17 per cent). The low level of EWCs reported by Irish MNCs is consistent with O'Hagan (2005) in an investigation of the implementation of the EWC Directive in Ireland, which found that out of a possible 40 MNCs stating their country of origin was Ireland, just five had established a EWC (Kerckhofs, 2002). She observed that compared to other member states this is a very low 'hit rate' (O'Hagan, 2005; 399). So again we find quite a high incidence of EWCs, but predominantly within foreign-owned MNCs. Couple this finding with the recent impact of the EU Information and Consultation Directive, it appears that foreign-owned MNCs are much more comfortable with these types of structures than Irish MNCs. One could argue that this is unsurprising given that these types of structures have very little tradition in Ireland. MNCs operating in the services sector were the least likely to have a EWC (28 per cent). This is unsurprising as MNCs operating in the manufacturing sector have a stronger tradition of representative structures than their services sector counterparts. Indeed one services sector MNC provided an insight into the workings of a EWC within the services sector:

> *"In terms of the EWC, we have one Irish representative but nothing ever comes about of it…No one wanted the position of Irish representative, the unions didn't even want to push it, in the end a manager took the position. The reason being that there is so many part-time workers and these workers don't want to be going away to England or wherever on their day off".*
> **UK Services MNC**

Those MNCs that did not have a EWC in place were asked if they anticipated one being established in the future; just 21 per cent indicated that a EWC may be established in the future. Thus it appears that the incidence of EWCs may have hit a peak with very little enthusiasm among MNCs that don't have such structures to introduce them.

Those MNCs which reported the presence of a EWC were asked about the nature of the EWC structure. As depicted by figure 6.9, almost seven in ten (69 per cent) provide information somewhat beyond that required or greater, with

27 per cent providing information considerably beyond that required and only 7 per cent providing information far beyond that required. Both Irish and European MNCs were less likely to provide information somewhat beyond that required or greater when compared to UK, US and rest of world MNCs. This finding contrasts with that of Waddington (2001) who suggested that the provision of 'useful' information and the occurrence of consultation are less widespread among MNCs based in the UK and the US than among companies headquartered in continental European countries (Marginson et al., 2004). Services sector MNCs provided slightly less information than MNCs operating in the other two sectors.

Figure 6.8 European Works Councils (EWC) by country of origin

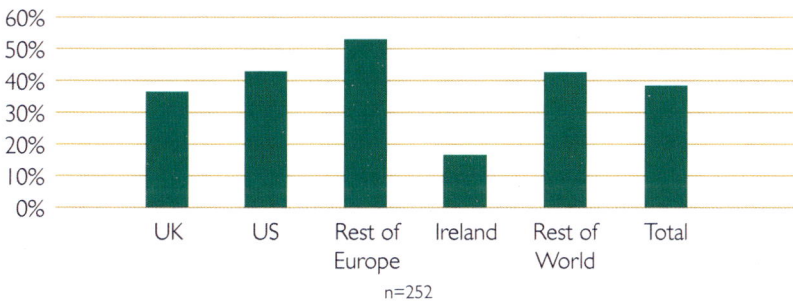

n=252

Figure 6.9 Provision of information and consultation with European Works Council

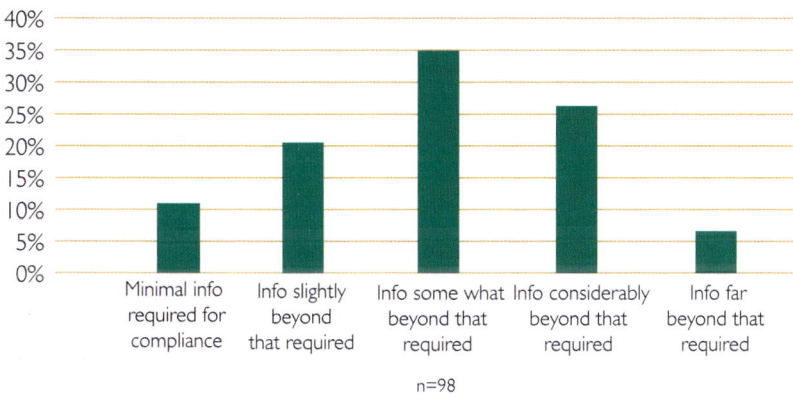

n=98

Conclusion

This chapter has reviewed the findings on employee representation and consultation in both foreign and Irish-owned MNCs operating in Ireland. What we found is that MNCs operating in Ireland are reporting relatively high levels of union engagement, with evidence of country of origin and sectoral effects. For example, we found high levels of trade union recognition amongst Irish, UK and European MNCs but low levels of recognition among US MNCs. Furthermore, manufacturing MNCs had a much higher propensity to recognise unions than MNCs operating in the services sector. Whilst Irish MNCs reported high levels of union recognition in Ireland, we identify a very different story abroad with a large number of Irish MNCs reporting non-recognition of unions in their foreign operations. Coupled with high levels of union recognition, we also found union density figures to be quite high. Strong collective bargaining coverage is also reported with it being highest in Irish, UK and European MNCs. There is also a sectoral effect with it being high amongst manufacturing MNCs. We also provided evidence of innovations with regard to collective employee representation in MNCs in Ireland. First, we saw a growth in non-union structures of employee representation, particularly over the past three years. Second, we found evidence of 'double-breasting', particularly among US MNCs. In terms of pay determination, a significant majority of MNCs used national level collective bargaining for the LOG and individual mechanisms for their managerial staff. Concentrating on the influence of national level agreements on pay in MNCs, we found differences between unionised and non-unionised MNCs. Unionised MNCs are much more likely to follow the terms of these national agreements whereas non-unionised MNCs are more likely to report paying above the terms of the agreements.

With regard to information and consultation, MNCs in Ireland reported high levels of information and consultation provision, with almost half reporting that the Information and Consultation Directive had initiated changes in employee consultation in their organisation. A significant minority of MNCs also reported having a European Works Council (EWC) in place, again with a discernible country of origin effect.

In conclusion, whilst we found relatively high levels of union recognition, union density and collective bargaining coverage, our findings suggest significant innovations in the area of employee representation and consultation.

ENDNOTES

[i]   This figure only relates to representation regarding the largest occupational group (LOG). That said, where unions are recognised the vast majority of members tend to be employees from the LOG.

[ii]   Not all MNCs are reporting for all Irish operations, a minority of MNCs only reported for a part or division only.

CHAPTER 7
Employee Involvement
and Communication

Joseph Wallace, Jonathan Lavelle, Anthony McDonnell
& Patrick Gunnigle

Introduction

Employee involvement is defined as any mechanism which provides for involvement in decisions affecting employees' jobs and immediate work environment, including formally designated teams, problem solving groups, attitude surveys, suggestion schemes, appraisal systems and meetings between managers and workers. The term employee involvement is one of a number used to describe employee engagement in the workplace. The most generic term used is "participation" but employee involvement and participation are frequently interchanged with one another. While participation is the more generic term, the use of a single term masks a wide variety of employee engagement options ranging across a continuum of worker control, industrial democracy, co-determination, collective bargaining, consultation, empowerment and employee involvement (Heller, et al., 1998). The differences in terms reflect a range of ideological perspectives from the left to the right and a concern with competing objectives. Writing of participation, Heller *et al.* (1998:1) note that "some proponents advocate it as a way of increasing productivity; others consider it to be desirable on a level of political democracy". These different orientations find expression in the distinct employment relations systems in which participation takes place. Thus, the industrial democracy/co-determination dimension is strongest in the Northern European context, most notably in Germany, Netherlands and Scandinavia. Employee involvement, on the other hand, is associated with the American and UK models of employment relations. Its introduction is at management's discretion, while industrial democracy and co-determination is legislatively based.

Irish contemporary trends: an overview

Ireland has seen considerable interest over the last 25 years in mechanisms for employee involvement, such as teamwork and for direct communications with employees. In an Irish context, direct forms of involvement have been favoured by the main Irish employers' organisation, the Irish Business and Employers Organisation (IBEC) and have been cited as examples of the development of partnership at the enterprise level (IBEC, 1999). This partnership contrasts with the representative forms of workplace partnership promoted by the trade union movement in Ireland. Involvement is direct, rather than representative, takes place at management's discretion and is task-based (Roche and Geary, 2002). In common with international trends, previous Irish studies have indicated an increase of direct and task-based forms of employee involvement in recent times. Roche and Geary (2001) note the growth in involvement and suggest voice mechanisms (team briefing, attitude surveys, employee involvement, suggestion schemes) in particular were more likely to be used in foreign-owned workplaces. Nor is such direct involvement confined to non-union establishments. Roche and Geary (1999:28) note that "direct employee involvement is common in unionised establishments and employers show a clear preference for this mode of collaborative production over partnership with unions".

Involvement and individualisation of the employment relationship

Communication and involvement schemes are synonymous with a more individualised approach to employee participation. In effect it involves direct engagement with employees, rather than through a representative forum. It is seen as reflecting the realities of changes to "new employment relations" in the last 30 years, in which trade unions have been in decline and with the representative systems of participation. As involvement is based on management discretion it reflects the need for organisational efficiency – in various guises - within a strongly competitive environment. Proponents of involvement claim it is designed to meet both employee and management needs. In this regard Heller *et al.* (1998: 1) note that between the ideological extremes discussed in the introduction above, one finds arguments for participation based on claims of "increased job satisfaction or loyalty to the organisation". They note that in so far as increased employee well being works to increase efficiency it does so through "indirect effect" (Heller et al., 1998: 1). Viewed in this way, within the continuum of participation, employee involvement straddles both the right and middle ideological terrain. It may provide improvements for both parties, leading to a win-win scenario. Not only is involvement distinguished because it is introduced at management's discretion, unlike collective bargaining and more developed forms of power–based participation, it is also distinguished by the issue of control over the final outcome. While management may decide to involve employees, they retain control over any action to be taken as a result of this involvement. Indeed it is this very control over action, which is, arguably, one of the strongest appeals involvement has for management over other forms of participation.

Trends and key issues in employee involvement

While there has undoubtedly been a growth in schemes to promote employee involvement since the 1970s, this can not be taken to imply that there is an evolutionary development over time. Instead interest in involvement tends to wax and wane in line with societal, competitive and economic factors. Jacoby (1997) notes that interest in involvement dates to the 1920s in the US being associated with "welfare capitalism". There are two main approaches that attempt to account for this variability in interest over time. Ramsay (1977) argues that involvement comes in "cycles" that coincide with the power of labour. He suggests that peaks of interest in involvement coincide with periods of labour strength and, when that power declines, interest in the latest fad quickly wanes. Marchington and Wilkinson (2005) have pointed out that the growth in interest in involvement since the 1970s can not be accounted for by the cycles approach. They have suggested a modified account based on a "waves" approach in which "patterns of EI [employee involvement] … owe as much to relations within management as they do to relations between management" (Marchington and Wilkinson 2005:401). A key driver of waves is the career aspirations of managers in various functions (Marchington et al., 1993; Marchington, (2005).

There are also a number of key issues around involvement generally and team work in particular. Firstly, introducing involvement may be risky for managers since it may raise expectations and lead to recriminations if they do not work out (Spreitzer and Mishra, 1999). Secondly, Marchington and Wilkinson (2005:412) note some studies that suggest line managers may find schemes a burden and that they "do not believe in the principles underlying direct participation – especially for more far-reaching schemes". Thirdly, the need for "champions" means that schemes are particularly vulnerable to changes in management personnel. Fourthly, there is a questioning of whether, and to what extent, involvement delivers real productivity benefits. While there are a number of studies which suggest benefits in some instances, these are not large, and there are methodological difficulties in establishing causation (Whitfield and Poole, 1997; Heller et al., 1998; Harley, 2005). Finally, there is a persistent questioning of the extent to which involvement delivers real discretion to employees as distinct from generating new forms of control and increased work intensification (Ezzamel and Willmot, 1998; Wilkinson, 1998; Ramsay and Scholarios, 1999).

Recent research claims employees tend to experience team working as a mixed blessing and conclude "in general, employees seem to welcome an increased latitude of decision making, yet have concerns about work intensification" (Benders, 2005:69). Summarising this more modest evaluation of involvement, Marchington and Wilkinson (2005) suggest that such a conclusion may not be earth shattering, but in a working environment where there is little opportunity to exercise discretion, it may improve working lives.

Team working and MNCs

It has long been noted that the country in which an MNC originates influences the way labour is managed in its international subsidiaries (Ferner, 1997). This is especially evident in the tendency for a decline in indirect participation associated with lower union recognition levels in American MNCs relative to Irish and European MNCs (De Vos, 1981; Gunnigle et al., 2005; Lavelle, 2008). However, these findings must be put in context of the likely interplay between differing voice mechanisms. Rather than being mutually exclusive, both direct and indirect forms of participation frequently co-exist in the same companies. Thus, Wood and Fenton-O'Creevy (2005:27) found that while the new employment relations thesis is confirmed when direct voice is used in isolation, "more often direct voice coexists with union and other representative channels". In this case it is the interplay between the differing voice mechanisms which becomes important (Wood and Fenton-O'Creevy, 2005). It has been accepted that there has been a growth in direct employee involvement; there is still uncertainty over the full extent of such schemes across MNCs and the extent to which MNCs lead the way in their introduction. It has been suggested there are higher levels of innovative forms of communication (typified by high levels of direct involvement) in American MNCs (Elger and Smith, 2005).

While it is widely accepted there has been a growth in direct communications schemes internationally and in Ireland, there is not a similar consensus on the incidence of team working. Benders (2005) notes the low incidence of socio-technical teams reported in the EPOC study conducted by the European Foundation for the Improvement of Living and Working Conditions. He contrasts that to the much higher 65 per cenfound in the 1998 (WERS) in the UK but notes this figure decreases progressively as one incorporates the extent of discretion given to these teams and only three per cent of teams could appoint their own leader. In Ireland, an early study in the mid-1990s by McCartney and Teague (1998) found teamwork in 27.5 per cent of establishments surveyed while the EPOC survey found team-based structures were present in 42 per cent of respondent organisations. The UCD survey conducted in 1996/1997 found a higher figure, with teamwork recorded in 59 per cent of workplaces (Roche and Geary, 1999). An IBEC (1999) survey indicated similar figures to the UCD results. It suggested that team working was the most extensive form of new work organisation and was present in 63 per cent of respondent companies.

In Ireland, Geary and Roche (1999) suggest "US-owned workplaces are considerably more likely to adopt "task-based" forms of collaborative management, as indexed by a higher incidence of such techniques as work teams,

Total Quality Management (TQM), and *ad hoc* task forces in all workplaces, as well as quality circles in unionised workplaces". Their UCD survey found that "US-owned workplaces were more than twice as likely to have had team-working and to have permitted individual employees discretion to organise their own work" (Geary and Roche, 2001:121).

As Benders (2005) has pointed out, part of the difficulty in establishing the extent of team working may relate to the definition of what constitutes a team. In order to limit terminological confusion our survey asked questions about the existence of both formally designed teams and problem solving groups. The survey results indicate that problem solving groups were the most common form of direct involvement being present in 74 per cent of firms (Fig. 7.1). In the UK survey, some 77 per cent of companies reported having problem solving groups – a figure comparable to the Irish one. Problem solving groups are seen as allowing for upward communication. As such groups involve efforts to tap into employee knowledge and skill, their high incidence is evidence of widespread management adoption of task-based involvement measures in MNCs in Ireland. There is, however a substantial degree of variation in the use of problem solving groups and teams across county of origin. Thus, at one end of the scale, 86 per cent of the Rest of World group had problem solving groups, compared to a low of 57 per cent in the UK grouping (Fig. 7.2). While not the country grouping with the highest usage, problem solving groups were present in 84 per cent of US MNCs and this compared to 74 per cent of the Rest of Europe and in 62 per cent of Irish organisations.

Figure 7.1 Forms of employee involvement

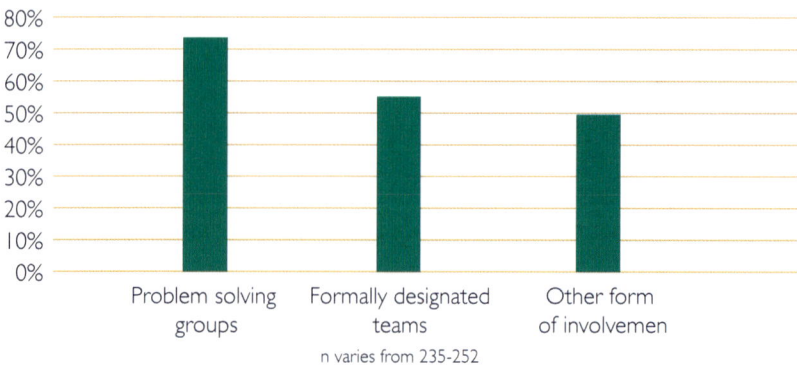

n varies from 235-252

The incidence of formally designed teams, at 54 percent, was lower than in the UCD and IBEC surveys referred to above – a somewhat surprising result given that MNCs are suggested to be leaders in their introduction (Fig. 7.1). The figure for formally designed teams in MNCs in Ireland is also much lower than the equivalent figure for the UK, where the parallel survey found that 73 per cent of MNCs had formally designed teams. This UK figure is some 19 percentage points higher than in Ireland. Thus, the reported use of teams (by all MNCs operating in Ireland) is substantially lower than in MNCs the UK. It is, however greater than the maximum 42 per cent reported by the EPOC study (see EFILWC, 1997) but marginally lower than the 59 per cent reported by the UCD survey (Roche and Geary, 1999). It is perhaps surprising, given the lead role attributed to MNCs in the introduction of innovative involvement mechanisms that the presence of team working was not found to be higher.

Despite impressions to the contrary, formally designed teams were not more likely to be present in US MNCs. The Rest of the World group (69 per cent) followed by the UK (57 per cent) and Rest of Europe (56 per cent) all reported greater usage than the 55 per cent figure for US MNCs. Only Irish MNCs (46 per cent) reported a lower usage of teams than US MNCs. This lower usage of teams among American companies was counterbalanced to some extent by US MNCs having a high usage of problem solving groups at 84 percent. However, even for problem solving groups, the MNC category with the highest usage was the Rest of the World group (86 per cent).

Figure 7.2 Presence of formally designed teams/problem solving groups by country of origin

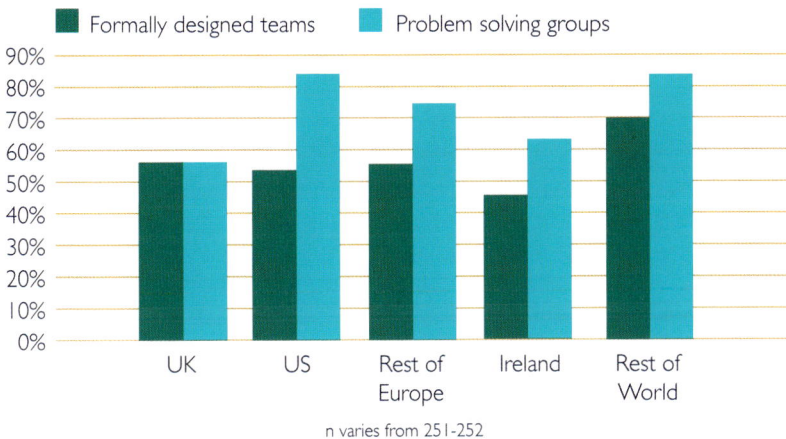

n varies from 251-252

Looking at sectoral variations for the two categories of problem solving groups and formally designated teams, there was a marked difference in the sectoral usage of problem solving groups, with 83 per cent of manufacturing companies having them as against 66 per cent in the services sector (Table 7.1). However, there was a slightly greater use of formally designed teams in the services sector (56 per cent) as against manufacturing (51 per cent). This is again a somewhat surprising result, given the developments in TQM, Just-In-Time (JIT) and World Class Manufacturing (WCM) which are predicated on team working and are generally associated with manufacturing industry. MNCs operating in a multi-sector context had the highest usage of formally designated teams at 61 per cent. They also had a high usage of problem solving groups with 83 per cent reporting their presence.

Table 7.1 Involvement across differing sectors

	Manufacturing	Services	Multi-sector
Formally designed teams	50%	56%	61%
Problem solving groups	82%	66%	83%

n varies from 251-253

In order to establish the extent of intra-firm uniformity/diversity in practices, respondents in firms with several sites in Ireland (possessing any form of involvement) were asked which of the following applied (with percentages given for each category of responses in brackets below):

- An identical or similar pattern exists across all or most sites (51 per cent).
- All or most sites have involvement systems, but they differ from site to site (35 per cent).
- Some sites have involvement systems while others do not (14 per cent).

These results indicate that just over half of the firms have a common approach to involvement across different sites, with a third having "hybrid approaches", namely involvement practices that differ from site to site. Dual systems, where some sites have involvement while others have none, are comparatively uncommon - being found in only 14 per cent of respondent organisations. In summary, while there is evidence in just over a third of cases of variation in forms of involvement within firms, the main thrust is towards common practices. Furthermore, involvement seems to beget involvement. This is indicated by the finding that the presence of involvement in some parts of the organisation is associated with the same or different forms of involvement in 86 per cent of cases. This may suggest a high degree of transference of systems within organisations, although detailed case studies would be necessary in order to explore this further.

Communications: an overview

There has been a continuing concern with communication in the management of people dating back to the human relations school, although this has more to do with the popularisation of that school than any developed theoretical exposition in that approach (see Rose, 1978). The notion that communications might be central in employment relations was derided by pluralist and radical writers of the 1960s and 1970s (see Fox, 1985). Despite this critical perspective, a concern with communications remained a staple of prescriptive writers (see Rollinson, 1993). The notion of communications also interacts with the concept of employee voice. The concern with employee voice can be traced to Freeman and Medoff (1984) who claimed that providing employees with a voice in the workplace can benefit both the organisation and employees. For employees, it can act as a vehicle to air grievances and communicate with management, whilst for employers it has the potential to improve productivity by decreasing quit rates and allowing for the development of an internal labour market within firms. Freeman and Medoff (1984) further argue that trade unions represent the best vehicle for workers to express their voice and essentially equate voice with union presence (see Willman et al., 2006).

This collectivist orientation is at odds with contemporary developments and trends, in which there has been a growth in direct forms of communication and a concomitant decline in representative or indirect forms of participation. Dundon et al. (2005:308) argue that the existing literature is excessively "union centred rather than examining a much broader involvement rubric". This is potentially a particular defect in the Irish context where union density has fallen by almost half since its high water mark of 62 per cent in 1980. Since then density has fallen consistently with density levels currently around 33 per cent (Central Statistics Office, 2008; Roche, 2008). This point is pertinent as union avoidance has been particularly evident in the MNC sector, particularly among those that established new sites in Ireland since the turn of the 1980s (Gunnigle, 1995; Roche, 2001; Gunnigle et al., 2005). Consequently, a focus on indirect forms of employee voice is inadequate.

As with involvement generally there is agreement internationally on the growth in direct forms of communications, including employee involvement in decision-making, empowerment and two-way communication. The growth in direct communications from the 1980s through to the end of the 1990s is clearly evident in the UK from the various WERS from 2004 and this is accompanied by a decrease in direct forms of participation (Culley et al., 1999; Millward et al., 2000; Marginson et al., 2007). Roehling *et al.* (2000) identify a consensus in published work on the emergence of a 'new employment relationship' characterised by a number of features. Prominent in these were employee involvement in decision-making, empowerment and two-way communication.

Communications in MNCs in Ireland

In Ireland, Gunnigle (1995) found a pronounced management focus on more direct communications with individual employees on green field sites. He notes the purpose of this was to inform employees of "market realities" as perceived by management and derived "more from a commercial imperative than from any widespread desire to increase employee involvement" (see Wallace et al., 2004:334). Geary and Roche (2001:111) note that evidence available as of 1996 showed "foreign-owned companies... place greater emphasis on direct communications...[and] were seen to have progressively given added emphasis to developing a direct relationship with their employees". Their UCD survey completed in 1996/'97 noted significant differences in a range of practices in MNCs when compared with Irish companies. During the period 1992 to 1995, "a substantial increase in direct written and verbal communication with employees" was noted as part of the Cranfield surveys (Gunnigle et al., 1997:198). That the growth in direct communication is part of a trend was shown by Morley *et al.* (2001), as they record a major growth in direct communication with employees over the course of the decade in the Cranfield surveys. Dundon *et al.* (2006) also record a growing preference for more communication and information-type channels of voice, rather than consultative-type mechanisms in a series of case studies.

Figure 7.3 below contains the responses to a question on the most common forms of communication present in the organisation in descending order of their presence. These vary from mechanisms that are likely to involve the one-way communication of information by management, to others which involve a two-way process of communication such as meetings. Questions on the presence of mechanisms for communication flow from employees to management, in the form of opinion and attitude surveys, were also asked.

The most common mechanism present was meetings between line managers and employees, with 98 per cent reporting such activities (Fig. 7.3). The use of newsletters and email to communicate information is the next most common mechanism, followed by the systematic use of the management chain. A company intranet was utilised in a high 78 per cent of organisations and meetings between management and the whole workforce were reported by 76 per cent of respondents. Attitude or opinion surveys are less common, used by two-thirds of firms, whilst suggestion schemes were utilised in only 55 per cent of companies.

Figure 7.3 Presence of differing forms of communication

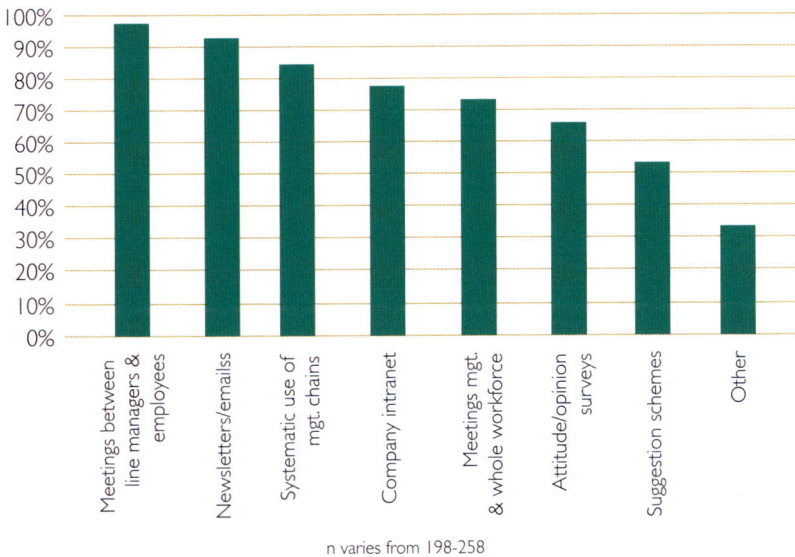

n varies from 198-258

There was a high level of usage of the most common three categories of communications mechanisms across all MNCs, irrespective of country of origin as shown in table 7.2. Multinationals from the US had a particularly high usage of meetings between management and whole workforce - with 90 per cent reporting the use of this mechanism. The Rest of the World group made the most frequent combined use of attitude/opinion surveys and suggestion schemes. Indeed, the Rest of the World Group had the highest usage, of any of the country/regional groupings, when all schemes were combined.   In comparison Irish MNCs made the least use overall of the six mechanisms (Table 7.2).

Previous research had suggested that US MNCs give particular emphasis to open door policies and to attitude surveys, which are sometimes seen as transference of sophisticated practices with their origins in welfare capitalism (Jacoby, 1997). Our findings do indeed establish that American companies make high usage of attitude and opinions surveys. Eighty-four per cent of US companies report having such schemes, by comparison with 71 per cent of UK companies and 59 per cent of Rest of Europe. However, the group with the highest usage was the Rest of World category with a 93 per cent usage. There was a dramatic difference in the use of attitude and opinion surveys between Irish MNCs and all foreign MNC groupings. Only one-third of Irish firms reported using these, while the corresponding figure for foreign companies as a whole was 74 per cent. Suggestion schemes were used in 59 per cent of US organisations, 49 per cent of UK companies and 52 per cent in the Rest of Europe grouping. Yet again the Rest of World category had the highest usage with 79 per cent and Irish MNCs had the lowest usage at only 44 per cent. The reasons for the lower usage of attitude/opinion surveys and suggestion schemes in Irish MNCs are unclear. It may be that Irish MNCS have less innovative approaches to employee involvement than foreign MNCs – in other words they are laggards in this regard. On the other hand it may reflect cultural factors, their perceived unsuitability given established employment relations mechanisms, or even scepticism at the utility of such schemes.

Table 7.2 Presence of forms of communication by country of origin

Communication mechanisms	Irish	UK	US	Europe	Rest
Meetings between line managers & employees	98%	97%	98%	98%	100%
Newsletters/emails	89%	91%	94%	97%	100%
Systematic use of management chain	70%	91%	87%	87%	87%
Company Intranet	67%	76%	85%	76%	86%
Meetings management &whole workforce	64%	76%	90%	63%	79%
Attitude/opinion surveys	33%	71%	84%	59%	93%
Suggestion schemes	44%	49%	59%	52%	79%

n varies from 254-258

Differences across sectors were minimal – with the usage of forms of communication being virtually identical in services and manufacturing. The most notable differences were the slightly higher utilisation of meetings between management and the whole workforce in manufacturing (79 per cent) as against services (72 per cent); and a higher usage of a company Intranet in services (83 per cent) as against manufacturing (69 per cent).

Comparative importance of differing communication mechanisms

The mere presence of a measure is not sufficient to establish its significance as it needs to be considered in conjunction with the importance attached to the mechanism. In order to test the relative importance of the differing mechanisms, respondents were asked which of the communication mechanisms were the most important. The responses to this question indicates that the more traditional mechanism of meetings between line managers and employees was considered the most important by a majority (52 per cent) of respondents (Fig. 7.4). This was followed by meetings between senior management and the whole workforce – 19 per cent of respondents considering these most important. Newsletters and emails and systematic use of management chain were in joint third place with just eight per cent nominating these categories (Fig. 7.4). A company Intranet was next – nominated by seven per cent of respondents. Only three respondents (one per cent) considered attitude and opinion surveys as the most important and no respondent identified suggestion schemes as the most important.

Figure 7.4 Most important mechanisms for involvement

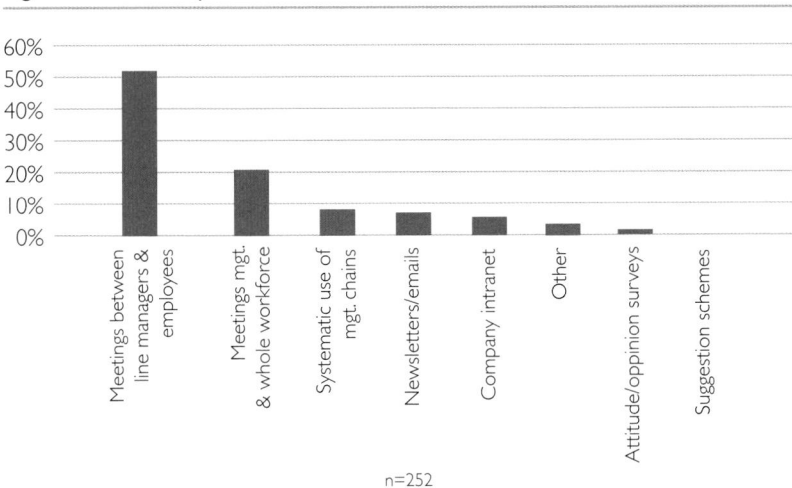

n=252

These results contrast somewhat with the UK findings where, in the parallel survey, some nine per cent of firms said that suggestion schemes, attitude surveys and open door were the most important communication mechanism. Even this nine per cent represented a low level. Commenting on these results Edwards *et al.* (2007:69-70) conclude "that mechanisms such as attitude surveys and open door schemes, which are sometimes seen as the more 'sophisticated' two-way communication mechanisms, receive relatively little emphasis". In summary, the greater use of attitude and opinion surveys by MNCs, particularly Rest of the

World and US MNCs, lends some support to the thesis that these innovative forms of communication are utilised more by foreign MNCs. However, the fact that very few companies reported these to be the most important mechanism qualifies that picture substantially.

Information communicated

It is not just the mechanisms of communication that are important but the information communicated. We review the findings in relation to foreign MNCs first, before reporting on the practices of Irish companies and comparing them to their foreign counterparts. Figure 7.5 contains details of the type of information communicated by foreign MNCs. In general, respondents indicated that a large percentage of companies (68 per cent) provide information on the financial position of the worldwide company in Ireland but a somewhat lower percentage provide information on investment (43 per cent) and staffing plans of the worldwide company (20 per cent).

Figure 7.5 Type of information communicated to employees (foreign MNCs only)

n=206

The country/region of origin breakdown indicates that a larger proportion of the American companies (80 per cent) provide information on the financial position of the company worldwide than the other groupings (Fig. 7.6). This supports the contention that US MNCs pay greater attention to communicating information on market realities. Information disclosure decreases significantly for all groupings when one looks at investment plans worldwide. While US MNCs continued to lead the way in this regard, information provision in this area was lower than for the equivalent information on Irish operations. Forty-seven per cent of US MNCs provided this information, a figure very close to that for the Rest of Europe, which disclosed this information in 44 per cent of cases. The UK figure was 35 per cent but only 23 per cent of the Rest of the World group disclosed information on worldwide investment plans. Information on staffing plans worldwide was the lowest category of information disclosed, ranging from 22 per cent for the Rest of Europe to only 15 per cent for the Rest of the World MNCs.

Figure 7.6 Information provided on company worldwide to employees on specified topics by country of origin

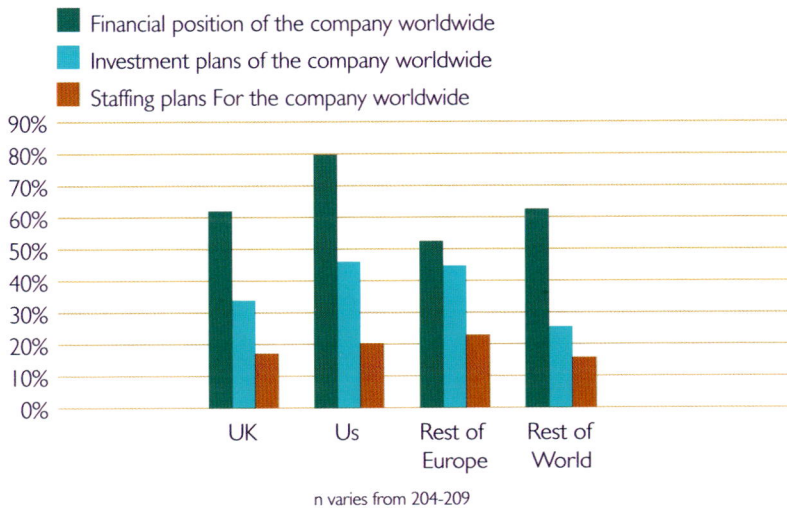

n varies from 204-209

Turning to the provision of information on operations in Ireland by foreign MNCs, it is unsurprising that this is generally higher than for information on worldwide operations (Fig. 7.7). For instance 71 per cent of all foreign MNCs provided information on the financial position of the company in Ireland. Although not directly comparable, these figures are much higher than those reported in the Cranfield-UL study (1999) where circa 45 per cent of companies provided information on financial performance to staff below the level of management (cf. Wallace et al., 2004). When it came to the provision of financial information on the position of the company in Ireland, 79 per cent of the Rest of World MNCs provided such information. By comparison the Rest of Europe grouping had the lowest with 63 per cent. US MNCs were the only grouping that provided less financial information on the Irish company compared with financial information provided on the worldwide company.

The communication of information on staffing plans in Ireland is much higher than staffing plans worldwide for all foreign MNCs and this may well reflect the greater immediacy that information on employment has for Irish employees. Information on staffing plans in Ireland was provided by over 60 per cent of US, Rest of World and Irish MNCs, with only the UK companies having a comparatively lower level at 46 per cent. The US companies led the way with 69 per cent reporting they provided information on staffing plans in Ireland.

American MNCs also led the way in the provision of information on Irish investment plans, with 72 per cent reporting they provided this information. The corresponding figure for the Rest of Europe was 68 per cent and Rest of World 62 per cent. Yet again, MNCs from the UK had the lowest reported disclosure, among foreign MNCs, at 59 per cent. All four foreign MNC groupings were more likely to provide information on investment plans and staffing in Ireland than provided this information on worldwide staffing and investment plans (Fig. 7.7).

Figure 7.7 Provision of information on the company in Ireland

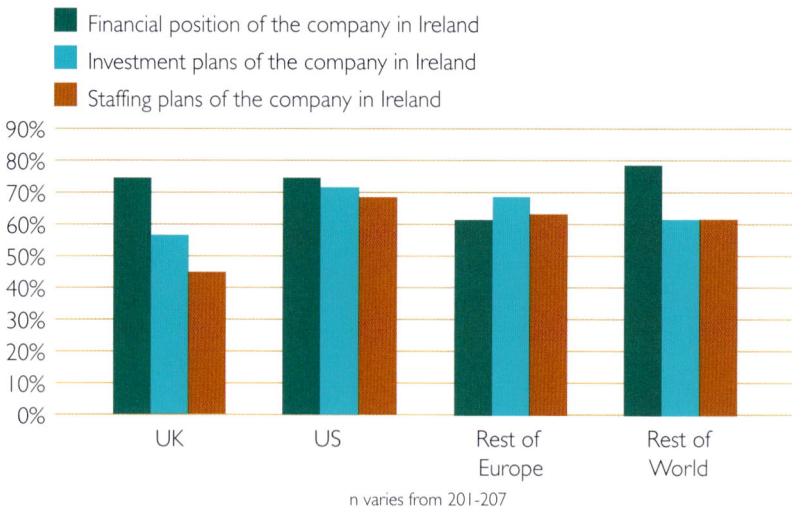

■ Financial position of the company in Ireland
■ Investment plans of the company in Ireland
■ Staffing plans of the company in Ireland

n varies from 201-207

For all foreign MNC groupings overall operating in Ireland, the provision of information on worldwide investment plans is significantly less than on Irish investment plans and this most likely again reflects the greater immediacy that Irish information has for Irish employees. However, there are variations across countries, with nearly 50 per cent of US MNCs providing information on investment plans worldwide, in contrast to some 35 per cent of UK firms and

23 per cent for the Rest of World MNCs (Fig. 7.8).

Figure 7.8 Information on investment plans worldwide (foreign MNCs only)

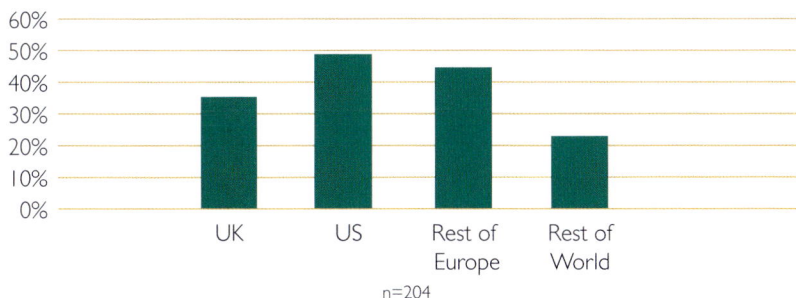

n=204

In foreign MNCs there were only minimal sectoral differences across manufacturing, services and multi-sector in relation to the provision of information on the financial position of the company in Ireland. However, there was a much higher provision of information on investment plans in Ireland in the manufacturing sector at 83 per cent. This compared with only 57 per cent in services and 59 per cent in MNCs in the multi-sector category. Differences were also evident across sectors in relation to the provision of information on staffing plans in Ireland. Seventy per cent of manufacturing companies provided this information as against 55 per cent in service companies, however surprisingly the highest figure was for the multi-sector category, 76 per cent of which reported providing this information.

Fig. 7.9 Provision of information by sector (foreign MNCs only)

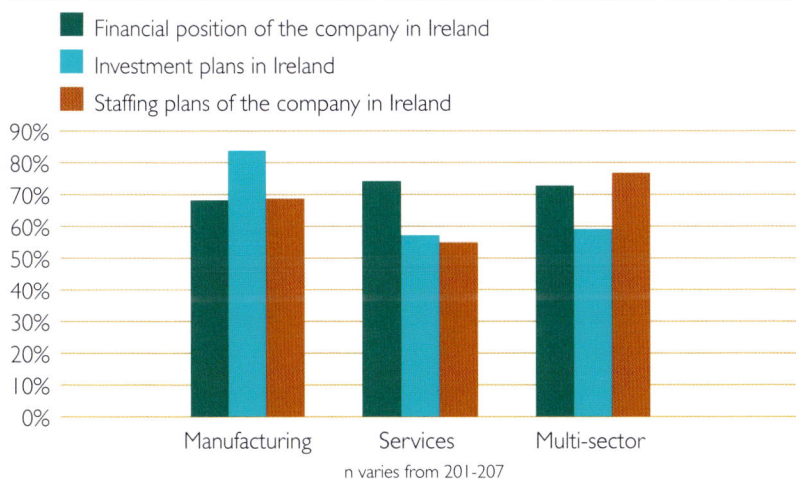

n varies from 201-207

Irish and foreign MNC information provision compared

For ease of comparison, we have separated out the information on Irish MNCs. It has long been considered that Irish MNCs lagged behind in information disclosure. A look at table 7.3 suggests a somewhat mixed picture. Irish MNCS are on a par with foreign MNCs when it comes to the provision of information on the financial position of the company in Ireland. Indeed they have the second highest disclosure of any grouping in this regard. However, they have by far the lowest disclosure in relation to both staffing and investment plans in Ireland.

Table 7.3 Information in Foreign and Irish MNCs Compared

Communication mechanisms	Irish	UK	US	Europe	Rest
Financial position of company in Ireland	76%	74%	74%	63%	79%
Investment plan of the company in Ireland	38%	59%	72%	68%	62%
Staffing plan for the company in Ireland	38%	46%	69%	64%	62%

n varies from 246-252

In Irish MNCs, there is a high propensity to provide information on the financial position of the company in Ireland across all sectors (Fig. 7.10). Indeed, all Irish MNCs in the multi-sector category provided such information, however as there were only six companies in that category no great significance can be read into this high figure. The services sector had the lowest overall provision of information, although in the case of staffing plans in Ireland the multi-sector was lowest with only one-third of Irish MNCs in that sector reporting they provided such information. This compared to 45 per cent in manufacturing and 36 per cent in the services sector.

Fig. 7.10 Provision of information by sector (Irish MNCs only)

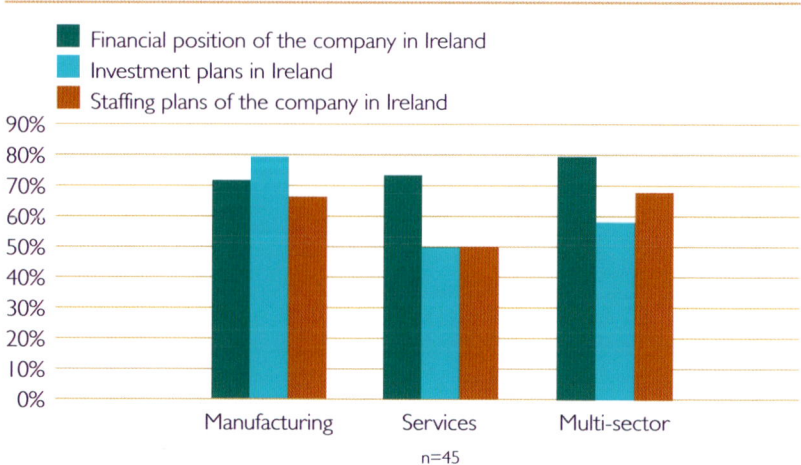

- Financial position of the company in Ireland
- Investment plans in Ireland
- Staffing plans of the company in Ireland

n=45

Human Resource Practices in Multinational Companies in Ireland: A Contemporary Analysis

Summary and conclusions

This chapter reviewed the general issues related to employee involvement and distinguished that process from other forms of employee participation. It is clear from the literature that there are complexities and subtleties in the debate on participation generally and employee involvement in particular. The survey results establish the range of involvement schemes in MNCs and provide room for subsequent reflection and further research on their meaning.

From the survey results, we see that there is a comparatively high usage of such mechanisms. Problem solving groups are present in nearly three-quarters of companies and these were the most common form of direct involvement. By contrast, formally designed teams were present in only 54 per cent of firms. This is much lower than the 73 per cent figure found in the equivalent UK survey but on a par with the 59 per cent level of teamwork found in the UCD study (Roche and Geary, 1999). Despite impressions to the contrary from previous research, formally designed teams were not more likely to be present in US companies. Only 53 per cent percent reported them as against the Rest of the World (69 per cent), Rest of Europe (56 per cent) and UK (57 per cent). Indeed only Irish MNCs (48 per cent) had a lower incidence of formally designed teams. In contrast to the low incidence of teams in US companies they had a high usage of problem solving groups, with 84 per cent of American MNCs reporting them. However, an even higher proportion (86 per cent) of Rest of the World companies has such groups. The figure for the Rest of Europe was by comparison 74 per cent and for Irish MNCs 62 per cent, with the UK group having the lowest usage at 57 per cent. There were also notable sectoral differences, with manufacturing companies having a higher incidence of problem solving groups than service companies. In contrast, and surprisingly, 56 per cent of services sector MNCs had formal teams as against 51 per cent in manufacturing.

The main communication mechanisms are the traditional ones of meetings between line managers and employees, meetings with the whole workforce and systematic use of the management chain. There is also a high level of usage of newer forms of communication via emails, newsletters and use of a company Intranet but a much lower usage of attitude and opinion surveys. Most strikingly 72 per cent of respondents identified meetings between line managers and employees, and meetings between senior management and employees, as being the most important involvement mechanism. Attitude and opinion surveys and suggestion schemes hardly registered in terms of a ranking of the most important mechanism, with only three respondents – one per cent of the total – suggesting these as the most important mechanism.

There is a comparatively high proportion of companies providing financial information on the company in Ireland (71 per cent) and worldwide (68 per cent). There is a substantially lower provision of information on investment plans (43 per cent) and staffing plans worldwide (20 per cent) than the provision of such information on Irish operations. In Ireland the equivalent information was investment plans (68 per cent) and staffing plans (63 per cent). American companies were to the fore in financial and investment information provision.

The overriding impression from the above data is that there is a substantial usage of employee involvement mechanisms in Ireland but that there is considerable variability across these mechanisms. There is also significant variation across country groupings and sectors. In some instances preconceived ideas are confirmed, as in the high usage of problem solving groups in US companies. In others, as in the lower presence of formally designated teams in US companies, these preconceptions are not confirmed. Nor is the view that US MNCs lead the way in the use of involvement schemes generally borne out, as the Rest of World group has the highest overall usage. While involvement is frequently presented as novel and new, the fact that meetings between management were the most common, and most important mechanism used, raises questions about that presumption. The fact that meetings are quite traditional techniques, and presumably have been used for a long time, must counsel some caution about a diagnosis of the importance of the new. There is of course room for further research on the interactions between the mechanisms identified in the survey. In this regard we expect further interrogation of the data will throw up interesting results. There will also be a need for case study research to determine how involvement works in practice and the extent of influence which it accords employees and the benefits it delivers to employers.

ENDNOTE

[i] There are two primary sources of data on trade union density in Ireland. The first is the Department of Enterprise Trade and Employment and is based on returns from unions themselves. The second draws on Quarterly National Household Surveys (conducted since the early 1990s). The latter indicate consistently lower levels of union density than the former. For more details see Roche (2008).

CHAPTER 8

Training, Development and
Organisation Learning

Anthony McDonnell, Jonathan Lavelle, Michael Morley
and David Collings

Introduction

Many commentators argue that one of the principal means by which firms can achieve differentiation and sustainable competitive advantage is through the effective management and development of their staff (Lowe et al., 2002, Caligiuri et al., 2005; Baron and Armstrong, 2007). This view resonates with the resource based view (RBV) which suggests that firms can gain a sustainable competitive advantage through the application of a bundle of valuable internal resources at the organisation's disposal (Penrose, 1959; Wernerfelt, 1984; Barney, 1991, 1995, 2001). This is based on the argument that human capital represents one of the few resources that are valuable, rare, inimitable and non-substitutable (see Barney, 1991 for greater exposition of the RBV). This line of reasoning follows that the traditional factors of production (e.g. raw materials and technology) are less of a competitive advantage as they are more easily substituted. For example, technology can be copied at a much quicker pace now, with product design to end product release times considerably quicker than in previous decades (Tiernan et al., 2006). However, by training and developing the firm's human capital firms will increase the bank of formal and tacit knowledge. These knowledge resources will be very difficult, if not impossible, to copy or mimic.

People possess human capital before they enter an organisation, but by investing in it further and creating the circumstances by which employees will activate their capital, management hope to achieve productivity, flexibility and performance benefits through improvement in employee skills and knowledge (Baron and Armstrong, 2007). However training and development is often merely used as an exercise in organisation rhetoric, for example: "people are our greatest asset and that is why we invest extensively in them" (Grugulis, 2007). However, the structure and content, as well as the impact of training and development mechanisms often vary considerably. Grugulis (2007: 3) notes that the level of training and development (T&D) which takes places varies greatly between organisations and sectors, some "do it extremely well but others are much less active". Indeed, there have been some cases of employers expecting their employees to pay for their own training meaning the cost burden of employee development is shifted from the employer to the employee. For example, *Ryanair* require their pilots to pay towards the cost of their training (Flint, 2004). However, most organisations are likely to provide some basic skills training, often due to legislative requirements, but the extent to which it goes beyond this in terms of developmental mechanisms is questionable. Despite the relatively common view that people represent one of a small number of intangible assets with the potential to provide continuing business success, there remains little reliable empirical evidence on the extent to which organisations develop their human talent. This deficit is particularly apparent with respect to MNCs.

This chapter explores T&D practices of MNCs in Ireland, focusing specifically on four key areas:

- The financial outlay on the training and development of the workforce.
- The extent to which MNCs operate formal succession planning and management development programmes, and whether these are global or local activities.
- The development tools being utilised to develop high-potentials/ senior managerial potentials.
- The practices used to facilitate organisational learning and knowledge diffusion between subsidiaries.

The chapter explores the use of expatriate assignments. This not only involves the provision of data on the use of traditional parent country expatriate assignments but also outflows from the subsidiary to other parts of the worldwide company including the parent country headquarters.

Training and development expenditure

The T&D spend MNCs made on all employees in the previous twelve months is used as a proxy measure for the extent to which a firm regards its human resources as an investment central to achieving organisational objectives. It has been noted previously that reliable data on this type of expenditure are not easy to come by, due in no small part to the complex structures of organisations (cf. Heraty and Morley, 2003; Edwards et al., 2007). This proved to be the case here with six indigenous and twenty-nine foreign-owned MNCs unable to even provide a range for their T&D expenditure. Despite this measure failing to illustrate the quality of T&D and excluding informal learning, it is particularly useful in highlighting the relative emphasis placed on T&D across organisations (Garavan et al., 2003). Furthermore, when combined with other training and development indicators, it is useful for providing insights into similarities, or differences, in how MNCs approach training and development overall (Edwards et al., 2007).

The findings show a mixed picture in terms of spending on T&D. Most respondents (57 per cent) categorised their training expenditure in the "greater than 1 per cent but less than 4 per cent" range. This was followed by 23 per cent of MNCs that indicated they spent "greater than 4 per cent" of their annual pay bill on training and development in the past year, while a further 20 per cent reported a spend of "up to 1 per cent". Unfortunately, there is little by way of a base in which to compare results. The most recent Irish *Cranet* data, whilst not directly comparable, showed more than a quarter of firms spent in excess of 4 per cent on T&D activities, close to 80 per cent indicated a spend of greater than 2 per cent (Morley et al., 2001). More recently, the biennial *Chartered Institute of Personnel and Development* (CIPD) national survey of T&D benchmarks found that the average T&D expenditure for firms with more than 50 employees equated to 3.17 per cent of total payroll costs (Garavan et al., 2008). This represented a decrease from the 3.85 per cent found in the 2001 study (Garavan and Heraty, 2001) and lags quite a considerable amount behind the EU average of 4.15 per cent (Garavan et al., 2008). This recent study also found that MNCs, which made up a small proportion of the sample, were the highest spenders on T&D with expenditure of just over 4 per cent of total employee costs. Although these are not directly comparable studies, the findings are broadly similar. However, this type of data is likely to be context and time dependent. By that we mean, where organisations find themselves in difficult operating conditions, the resources allocated for development are likely to be much reduced. Furthermore, it is interesting to note the whole figures provided in these other studies because a significant number of respondents here were only able to provide a range of spending. They found it extremely difficult to be tied to an absolute figure.

Figure 8.1 Training and development expenditure in MNCs

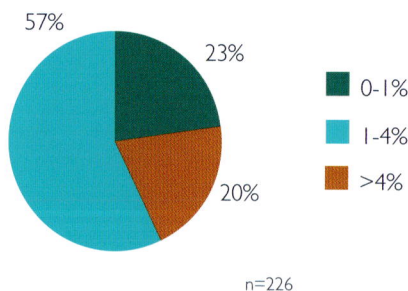

n=226

Figure 8.2 illustrates the T&D spend by country of origin. The biggest spenders (i.e., those with T&D spend of more than 4 per cent) were US MNCs (27 per cent) followed by the UK and European MNCs (both 23 per cent). Smaller numbers of indigenous MNCs (17 per cent) were shown to spend in excess of 4 per cent vis-à-vis MNCs of other national origins. This may be somewhat surprising given that indigenous MNCs are talking about T&D in their home operations, where MNCs have traditionally focused greater resources. For example, in the comparative study of MNCs in the UK, UK-owned MNCs were found to have particularly high levels of T&D spend. Edwards and colleagues (2007) suggest this may be due to the fact that they were reporting on their home operations. However as noted earlier, studies on T&D activity in organisations in Ireland have shown them to be relatively low spenders. Another possible reason relates to sector. Large numbers of indigenous MNCs are located in the more low-technology, traditional sectors (e.g. food and retail). Consequently they may be less likely to invest large amounts in the development of staff involved in low skills activities. Overall, minimal country differences were found which differs from the comparative study in the UK. Edwards *et al.* (2007) found US-owned MNCs as having the fourth highest T&D spend, with German, French and British MNCs being the highest T&D investors (Edwards et al., 2007). The high spend of German-owned organisations is not surprising as they are believed to be some of the largest investors (Mabey and Ramirez, 2004), largely due to German vocational system of work and German firms' focus on product differentiation (Edwards et al., 2007). Unfortunately, we are unable to provide evidence of these potential effects here due to small cell sizes, both French and German MNCs are incorporated in the 'Rest of Europe' category.

Figure 8.2 Training and development expenditure by country of origin

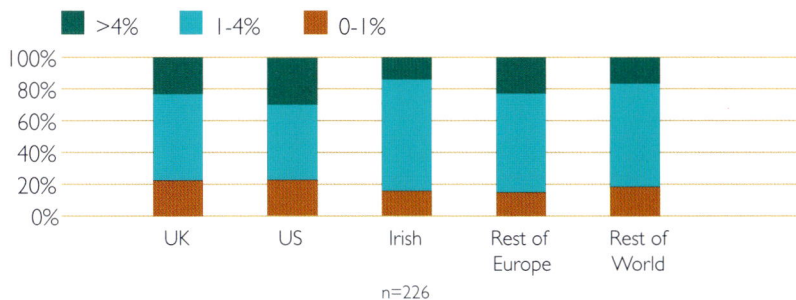

n=226

Sectoral differences are highlighted in figure 8.3. Significant differences clearly emerged - with multi-sector MNCs (45 per cent) the most likely to report a spend in excess of 4 per cent on T&D activities more than either manufacturing MNCs (15 per cent) or services sector MNCs (25 per cent). While some caution is needed in interpreting the multi-sector finding due to the smaller cell sizes, it may be linked to the size of these organisations. In addition, further detail would need to be provided on the actual activities of the organisation. For instance, the MNC may have a research and development wing, manufacturing operations and support activities (e.g. call centre) meaning there may be considerable need for a diverse array of training and development interventions.

Figure 8.3 Training and development expenditure by sector

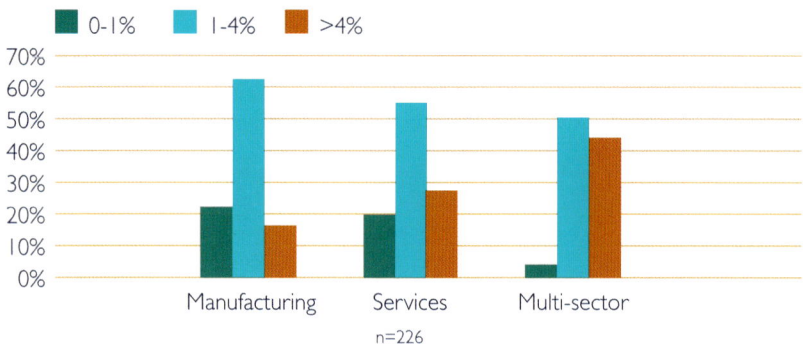

The key group

In chapter three, it was established that 52 per cent of MNCs reported the identification of a key group. The exploration of such a group is an innovative development and has much resonance with the emergent field of 'talent management'. The key group can be categorised as a critical talent pool (see Boudreau and Ramstad, 2005, for discussion on talent pools) who are particularly important to the achievement of an organisation's corporate strategy. In addition to exploring the identification of such a group, we also established if there was a specific development programme in place for the key group. Of those firms that identified a key group, some 57 per cent reported the presence of a specific development programme for these particular employees. Interestingly these findings were significantly different to the study of MNCs in UK (Edwards et al., 2007). There only 38 per cent of MNCs had a specific key group development programme. The authors argued that this may suggest that in the majority of companies the key group are not treated as a specific group for development purposes (Edwards et al., 2007). However, we find that such a contention may not be as straightforward and is worthy of further investigation to establish the reasons behind such a difference.

Irish-owned MNCs (64 per cent) were the most likely to indicate a specific development programme for their key group. This may possibly be explained by the fact that this refers to the organisation's home operations. Previous studies have suggested that "key strategic activities are highly concentrated in the home base" (Edwards and Ferner, 2002: 97). While this effect did not emerge in respect to T&D expenditure it may indicate that MNCs are appropriating their resources to a greater extent. It has been suggested given the increasing financial constraints being placed on organisations, they may seek to focus their resources more appropriately (Boxall and Purcell, 2000; Huselid et al., 2005). This is again linked with 'talent management' which has seen some researchers argue for development efforts to be primarily placed on those employees who have the greater impact on organisational success (Boudreau and Ramstad, 2005, 2007; Collings et al., 2008a).

Figure 8.4 Presence of key group development programme by country of origin

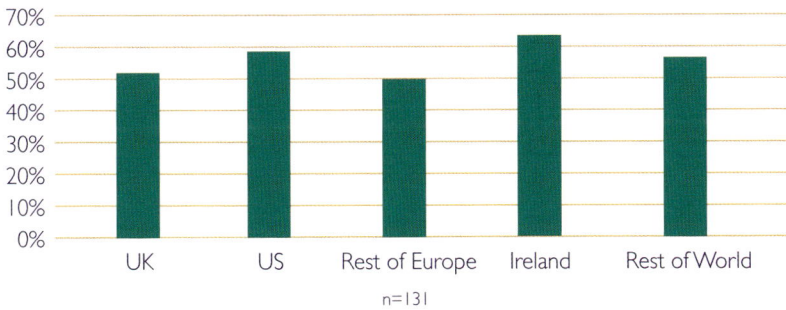

n=131

Figure 8.5 Presence of key group development programme by sector

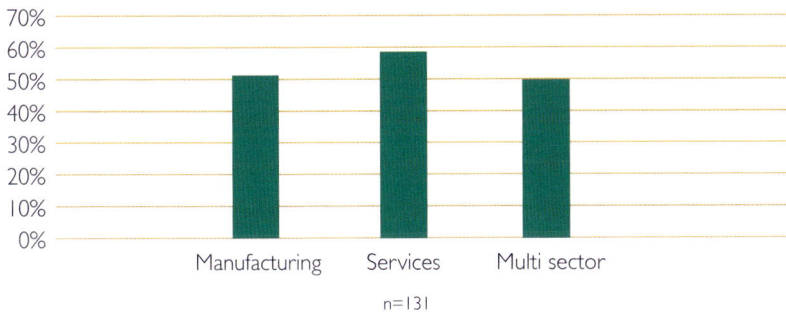

n=131

The sectoral findings are highlighted in figure 8.5 and follow the earlier result with respect to T&D expenditure. Multi-sector MNCs (64 per cent) were the most likely to provide a key group development programme, followed by MNCs in the services sector (60 per cent). Manufacturing sector MNCs (51 per cent) emerged as the least likely to have a formal development programme for the key group. The lower numbers of manufacturing firms with a development programme may be somewhat surprising. A possible explanation is that there are a relatively significant proportion of manufacturing MNCs involved in the lower-value activities such as food processing.

Succession planning

A further source of talent in organisations (other than key functional employees, i.e. the key group) is managerial talent. This is arguably ever-more critical for MNCs. Collings *et al.* (2008a) argue that a large part of success in the global business environment will be driven by a small number of high potential, exceptional performers, principally managerial employees who fill key strategic positions within the MNC's global operations. "One firm resource required in the implementation of all strategies is managerial talent" (Barney, 1991: 106). With shortages of internationally competent managers being reported in MNCs (Scullion, 1994; Suutari, 2002; Sloan et al., 2003; Scullion and Collings, 2006), a "straightforward case can be made that today's businesses actively need to select and prepare high-potential employees to manage in complex environments" (Burke, 1997: 18).

Succession planning involves the systematic identification and development of an organisation's internal talent. The principal aim here is the identification and subsequent nurturing of managerial talent to ensure there will be sufficient numbers of employees available to assume senior roles when required. The study showed that almost two thirds of all MNCs have a formal system of succession planning covering some or all of the Irish operations, an identical result to the parallel UK study (Edwards et al., 2007). This means that some 35 per cent of MNCs do not undertake succession planning, although a number of respondents, predominantly Irish-owned MNCs, suggested succession planning was conducted on an informal, ad hoc basis:

> We don't have a specific, formalised succession planning system in place, however we do it informally in that senior management look at employees who they view as being of future management potential, however this process is by no means formal
> **HR Director, Irish-owned, services sector MNC.**

> We have no formal system [succession planning] in place but there is an informal system. We always look to promote from within, this is something

we do first. We will see if there is someone internal who might be able to do the role
HR Director, US-owned, services sector MNC.

Whilst we do not have a formal succession planning policy in place it is talked about a lot by management, however there is no formal process in place although it would be regarded as quite important
HR Manager, Irish-owned, services sector MNC.

The efficacy of conducting succession planning on an informal basis is questionable. Organisations with formal succession planning may benefit from improved retention rates through the establishment of a career ladder, as well as the creation of a 'line of sight' so that employees can see how they may progress in the organisation (Reilly et al., 2007). If systems are unstructured and *ad hoc* for the identification of managerial talent, it is likely that development and talent availability issues will emerge as indicated in the following quote:

One of our major concerns is the lack of succession planning. We have made a very conscious decision to look at putting a formal system in place as many of our directors who were involved in the set up of the company are now getting old. We do not have natural successors to them which is an issue
HR Manager, Irish-owned construction sector MNC.

Figure 8.6 Global or local succession planning

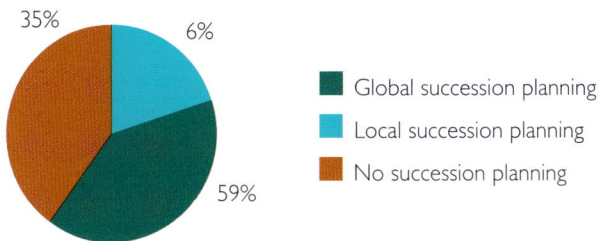

Where succession planning was indicated to be in situ, a clear majority (90 per cent) reported it was a global system. This means that only 10 per cent of those with succession planning systems indicated they were specific to the Irish operations. Figure 8.6 illustrates the overall findings per use of succession planning. Some 59 per cent have a global system, 6 per cent a local plan, while 35 per cent do not undertake formal succession planning in any capacity in the Irish operations. These results are similar to that found in the UK study which overwhelmingly indicated that the system found to be in place was global in its reach (Edwards et al., 2007).

It has been suggested that talent pipelines are increasingly being coordinated on a global level (Sparrow et al., 2004; Stiles et al., 2006; Sparrow, 2007; Stahl et al., 2007; Briscoe et al., 2008). The reasons proposed include the need to move away from a headquarters perspective, the potential to gain from scale economies, and the potential of global networks to transfer practices between operations (Sparrow et al., 2004). In addition, the RBV suggests that MNCs can gain a global competitive advantage from their internal resources but only if the knowledge and capabilities possessed by these are leveraged appropriately across the organisation (Harvey et al., 2000). Evans *et al.* (2002) argue that MNCs operating a localised system are likely to be unaware of where their best talent is located. Taking this into account and the very small numbers with local systems, we provide country of origin and sectoral breakdown in terms of having a global system and not being covered by a global system (includes no succession planning and those firms with a global system).

US-owned MNCs were the most likely to have a global system of succession planning (67 per cent) followed by the rest of World category (59 per cent), Europe category (56 per cent) and UK-owned MNCs at 54.5 per cent. Indigenous MNCs (48 per cent) were the least likely to indicate global succession planning takes place. The study of MNCs in the UK found US-owned MNCs were the most probable to undertake succession planning with Japanese organisations the least likely (Edwards et al., 2007). Due to a near total failure to attract Japanese (and indeed other Asian investment) firms to Ireland, we were unable to explore this trend.

Figure 8.7 Global succession planning by country of origin

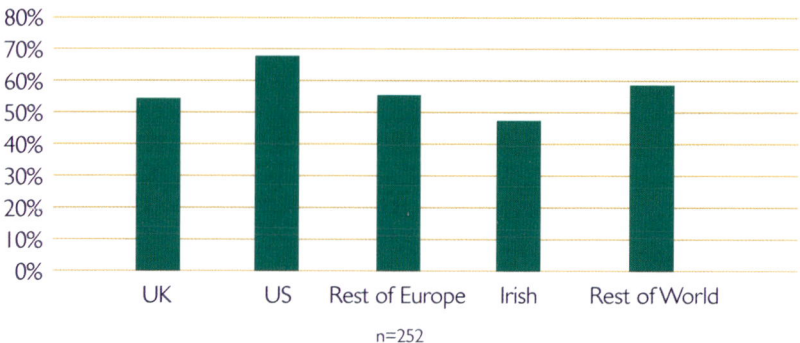

n=252

Few differences were found according to whether the MNC operates in manufacturing or services sectors. Both were quite similar in terms of whether these MNCs were covered by global succession planning (59 per cent of services sector MNCs are versus 55 per cent of manufacturing MNCs). The one point of note was that multi-sector MNCs (71 per cent) were significantly more likely to have a global system.

Management development

Detail is now provided on the extent to which MNCs provide high-potentials with a formal management development programme. With MNCs reporting shortages of managers, particularly those with international experience and competencies (cf. Scullion, 1994; Gregersen et al., 1998; Suutari, 2002; Collings et al., 2007), one may expect the development of managerial cadres to become ever-more important. In recent years, it has even been suggested that management development represents the "new organisational wealth", due to the integral role management play in unlocking the benefits of investing in both human and material capital (Heraty and Morley, 2003: 60).

It is one thing recruiting good quality employees but these also need to be developed.

> It is not enough to simply buy talent, it is essential to develop talent as well, not least because it is easier to inculcate brand values in workers or players who come through the organization: they will acquire the valuable contextual talent as part of the development process
> **Brady et al., 2008:69.**

Almost three quarters of all MNCs (72 per cent) indicated the use of a high-potential development programme. Once more, it was clear that the majority of these programmes were global in their focus. Some 80 per cent reported this to be the case. Overall these results showed that almost three in ten MNCs do not have a development programme for high-potentials, at least on a formal basis. Similar to our findings with respect to succession planning, a number of MNCs suggested that a formal programme was currently under consideration or in its infancy stage of development. The following quotes are indicative:

> We have no hard and fast programme in place but it was something we looked at introducing last year but it has been forgotten about since we first looked at introducing a programme
> **HR Manager, Irish-owned, traditional manufacturing MNC.**

We do not have a high potential management development programme. However it is currently being developed and will be implemented in this site and our 2 UK sites (i.e. same division). Currently external qualifications are used on an ad-hoc basis for managers
Senior HR officer, Irish-owned, traditional manufacturing MNC.

In addition, these findings highlighted that there are slightly more MNCs with a development programme for their high-potentials than those with succession planning – one of the primary tools for identifying high-potentials. The authors question the effectiveness and sensibility of such a situation and it begs the question, are resources being targeted appropriately? For instance, Boudreau and Ramstad (2005, 2007) assert that the failure of organisations to have a formal framework to identify talent pools means organisations are likely to invest too much in non-core pools and fail to appropriate resources in those which are pivotal.

As with succession planning, nationality and sectoral variations were analysed according to those with and without a global programme for high-potential development. Substantial differences were found between Irish-owned MNCs and foreign MNCs. This varied from the findings of the parallel UK study which found a similar pattern of use of management development across all nationalities (Edwards et al., 2007). Specifically, it was found that 73 per cent of the rest of world category utilised a global programme, followed by 64 per cent of US MNCs, 53 per cent of European firms, 48.5 per cent of UK-owned with indigenous MNCs once more the least likely to indicate the formal use of a global high-potential development programme.

These findings coupled with those on succession planning demonstrate that indigenous MNCs tend to be somewhat less developed in terms of formalised talent identification and development systems and programmes. This provides some support from previous case study work on Irish-owned MNCs that noted an *ad hoc* approach to management development (see Scullion and Donnelly, 1998; Donnelly, 1999; Scullion, 1999; Monks et al., 2001; Loane et al., 2004).
At the same time, this case-based research showed indigenous MNCs as increasingly concerned about the development of managerial cadres. This may be the case here also with some firms being quite formal in their approach and others being far less advanced.

Consistent with the findings to date, multi-sector MNCs (79 per cent) were found to be considerably more likely to have a formal global management development programme than manufacturing (45 per cent) and services sector MNCs (60 per cent). These quite stark differences are at odds with the results from the UK study on MNCs which found little evidence of a sectoral variation regarding management development programmes (Edwards et al., 2007).

Figure 8.8 Global management development by country of origin

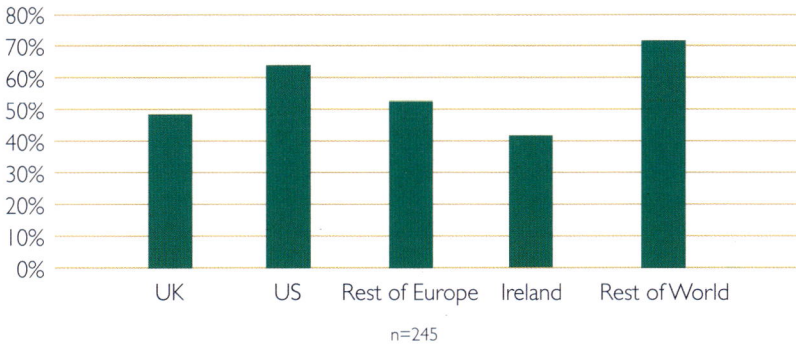

n=245

Next we detail the substance of these programmes. Many of these mechanisms are designed to give high-potentials the skills and competencies to manage in global markets.

- Long-term international assignments
- Short-term international assignments
- Formal global management training
- Assessment of performance against a set of global management competencies
- Qualifications programmes (e.g. MBA)

These developmental tools were only asked of those who indicated the use of a formal programme. It is possible that some organisations may use these mechanisms in an informal manner. However the aim of this study was to capture those that systemically use such development mechanisms. The development mechanism being used by the greatest number of MNCs is what may be characterised as traditional qualifications programmes (e.g. MBA). Almost nine in ten (89.4 per cent) MNCs reported some level of utilisation of this development tool. This is followed by the assessment of performance against global management competencies (78 per cent), formal global management training (76 per cent), short-term international assignments (74 per cent) and finally long-term international assignments (65 per cent).

As has been endemic in the country of origin effects to date, it was US-owned MNCs that emerged as the highest users of all five mechanisms. Also worthy of note was the low utilisation of international assignments amongst UK

MNCs. The close geographical proximity may explain the low level of utilisation of expatriate assignments as a development tool. UK and Irish managers are likely to have broadly similar skill sets and consequently the use of expatriate assignments in the Irish operations may not be seen as particularly useful. Previously, Mabey and Ramirez (2004) classified UK firms as one of the lowest investors in management development and the findings here may, in part, reflect this pattern.

Figure 8.9 Utilisation of management development mechanisms

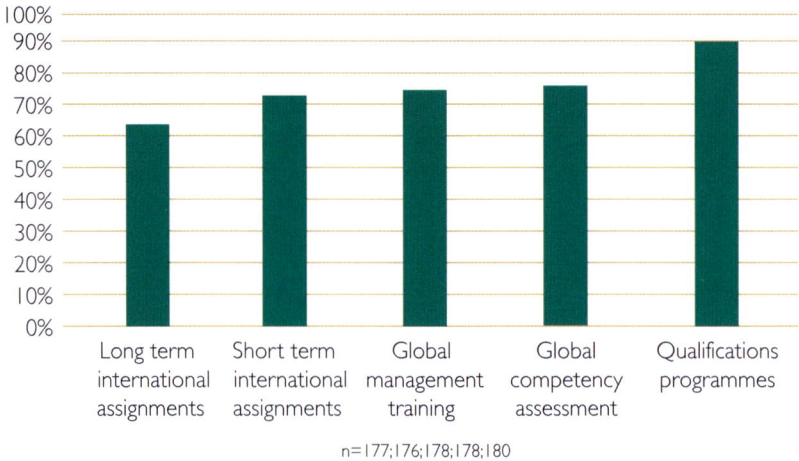

n=177;176;178;178;180

While it was useful to note the number of MNCs using the above mechanisms, it was particularly worthwhile to explore the actual level of utilisation of each of these development interventions. This incorporates a five point scale from '1 = not used at all' to '5 = used very extensively'. The assessment of performance against global management competencies emerged as the most extensively used, some 53 per cent of MNCs reported that it was utilised quite or very extensively. This was followed by the more traditional development mechanism of qualifications programmes (36 per cent reported it was used quite or very extensively). The least utilised mechanisms that emerged were short and long term international assignments. Only 16 per cent of MNC reported the extensive use of short term assignments and this fell to 12 per cent for long term international assignments. This low level of use amongst expatriate assignments is not particularly surprising when one considers the extant literature cites increasing repatriation concerns as well as dual career and family issues as making people less likely to accept foreign secondments (Scullion and Collings, 2006).

Table 8.1: Development mechanisms used by country of origin

	Short term international assignments	Log term international assignments	Global management trainingq	Global competency assessment	Qualifications programmes
UK	50%	43%	64%	82%	86%
US	83%	74%	90%	87%	94%
Rest of Europe	76%	64%	74%	70%	88%
Ireland	72%	72%	56%	67%	83%
Rest of World	58%	33%	58%	67%	83%

Valid n = 177; 176; 178; 178; 180.

Figure 8.10 Frequency of use of management development mechanisms

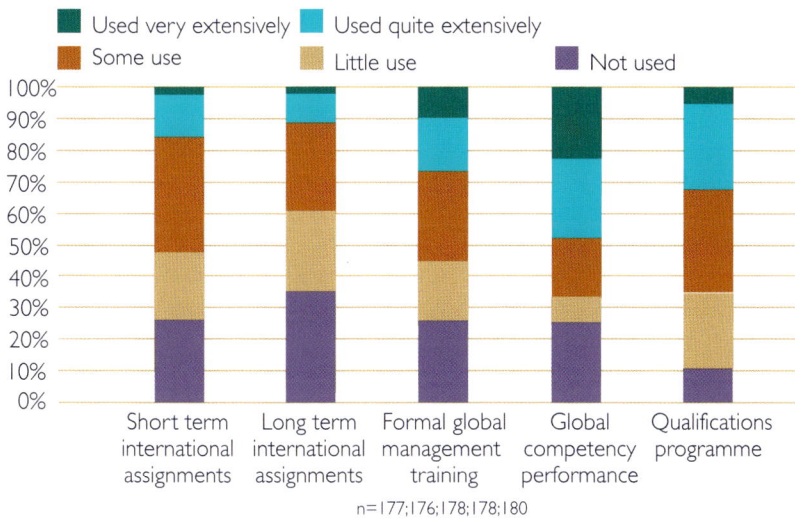

n=177;176;178;178;180

We found some variations between MNCs of different nationalities concerning how extensively these management development methods were used. For example, two thirds of US MNCs made extensive use of global management competencies, a substantially higher figure than the 46 per cent of UK MNCs that stated use of the same measure. The UK study found the use of global competencies to be highest amongst French MNCs followed by US firms, both of which were significantly higher than MNCs of all other nationalities (Edwards et al., 2007).

Overall the level of utilisation of each development mechanism appeared as quite low. The authors suggested that the reasoning behind this may be that MNCs favour a multi-faceted development approach. By that, we mean that they are inclined to use a greater range of development interventions than having a heavy reliance on one or two. They may feel that such an approach may be more useful in providing their high-potentials with a broader organisational overview which is cited as a key part of the development of high-potentials, in addition to a 'global mindset' (Briscoe and Schuler, 2004; Osland et al., 2006). This suggestion is given some support by the results which showed 44 per cent of MNCs used all five of the aforementioned mechanisms, 37 per cent used three or four of them, 10 per cent used three while the remaining 9 per cent used two or less.

Figure 8.11 Number of management development mechanisms utilised

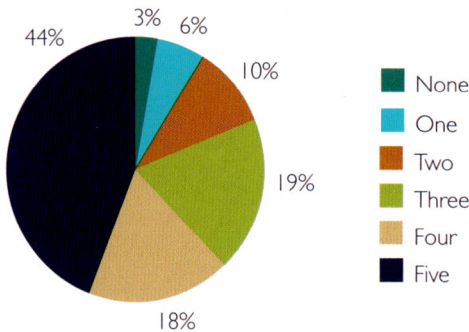

The most noticeable finding according to country of origin was that US MNCs were substantially more likely to report using all five development mechanisms (57 per cent) followed somewhat surprisingly by indigenous MNCs (40 per cent). 89 per cent of multi-sector MNCs reported the use of four or five mechanisms, while somewhat surprisingly in the context of the previous findings outlined manufacturing sector MNCs were more likely to use greater numbers of the aforementioned mechanisms than services sector MNCs.

Organisational learning and knowledge diffusion

Next, we turn to the concept of organisational learning which continues to be an area of research interest due in no small part to the increasing importance of creativity and innovation. This coupled with the ultra-competitive global business environment, makes organisational learning particularly important to MNCs. Organisational learning in MNCs has been defined as, "some combination of improving actions and acquiring new knowledge, whether it is new products or processes that are of strategic importance to the multinational firm" (Saka-Helmhout, 2007: 295). While organisational learning has been considered by academics for some time now, it is an area characterised more by conceptual rather than empirical work. This may be viewed as surprising considering the suggestion that firms which engage in effective organisational learning can achieve sustainable competitive advantage (Moingeon and Edmondson, 1996). It has been suggested that a major advantage of MNCs are the synergies that can be developed from cross-border creation, accumulation and sharing of knowledge (Bartlett and Ghoshal, 1989; Gupta and Govindarajan, 1991). MNCs possess great potential in exploiting market conditions from accumulating information in the different markets in which they operate and transforming this into organisational knowledge (Macharzina et al., 2001; Taylor, 2006).

Evidence is provided here on whether MNCs have a formal policy for organisational learning and also the extent to which there are practices in situ to facilitate organisational learning.

Figure 8.12 Formal organisation learning policy by country of origin

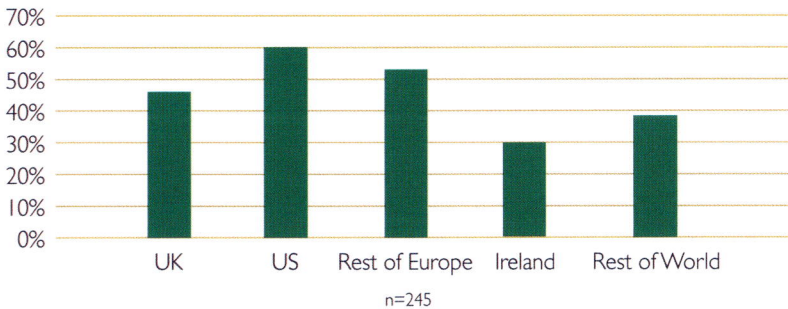

n=245

Just less than half (49 per cent) of all MNCs reported a formal policy for organisational learning in some/all of their Irish operations. The existence of such a policy may be construed as a proxy measure for indicating the value placed on organisational learning by MNCs. This policy, where in place, emerged as being predominantly global in focus (88 per cent) rather than specific to the local Irish operations (12 per cent). This is as expected because a global organisation learning policy "may have a role to play in co-ordinating learning processes internationally that encourage knowledge diffusion or the collaborative development of knowledge across borders" (Tregaskis et al., 2008: 13). Some distinct country of origin variations also seemed to emerge. Figure 8.12 shows that US-owned MNCs (59 per cent) were the most likely to report a formal policy with indigenous MNCs (30 per cent), by some considerable distance the least likely. This may be due to foreign MNCs having a longer history of internationalisation than Irish MNCs and are more advanced in seeking to gain from the potential benefits that may arise through the diffusion of knowledge across their international network of operations.

There are various means by which organisational learning can be facilitated within MNCs. One of the most traditional methods of transferring knowledge in MNCs is through international assignments, which can take the form of expatriate deployment both into and out of the firm's operations across different countries (Galbraith and Edstrom, 1976; Edstrom and Galbraith, 1988; Bartlett and Ghoshal, 1995; Berthoin Antal, 2000; Kidger, 2002). Expatriates develop knowledge banks from exposure to different situations and cultures and this can be used to benefit the rest of the MNC (Kamoche, 1997). Further to international assignments, there exist structural devices which can aid organisational learning, including international project groups and steering committees (Kets de Vries, 1999; Gupta and Govindarajan, 2000; Mendez, 2003; Frost and Zhou, 2005). These can offer a different learning experience to that of the international assignment. For instance, Kidger (2002) suggests international project groups are particularly useful in the development of global innovation whilst also taking account of the local needs. This study explored the use of five mechanisms:

- Expatriate assignments
- International projects groups or task forces
- International formal committees
- International informal networks
- Secondments to other organisations internationally (e.g. to suppliers, customers, universities or private R&D companies)

Figure 8.13 Organisational learning mechanisms used

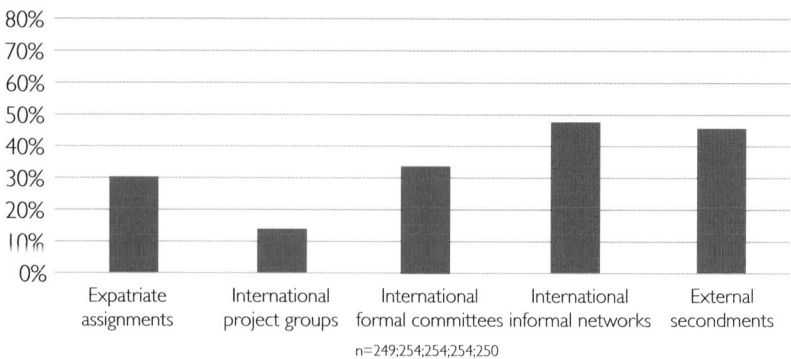

n=249;254;254;254;250

As figure 8.13 illustrates, there was widespread variation across the five mechanisms. The most used mechanism for organisational learning was international informal networks (76 per cent), followed by international project groups/task forces (69 per cent), expatriate assignments (59 per cent), and international formal committees (50 per cent). Secondments to external organisations internationally (e.g. to suppliers, customers, universities and private research and development facilities) were reported as the least utilised (22 per cent).

Relatively large numbers of MNCs indicated multiple mechanism use. 14 per cent reported the use of all five mechanisms, 23 per cent utilise four, 24 per cent avail of three, 17 per cent use two mechanisms, 7 per cent only utilise one with the remaining 15 per cent failing to use of any of these organisational learning practices. This is almost double the figure found in the UK study in regard to MNCs that fail to use any (Edwards et al., 2007), Consequently, over six in ten MNCs have adopted more than three mechanisms for the facilitating organisational learning.

We discovered that although not the most commonly used, international project groups/task forces were reported as the most important organisation learning mechanism used. Four in ten respondents indicated this to be the case. This was followed by 28 per cent of respondents that cited international informal networks, slightly ahead of the 24 per cent who chose expatriate assignments as the most important aid for organisation learning between operations. Less than one per cent indicated external secondments, the remaining 7 per cent indicated international formal committees were the most significant.

Once again US MNCs (74 per cent) emerged as the most likely to utilise at least three of these mechanisms, followed by 61 per cent of European MNCs. Differences between manufacturing and services sector MNCs were miniscule, both were found to be less inclined to use 3 or more of the aforementioned mechanisms than multi-sector MNCs.

Diffusing knowledge through expatriates

In the previous section it was noted that expatriate assignments may be used as a means of transferring knowledge in MNCs. Edstrom and Galbraith (1977) reported that expatriates are used for three primary reasons. Firstly, to fill a position. Secondly, to develop individual employees and organisational development. Thirdly, for knowledge transfer, control and coordination of operations. Our findings were able to provide some support for these contentions. A total of 58 per cent of all MNCs testified that expatriates are used for organisational learning purposes, while 73 per cent reported the use of short term international assignments and 63 per cent reported the use of long term international assignments for management development purposes.

We now provide some evidence on the use of expatriate assignments. Traditionally, parent country nationals (PCNs) have been the predominant form used by MNCs but in more recent times it was suggested that there have been increases in the number of inpatriates and third country nationals (TCNs) (see Scullion and Collings, 2006). Inpatriates refer to staff who are seconded from subsidiaries to the parent company headquarters while TCNs refer to employees whose national origin is not the same as the parent company or host country. However, there is a lack of survey evidence on the extent to which these types of assignments are being used.

Firstly we turn to foreign-owned MNCs. Some 44 per cent have PCNs and 30 per cent have TCNs currently on long-term assignments in the Irish operations. In terms of the numbers of expatriates in each operation, it was found that 84 per cent of firms with PCNs have between one and five, the remaining 16 per cent reported more than six PCNs. A total of 72 per cent of MNCs with TCNs employ between one and five, the remaining 28 per cent have greater than six. The median number of parent country expatriates was 2, the corresponding figure for third country expatriates was 3. This reinforces Collings et al.'s (2008b) assertion that the use of TCN expatriates is under estimated in the literature. The comparative UK study found the median number of parent country and third country nationals to be the same (3) indicating that the expatriate population is no longer dominated by parent country nationals (Edwards et al., 2007), a finding that is supported by these data.

A number of national differences were also found, US-owned firms (41.5 per cent) were the least likely to have PCNs in the Irish operations. The most likely being the rest of the world category (54 per cent), followed by UK-owned (48 per cent) and European MNCs (43 per cent). Considerably different findings were found with respect to TCNs. Here, US-owned MNCs (33 per cent) were the most likely to have TCNs in their Irish sites, followed by European MNCs (30.5 per cent) and UK MNCs (19 per cent). The rest of the world category (17 per cent) had the lowest incidence of TCNs.

Foreign MNCs were also asked to indicate the number of expatriates from the Irish operations working on expatriate assignments in the corporate headquarters (inpatriates) and in other parts of the worldwide company (third country outflows). Almost five in ten MNGs (46 per cent) indicated there are employees from the Irish operations on assignment somewhere in the worldwide operations (either to the parent country or third country operations). Conversely almost 54 per cent of foreign MNCs do not have any employees from Ireland on assignment in their global operations. A quarter of all Irish operations reported inpatriates, with 38 per cent reporting outflows to operations outside of the parent country. More specifically, the results show 21 per cent of firms only have outflows to third country operations with 9 per cent only with staffing flows to the parent country headquarters. The remaining 16 per cent currently have staff from the Irish operations in both the parent country headquarters and other worldwide subsidiaries.

Table 8.2: Staffing outflows from the Irish operations

	n	Percent
Inpatriates	51	25%
Third country nationals	76	38%
Inpatriates and/or third country nationals	93	46%

In terms of the numbers on assignment in the parent country headquarters, we found a range of between one and thirty. Although a considerable range, the majority (71 per cent) reported between one and three inpatriates. Turning to third country outflows, we found a slightly smaller range of one to twenty. 65 per cent of MNCs with third country outflows reported having one to three expatriates on foreign assignment from the Irish operations.

US-owned MNCs (56 per cent) represent the country category which were the most likely to indicate expatriates from the Irish operations being on assignment somewhere in the worldwide company. UK-owned MNCs were the least likely, with just a quarter having staffing outflows from the Irish operations. Taking these results as a whole, they are shown to contrast with the more general literature on expatriation which has suggested US MNCs are less likely to use expatriates than MNCs of other nationalities (Harzing, 2001). This may possibly be explained by the fact that inpatriates and TCNs are less likely to be utilised for control purposes and hence their use may be premised on development and knowledge transfer objectives. However these reasons are tentative as the motives of assignments were not explored here.

Turning to Irish-owned MNCs, we found that 73 per cent currently have PCNs working in their foreign subsidiaries. 60 per cent of these involve between one and five PCNs in their foreign sites, 40 per cent have in excess of six, the median number being 5. On the other hand, only 38 per cent of Irish MNCs indicated they have expatriates from their foreign operations working on long term assignments in Ireland. Due to the lateness by which Irish firms internationalised, indigenous MNCs may be somewhat behind the curve with regard to the use of inpatriate assignments which are useful in embedding employees from outside of the MNCs' national origin into the organisation and at the same time providing them with defined career paths, facilitate the learning of organisational cultures, values and decision making processes (Harvey et al., 2001). The median number of these expatriates was 3, while 53 per cent of those indigenous MNCs indicating inpatriates had five or less.

Conclusion

This chapter summarised the training and development and organisational learning policies and practices of MNCs in Ireland. The findings showed that the majority of MNCs spend between one and four per cent of their annual pay bill on training and development activities for their workforce. An interesting result was the difficulty of respondents in providing a specific figure on T&D expenditure whilst a significant number were even unable to provide a range for this spending. A substantial number of firms were shown to have systems of succession planning in place, of which an overwhelming majority were global in scope. A majority of firms also indicated they have a formal management development programme for their high-potentials, although the numbers were slightly less than those with succession planning systems. Once again, these tended to be global in reach rather than locally specific. These findings corroborate existing researching suggesting talent pipelines are increasingly being coordinated on a global basis (cf. Sparrow et al., 2004; Stiles et al., 2006; Sparrow, 2007; Stahl et al., 2007; Briscoe et al., 2008). These findings may also indicate that localisation represents a key element of the globalisation strategy in a significant number of MNCs. Localisation is taken to mean the systematic investment in the recruitment, development and retention of local (host) employees (Evans et al., 2002).

MNCs were also shown to make use of a diverse range of development interventions for their high-potentials. The provision of such opportunities will arguably place these MNCs in a much stronger position to retain these employees vis-à-vis those MNCs which do not (Windolf, 1986; Boxall and Purcell, 2003). Elsewhere, it has been reported that high-potentials expect top management to pay close attention to their development and career progression (Stahl et al., 2007). Furthermore, it has been argued that MNCs need to move away from a sole focus on PCNs and include host country staff so as to enhance the quality of their international staff (McPherson and Roche, 1997).

Organisational learning also emerged as an area of significant activity amongst MNCs in Ireland. We found that almost half of these organisations have a formal policy for organisational learning. Substantially more MNCs indicated the use of mechanisms to facilitate organisational learning between cross-country operations. This suggests informal mechanisms as well as formal ones play a crucial role in the creation of new organisational knowledge and the diffusion of this knowledge across the global organisation.

This study also found that expatriate assignments remain popular although possibly on a downward trend. The findings suggest that there is an emergent portfolio of global staffing options open to and being utilised by MNCs. In addition to the more traditional parent country expatriate assignment, it emerged that inpatriates and third country expatriates now play a key role in MNCs. This provides support for the argument put forward by Harvey and colleagues (2001) that the traditional and unidirectional models of global staffing are becoming less appropriate for organisations operating in the global sphere.

Some interesting variances were noted with respect to country of origin and sector. US-owned MNCs tended to be the most developed and formalised with respect to T&D and organisational learning. For example, there were a greater proportion of US MNCs who spent in excess of 4 per cent of their annual pay bill on T&D for the workforce. They were also the most likely to undertake succession planning, management development and organisational learning. Previous research suggested T&D of host country employees was not an area where they were particularly known for (Russ-Eft et al., 1997). Bartlett and colleagues (2002) in their study of US MNCs in East and Southeast Asia also found them to be the leading players in respect to T&D. They argued that it may reflect "the changing strategic focus of US companies and a renewed emphasis on quality, service, and related objectives" (Bartlett et al., 2002: 400). The finding that indigenous MNCs tended to be the least likely to have formal T&D interventions was unsurprising, due in no small part to their late internationalisation. In addition, Irish-owned MNCs may be constrained by their financial resources. Indigenous MNCs tend to be small to medium sized firms by international standards and thus may not have the financial muscle that the larger, more mature MNCs may have. This supports the argument of Tregaskis and colleagues (2001: 45) that "larger organisations, by their very nature and structure can offer, a wider range of career development opportunities and are also more likely to have the resources to invest in sustaining an internal labour market".

Sector was interesting in that it was MNCs classified as multi-sector which tended to be the most likely to have the various policies and practices that were investigated in situ. Manufacturing sector MNCs tended to be the least likely to have formalised succession planning and management development programmes for their high-potentials. It would be worthwhile exploring these sectoral variations in greater detail by more specific activities something which can be found at the end of the book in regard to specific articles currently in process and/or have been published.

CHAPTER 9
Managing Across Borders:
Autonomy Coordination and Control in MNCS

Anthony McDonnell, Ryan Lamare and Jonathan Lavelle

Introduction

This chapter investigates the degree of influence and the extent of discretion of local management within the overall corporate framework of MNCs. Some questions that will be addressed in this chapter include the following: are managers in foreign-owned MNCs simply executors of HR and ER strategies conceived and created at higher levels? Or do they play a more strategic role, with autonomy to adjust HR and ER strategies and policies to the local context, and to change and develop the mandates for their firms beyond those initially envisaged at corporate level? The chapter also uniquely focuses on Irish-owned MNCs that have established international operations and the autonomy afforded to these foreign subsidiaries by the Irish headquarters[i].

In HR and ER, as in most other management spheres, the approach adopted by MNCs may range from reliance on the application of standard policies across operating units in different countries, to allowing extensive local autonomy for national management teams to develop their own HR/ER polices and practices. Standardisation is regarded as optimal where MNCs engage in similar activities in different countries, while local autonomy may best apply where the nature of a MNCs' activities in different countries vary considerably (Edwards and Zhang, 2008). Of course there are also intermediate possibilities, which concurrently seek to achieve elements of both centralisation and devolved autonomy (Edwards et al., 2007). An example might be the utilisation of broad policy frameworks that map out general guidelines but allow for local autonomy with respect to implementation and execution. We also know that MNCs can change their stance over time, involving either an increase or decrease in local managerial autonomy. For example, a recent case study investigation found that the Irish subsidiaries generally operated with high levels of autonomy but also noted a trend toward greater centralised control from the corporate base, particularly with respect to the monitoring of headcount and greater budgetary control, often related to Irish operations' moving 'up the value chain' (i.e. engaging in higher value-added activities (Gunnigle et al., 2004)). By and large, one would expect to find greater local autonomy in HR/ER compared to other management spheres (e.g. production or finance), given that HR/ER tends to be more institutionally embedded and sensitive to particular national characteristics, such as labour legislation, labour supply and trade union organisation (cf. Rosenzweig and Nohria, 1994).

Local managerial autonomy and standardisation

We now consider the evidence on patterns of standardisation and local autonomy across a range of employment practices, and investigate the extent to which the nationality of the MNC and the sector it operates in are useful in accounting for variation in the overall degree of discretion. Specifically, our survey investigated the extent of management discretion in four substantive areas of HR policy:

a) Pay and performance management
b) Employee representation and consultation
c) Employee involvement and communication
d) Training, development and organisational learning

Within each area, a number of discrete policy issues were identified and respondents were then asked to indicate their level of discretion on a five-point scale from 'no discretion' (i.e. must implement policy set by a higher level) to 'full discretion' (i.e. can set own policy). A sixth option was also provided, namely that the level of discretion varies widely across the different operations (i.e. no typical situation exists). This option was selected in only a small number of cases and is not included when mean values are provided. Clearly, this domain is one where the data from foreign and Irish-owned MNCs must be analysed separately. Among foreign-owned MNCs, our data identify the extent of local autonomy **afforded** to local management from higher levels, while in indigenous MNCs the data inform the level of discretion **granted** to their overseas subsidiaries. We therefore consider foreign and Irish-owned MNCs separately, but also make some brief comparisons where appropriate.

By way of structure, we will explore the discretion according to each of the aforementioned substantive HR areas while keeping the indigenous and foreign-owned MNC findings separate. This will allow use explore whether the key HR/ER decisions are taken locally or at higher international levels. In the words of a comparative study of MNCs in Canada, "are managers within foreign-controlled MNCs merely agents of global firms – simple executors of strategies crafted elsewhere – or are they strategic players, with the autonomy to adjust to local contexts and to develop visions of the activities of their firms that supersede original MNC strategies?" (Bélanger et al., 2006: 30).

Evidence of differences according to the MNCs' country of origin and sector will also be provided. There has been much research that shows "multinationals appear to follow the tracks of coordination and control in which they have become embedded in their country of origin" (Harzing and Sorge, 2003: 187). Sector has also emerged as key variable with Fenton-O'Creevy et al. (2008) suggesting that services sector MNCs are more likely to be locally adapted compared to manufacturing MNCs. Consequently, services sector firms may be expected to be less subject to central control.

Discretion over pay and performance management

Foreign-owned MNcs

The results showed that local management in a significant number of MNCs have discretion in the area of pay and performance management. With respect to relating pay levels of the MNCs' Irish operations to market comparators, it was found that almost one-third of MNCs reported full discretion (i.e. they had the discretion to set their own policy). A further 50 per cent indicated having some or quite a lot of discretion. A further 10 per cent indicated they had no discretion in regard to this aspect of pay. As demonstrated in Table 9.1, levels of discretion were broadly similar across each of the other five specific aspects that were investigated, although there tended to be greater numbers which reported no discretion. For instance, 32 per cent reported no discretion over employee share ownership schemes, 24 per cent in regard to performance appraisals for managers, 20 per cent with respect to performance appraisals for the LOG and 17 per cent over variable pay for managers. Furthermore, some 10 per cent reported no discretion over variable pay for the LOG while 34 per cent indicated full discretion. Thus, discretion levels tend to vary between MNCs rather than being polarised between high and no discretion. Few organisations reported that there was no typical situation between the firms Irish operations (i.e., discretion varied between the different Irish sites).

Table 9.1 Discretion over pay and performance management

	Relating pay to market comparators	Employee share ownership	Performance appraisal for managers	Performance appraisal for LOG	Variable pay for managers	Variable pay for LOG
No discretion	10%	32%	24%	20%	17%	10%
Little discretion	8%	17%	14%	7%	15%	10%
Some discretion	23%	12%	14%	17%	21%	20%
Quite a lot of discretion	28%	17%	15%	15%	24%	25%
Full discretion	32%	22%	34%	39%	23%	34%
No typical situation	-	2%	1%	2%	1%	2%

n = 199; 60; 182; 149; 185; 136.

Respondents were also asked, "over the last three years, to what extent has the discretion of your Irish operations in setting HR policy relative to higher levels of your worldwide company increased or decreased in the following HR areas"? A five point scale was used from $1 = significantly\ decreased$ to $5 = significantly\ increased$. No MNCs reported that the Irish management's autonomy had significantly decreased over pay and performance management: 7 per cent stated there had been a decrease and 49 per cent said that no change had taken place. Some 32 per cent stated there had been an increase in their autonomy over pay and performance management policy vis-à-vis higher organisational levels, whilst the remaining 12 per cent reported there had been a significant increase.

Sectoral variations were relatively minimal with broadly similar discretion levels reported against each of the aforementioned aspects pay and performance management. The main difference tended to be in regard to multi-sector MNCs who were more likely to report no discretion with the exception of employee share ownership schemes. By way of example, some 38 per cent of multi-sector MNCs reported no discretion over the performance appraisal system for managers, while 25 per cent noted full discretion. This compared to some 19 per cent of services sector and 27 per cent of manufacturing sector MNCs that stated they had no discretion. At the same time, 39 per cent of services sector MNCs and 28 per cent of manufacturing firms had full discretion. These findings were broadly characteristic across each of the other pay and performance management policy areas investigated. Manufacturing MNCs were also considerably more likely to report that there had been no change in the discretion of Irish management over pay and performance management policy in the previous three years (64 per cent versus 44 per cent of services sector firms and 43 per cent of multi-sector MNCs).

Figure 9.1 Discretion over pay and performance management by country of origin

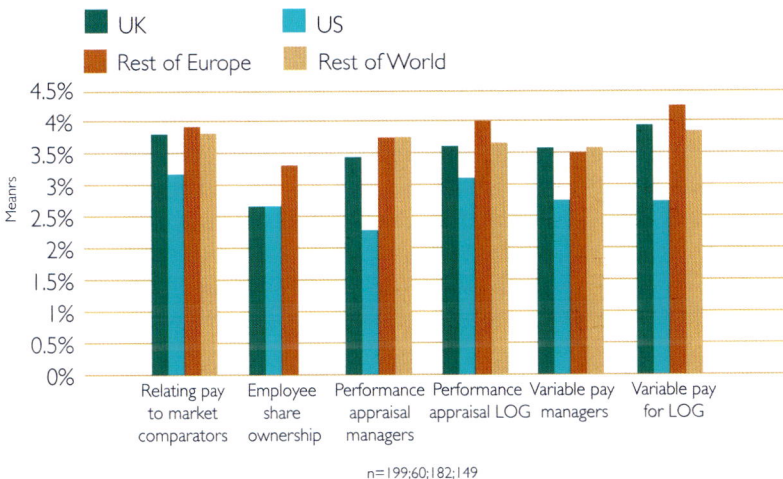

n=199;60;182;149

Nationality effects also emerged with local management in US-owned MNCs the least likely to indicate they have full discretion over each of the explored pay and performance management areas. UK-owned, European MNCs and those firms classified as rest of the world all reported greater levels of discretion over pay and performance management systems and policies. US firms were also shown to have the lowest mean scores in terms of discretion afforded to the Irish operations across each aspect of pay and performance management with the exception of employee share schemes.

Further, US MNCs were also the most likely to have stated that discretion decreased over pay and performance management policy in the previous three years. Some 5 per cent of US firms reported that higher organisational levels had significantly reined in on the autonomy afforded to local management. A further 27 per cent stated that the autonomy of the Irish subsidiaries had decreased and 40 per cent reported that there had been no change. This meant 29 per cent reported an increase of some form with respect to autonomy over pay and performance management policy.

Indigenous MNCs

Figure 9.2 Discretion afforded to indigenous MNCs over pay and performance management

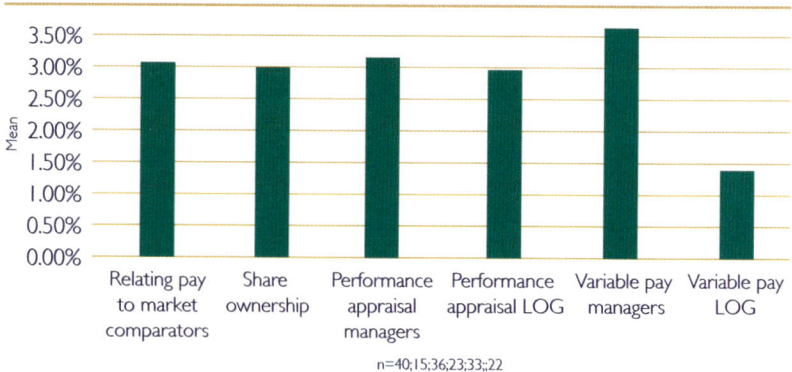

n=40;15;36;23;33;:22

As depicted by Figure 9.2, Irish-owned MNCs were shown to afford relatively low levels of discretion to their foreign operations. This was particularly pronounced with regard to share ownership where 87 per cent of Irish MNCs reported that their foreign operations had no discretion. This equated to a mean score of just 1.33. Indigenous MNCs reported the highest level of discretion (mean score of 2.87) was afforded to their foreign operation's with regard to performance appraisals for the LOG. Greater numbers of multi-sector, indigenous MNCs were found to report that no discretion was afforded to their foreign operations. Specifically, six in ten multi-sector firms reported that their foreign operations had no discretion over the performance appraisal system for managers, compared to 33 per cent of services sector and 30 per cent of manufacturing MNCs.

With respect to whether there had been a change in the discretion afforded to the foreign operations of Irish-owned MNCs, in the three years previous to the study, a similar result to that highlighted about foreign-owned MNCs was found. Most indigenous MNCs stated that there has been no change (49 per cent), whilst 44 per cent stated they had provided subsidiary management with greater levels of autonomy over pay and performance management. This may be related to the age of the foreign operations. Greater corporate control may be expected in the early years of subsidiary establishment than in a long-standing site. Fenton-O'Creevy *et al.* (2008) suggest that the older the subsidiary, the less important centralised control is because the MNC has had sufficient time to socialise the operation into the corporate culture. On the other hand, Ferner *et al.* (2007) suggest that central control could also increase over time, particularly in regard to acquired operations. This is related to corporate management increasing its hold over the acquired firms management structure.

Comparing the headquarters perspective (Irish-owned MNCs) and the subsidiary perspective (foreign-owned MNCs) regarding discretion there appears to be somewhat of a consistent pattern. A number of subsidiaries of foreign-owned MNCs reported low levels of discretion over policies on pay and performance management; whilst senior management in Irish MNCs reported that they afforded low levels of discretion to their foreign operations over the same issues. This was particularly evident with regard to policies over share ownership schemes. These findings would suggest that policies regarding pay are centralised and thus MNCs are unwilling to afford large amounts of autonomy to subsidiaries to make decisions over such issues. Considering the growing concerns over financial issues, it was not surprising to see relatively low levels of discretion over such issues.

Discretion over employee representation and consultation

Foreign-owned MNCs

The levels of discretion afforded to the Irish management of foreign-owned MNCs were far higher in regard to decisions over trade union recognition, the extent of union involvement in decision-making and employee consultation than with respect to each of the aforementioned performance management measures. In fact, across each of the three measures here, in excess of half of the foreign MNCs reported full discretion. Indeed a mere 4 per cent reported that they had only a little or no discretion over employee consultation and 7 per cent with respect to the extent of union involvement in decision-making. There were a somewhat greater number of MNCs (21 per cent) who reported no or a little discretion over whether to recognise a trade union. Again, there was a fairly common approach taken across all of the Irish sites as less than 3 per cent indicated that there was no typical situation for all Irish operations.

Table 9.2 Discretion over employee representation and consultation

	Trade union recognition	Extent of union involvement in decision-making	Employee consultation
No discretion	15%	1%	1%
Little discretion	6%	6%	3%
Some discretion	13%	13%	15%
Quite a lot of discretion	13%	20%	24%
Full discretion	51%	58%	56%
No typical situation	3%	3%	1%

n = 191; 111; 183.

As with pay and performance management, respondents were asked to indicate whether their discretion over employee representation and consultation matters had changed in the previous three years. It was found that 66 per cent reported no change, while 4 per cent indicated diminished autonomy. The remaining 30 per cent stated there had been an increase of some form in regard to their autonomy over employee representation and consultation.

Sectoral variations were almost non-existent in regard to discretion in this area and whether there had been a change in the previous three years. The one exception was in relation to subsidiary discretion over trade union recognition. Multi-sector firms (33 per cent) were found to be considerably less likely to report full discretion over trade union recognition than MNCs in the services sector (53 per cent) and manufacturing (52 per cent) firms. With respect to employee consultation and the extent of union involvement in decision-making, the differences found between sectors were less than six percentage points.

Similar to the findings on pay and performance management some clear country of origin effects emerged with subsidiary management in US-owned MNCs the least likely to indicate they had full discretion over the three measures of employee representation and consultation. Whilst 74 per cent of European

MNCs, 66 per cent of UK-owned firms and 42 per cent of the rest of the world MNC category stated that they held full discretion over trade union recognition, while only 32 per cent of US MNCs held full discretion. Across the other two measures, US-owned firms were found to be less likely to report full discretion although the numbers were higher than with respect to trade union recognition (46 per cent reported full discretion over union involvement in decision-making and 51 per cent over employee consultation). The average levels of discretion afforded to local management by country of origin are illustrated in Figure 9.3. No noticeable country of origin differences were found with respect to a change in discretion over employee representation and consultation issues in recent times.

Figure 9.3 Discretion over employee representation and consultation by country of origin

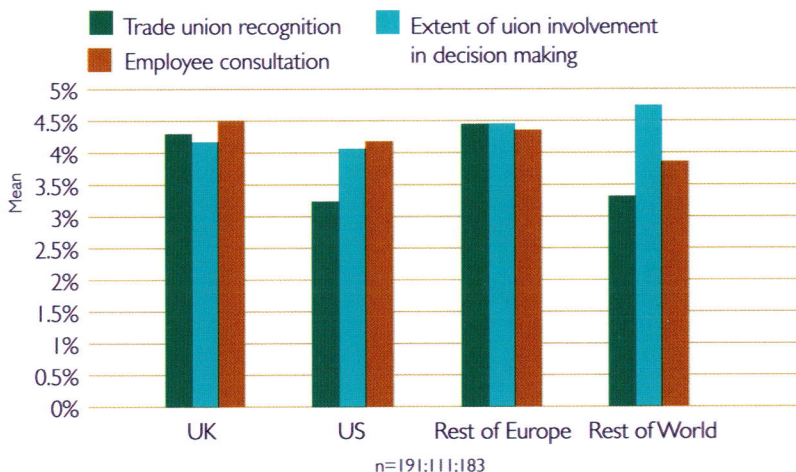

Indigenous MNCs

Irish-owned MNCs were asked to what extent they afforded discretion to their foreign subsidiaries over the same employee representation and consultation measures. As depicted by Table 9.3, Irish-owned MNCs appeared to afford low levels of discretion over the same three policy areas to their foreign subsidiaries, particularly with regard to union recognition, which the following quite may be taken as indicative of this:

> To involve unions in any decision making you would need to get the approval of the headquarters. Trade unions would not be involved in decision

making in this company
HR Manager, Irish-owned, manufacturing MNC.

The discretion provided to local managers on trade union recognition was shown to have a mean value of 2.95, 3.22 in relation to the extent of union involvement in decision-making and somewhat higher at 3.28 for employee consultation. Table 9.3 shows that firms reported varying discretion levels with each category of response relatively even rather than there being polar values of no discretion and full discretion.

Table 9.3 Discretion afforded to foreign subsidiaries of Irish-owned MNCs

	Trade union recognition	Extent of union involvement in decision-making	Employee consultation
No discretion	30%	21%	21%
Little discretion	10%	15%	10%
Some discretion	10%	9%	10%
Quite a lot of discretion	27%	24%	26%
Full discretion	18%	27%	26%
No typical situation	7%	6%	7%

n = 41; 32; 39.

Almost three-quarters (74 per cent) indicated that there had been no change in the discretion provided to management of foreign subsidiaries over these matters in the previous three years. Some 7 per cent stated the afforded discretion had decreased while the remaining 19 per cent indicated there had been an increase.

Sectoral differences did not substantially emerge although indigenous MNCs operating in the services sector (33 per cent) were shown to be somewhat more likely to report no discretion over trade union recognition compared to manufacturing (20 per cent) and multi-sector (29 per cent) firms.

What is interesting is the contrast between the headquarters perspective (Irish MNCs) and the local operations perspective (foreign MNCs), as noted in both tables 9.2 and 9.3. On the one hand, the Irish operations of foreign-owned MNCs reported high levels of discretion/autonomy whilst senior management in the headquarters for Irish MNCs noted that they afford low levels of discretion to their foreign subsidiaries. How do we reconcile these differences between the two perspectives? Was it the case that subsidiaries were over-estimating their autonomy with regard to employment relations? Or perhaps managers at the headquarters level reported higher levels of control than there actually was? The extant literature suggests that there is a high level of devolvement of HRM to the local level (Rosenzweig and Nohria, 1994), particularly with regard to employee representation (Ferner, 1997). Furthermore Gunnigle et al. (2005) noted that decisions regarding trade union recognition at newer sites of US MNCs operating in Ireland were taken or driven by local management, albeit in the knowledge that corporate headquarters would be in favour of the decision. Thus, it may be more likely that the headquarters perspective is over-estimating its power on employee representation and consultation matters in its foreign operations. Future studies may look to gain an additional perspective from the foreign operations of indigenous MNCs.

Discretion over employee involvement and communication

Foreign-owned MNCs

The results of this survey indicated that in the vast majority of instances local operations of MNCs operating in Ireland considered that they had either total or wide discretion in the task based aspects of employee involvement in work processes and suggestion schemes. Discretion was also reported to be high in the provision of information to employees. This high degree of discretion corresponds to the high levels of discretion perceived to exist over employee representation and consultation issues previously described. The high levels of discretion may reflect the fact that direct forms of communication and involvement are within management control and are largely non-controversial. Thus, high levels of discretion over meetings, likely to deal with task-related matters and be relatively standard practice, were found. Full discretion was reported by more than half of all MNCs across three of the four aspects of employee involvement and communication. Greater limitations were placed on discretion where attitude and opinion surveys were involved. A little over a quarter (27 per cent) reported full discretion whilst 40 per cent reported only a little or no discretion over attitude or opinion surveys. In addition, the mean value for local management autonomy over attitude and opinion surveys was 3.13 compared to 4.27 for the provision of information to employees, 4.38 over suggestion schemes and 4.43 with respect to the involvement of employees in the work process. This may be due to companies conducting mandatory cross-national surveys within the organisation, although in some instances conducting such surveys may be potentially more controversial and require higher-level authorisation. Similar results emerged here, as to the previous HR areas, with respect to whether there was a change in the autonomy provided to local management. Some 62 per cent indicated that there had been no change, 31 per cent said that there had been an increase, whilst 7 per cent suggested that they had witnessed a decrease in their autonomy over employee involvement and communication.

Table 9.4 Discretion over employee involvement and communication

	Employee involvement in work process	Attitude/opinion surveys	Suggestion schemes	Provision of information to employees
No discretion	2%	20%	3%	1%
Little discretion	2%	20%	2%	3%
Some discretion	9%	14%	7%	15%
Quite a lot of discretion	25%	19%	31%	31%
Full discretion	62%	27%	57%	50%
No typical situation	-	-	-	-

n = 205; 153; 110; 197.

Figure 9.4 Discretion over employee involvement and communication by country of origin

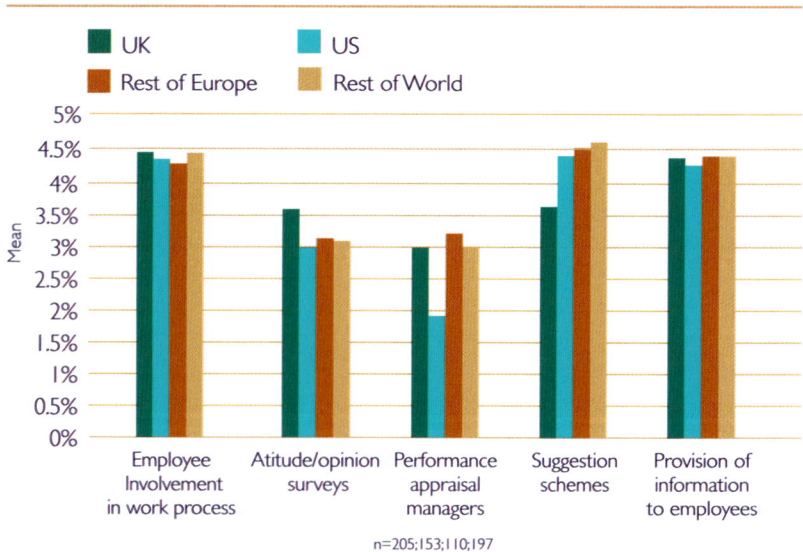

n=205;153;110;197

Few differences emerged in regard to sectoral differences with the average discretion values according to each aspect of employee involvement and communication were quite small. Some differences emerged with respect to the

MNCs' country of origin. US MNCs tended to report lower levels of local management discretion however, this was not the case across each of the measures and the differences were less apparent relative to the findings on pay and performance management and employee representation and consultation. The more pronounced difference was with respect to suggestion schemes and it involved UK-owned MNCs being quite different to the other three categories of foreign-owned MNCs. Specifically, UK MNCs were found to have a mean discretion score of 3.71 compared to 4.42 for US-owned firms, 4.55 for European MNCs and higher again for the rest of the world category (4.6). Changes in discretion in the previous three years did not emerge as particularly distinctive across the different sectors or nationalities.

Indigenous MNCs

Overall, Irish headquarters managers reported their overseas operations had somewhat less discretion than that reported by the subsidiary managers of foreign operations in Ireland. Whilst 50 per cent or more foreign-owned MNCs indicated full discretion across three of the four employee involvement issues, the largest number of indigenous MNCs that reported full discretion was 41 per cent in respect to suggestion schemes. Thus, lower discretion was reported in the areas of work process involvement, the provision of information and the use of suggestion schemes. The one exception was in regard to attitude/opinion surveys where the mean discretion value afforded to the foreign operations of Irish-owned MNCs was 3.14, 0.02 higher than that found with respect to the autonomy afforded to local managers in foreign-owned firms.

Table 9.5 Discretion Irish MNCs afford its foreign subsidiaries over employee involvement and communication

	Employee involvement in work process	Attitude/opinion surveys	Suggestion schemes	Provision of information to employees
No discretion	12%	29%	18%	15%
Little discretion	10%	7%	12%	7%
Some discretion	12%	7%	12%	17%
Quite a lot of discretion	29%	36%	18%	27%
Full discretion	38%	21%	41%	34%
No typical situation	-	-	-	-

n = 42; 14; 17; 41.

As per previous results, 62 per cent of indigenous MNCs reported that there had been no change in the autonomy afforded their foreign operations over employee involvement and communication matters during the three years previous to this study. Three in ten MNCs reported that the discretion afforded the foreign arms of the indigenous MNC had increased or significantly increased, while 7 per cent stated that it had decreased.

Some sectoral differences emerged with regard to the numbers reporting full discretion: however, due to the very small numbers of indigenous MNCs with attitude/opinion surveys (n=14) and suggestion schemes (n=17), interpreting these as being in any way concrete is not advisable. In regard to the provision of information of employees and the involvement of employees in the work process, significantly greater numbers of services sector MNCs reported full discretion vis-à-vis manufacturing and multi-sector firms. For instance, 48 per cent of Irish-owned services sector firms reported full discretion over the involvement of employees in the work process compared to 29 per cent of multi-sector and 20 per cent of manufacturing MNCs.

Discretion over training, development and organisational learning

Foreign-owned MNCs

Almost 8 in ten foreign-owned MNCs (79 per cent) reported having quite a lot or full discretion over the training and development policy in the Irish operations (see Table 9.6). A mere 1 per cent stated that they had no discretion whatsoever over this policy area. Indeed high levels of discretion were also reported across the other two policy areas. Some 57 per cent of foreign MNCs reported quite a lot or full discretion over the organisational learning policy: the comparative figure for succession planning was 48 per cent of MNCs. In terms of mean scores, far greater discretion seemed to have been afforded to local management over the training and development policy (mean of 4.14) compared to the organisation learning policy (mean of 3.71) and succession planning (mean of 3.47). Considering these tend to be global policies, the lower discretion values are unsurprising. The comparative study of MNCs in the UK also found higher discretion levels over the overall training and development policy than on succession planning (Edwards et al., 2007).

With respect to changes in discretion over the previous three years, it emerged that 37 per cent reported an increase or significant increase from higher organisational levels, 46 per cent said there had been no change, whilst the remaining 17 per cent stated there had been a decrease.

Figure 9.5 illustrates the level of discretion (mean scores) by industrial sector. What emerged was that manufacturing MNCs had higher levels of discretion over training and development policy and the policy on organisation learning although services sector firms were shown to have greater levels of autonomy over succession planning. Of interest was the finding that greater numbers of services sector MNCs (47 per cent) reported an increase or significant increase in discretion over training, development and organisation learning areas than manufacturing (29 per cent) and multi-sector (29 per cent) MNCs.

Table 9.6 Discretion over training, development and organisational learning

	Training and development policy	Organisation learning policy	Succession planning
No discretion	1%	3%	4%
Little discretion	5%	9%	18%
Some discretion	15%	30%	29%
Quite a lot of discretion	35%	29%	23%
Full discretion	44%	28%	25%
No typical situation	-	-	1%

n= 210; 106; 140.

Figure 9.5 Discretion over training, development and organisational learning by sector

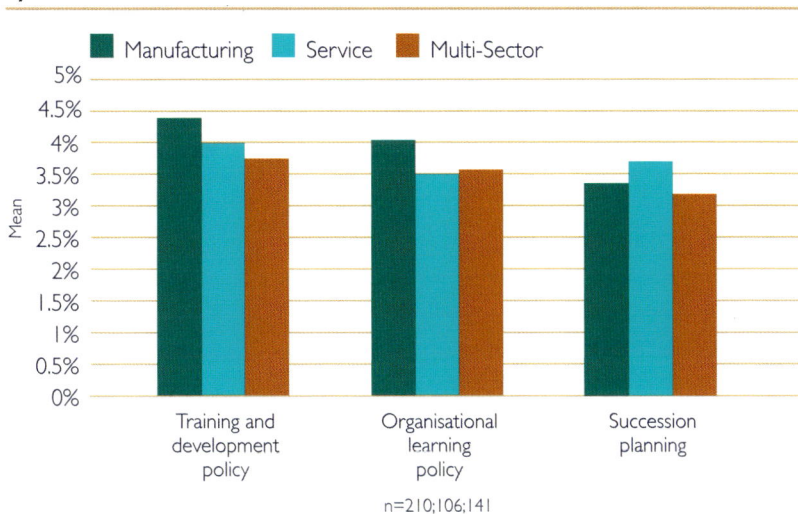

n=210;106;141

Consistent with previous findings, US-owned MNCs emerged as the least likely to provide discretion to local managers over these three measures. These variations, according to the mean scores, are illustrated in figure 7.11. In addition to the mean values, US MNCs were found to be considerably less likely to state full discretion was afforded over the training and development policy (32 per cent), organisation learning policy (15 per cent) and suggestion planning (18 per cent). No substantial differences emerged with regard to whether there had been a change in the discretion afforded to local management over the previous three years. Most respondents reported that there had been no change or that there had been an increase.

Figure 9.6 Discretion over training, development and organisational learning by country of origin

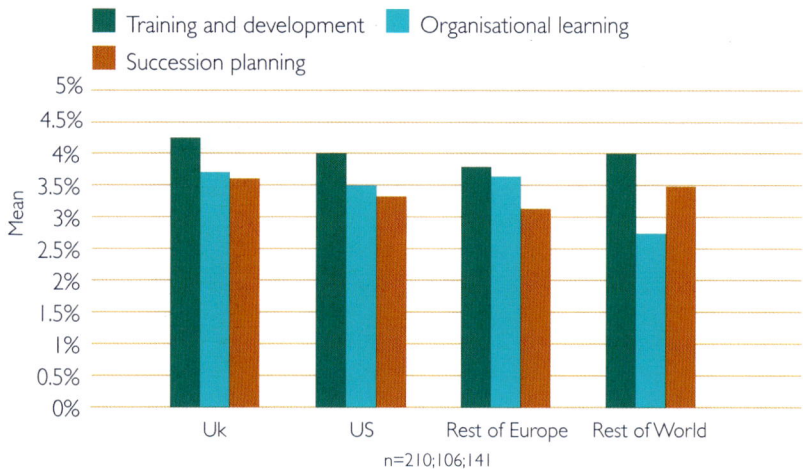

n=210;106;141

Indigenous MNCs

Whilst a clear majority of Irish-owned MNCs (64 per cent) reported that their foreign subsidiaries had quite a lot/full discretion over training and development policy, they emerged as less likely to report high discretion levels compared to what local managers in the foreign-owned MNCs answered. The level of discretion afforded to foreign managers was particularly low in regard to succession planning where the mean value was 1.75. The results were considerably more polarised. Significant numbers reported, at the one end, no or a little discretion and, on the other end, quite a lot or full discretion.

Some 44 per cent of indigenous MNCs stated that the level of autonomy provided to management in their foreign operations over training, development and organisational learning had increased or significantly increased in the past three years. A further 51 per cent stated there had been no change and the remaining 5 per cent said that their foreign operations had less discretion.

Sectoral variations were minimal in terms of indigenous MNCs that reported quite a lot or full discretion over the three aspects measured, although multi-sector (67 per cent) were far more likely to have reported an increase in discretion in the recent past vis-à-vis services sector (46 per cent) and manufacturing (27 per cent) MNCs. However, one needs to exert great care when considering these outcomes as the number of Irish-owned MNCs with succession planning and organisational learning policies was low.

Table 9.7 Discretion over training, development and organisational learning

	Training and development policy	Organisation learning policy	Succession planning
No discretion	17%	18%	44%
Little discretion	12%	27%	20%
Some discretion	5%	9%	16%
Quite a lot of discretion	32%	18%	12%
Full discretion	32%	27%	8%
No typical situation	2%	-	-

n= 40; 11; 25.

Staffing the top management team: the extent of social control

A related issue for MNCs that seek to diffuse global HR/ER policies (i.e. standardised policies), is the means by which it can be achieved. Scullion and Starkey (2000) differentiate between 'structural' and 'social' control. Structural control emphasises the use of formal international structures and monitoring processes to ensure the implementation of centrally determined policies. These were dealt with substantially in chapter four. In contrast, social control focuses on diffusing the company's culture and values throughout its international operations via more informal networks and, most significantly, through the deployment of home country nationals in foreign subsidiaries (cf. Bartlett and Ghoshal, 1998; Harzing, 1999, 2001).

Our study investigated how many of the five most senior management positions in the Irish operations were currently filled by managers who previously worked in the home country. Due to the nature of this survey, data were only available for foreign-owned MNCs. Just less than half (47 per cent) reported that they had at least one manager with experience of the home country operations among the five most senior positions in the Irish operations. This was slightly higher than the findings of the UK research team, where the equivalent figure was 45 per cent (Edwards et al., 2007). The deployment of such managers was broken down as follows: 18 per cent of companies reported one member of the top management team (TMT) had previous experience in the home country, 9 per cent reported two, 8 per cent had three, 4 per cent reported five, whilst 8 per cent revealed that each of the TMT had previous experience of working in the parent country.

Figure 9.7 Percentage of top management team with experience of working in the parent country

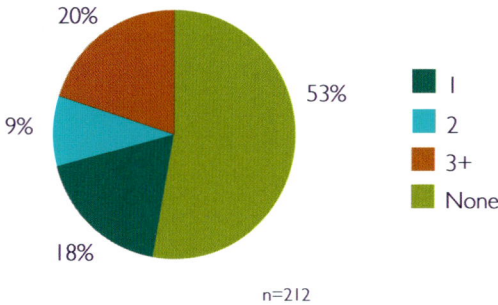

n=212

When we look at the impact of ownership, US-owned firms were least likely to report that the TMT for the Irish operations had previous home country work experience. The differences were quite stark as illustrated in Figure 9.8. UK-owned MNCs (71 per cent) were much more likely to select TMT members with home country experience, followed by European MNCs (57 per cent), the rest of world category (43 per cent) and finally US-owned firms (34 per cent). This finding may plausibly be linked to the geographical proximity of the UK making it less expensive to provide employees with home country experience. These findings are broadly in line with Thompson and Keating's (2004) study of executive staffing practices in Irish subsidiaries of foreign MNCs and indeed the broader literature on international staffing (Harzing, 1999; Scullion and Collings, 2006).

The traditional view has been that MNCs have parent country nationals or people with experience of the parent country in the key management positions of their foreign operations. This view is aptly captured by the HR manager of one German-owned manufacturing MNC:

They [HQ] would only fill the general management's position with a German, [Name] has been working for the company even though he wasn't qualified for the position: they [Germans] still would not give it to anyone else.
HR Manager, German-owned, manufacturing MNC

However, the evidence has shown that such a view were not as widespread as may be believed. Indeed, we captured some qualitative comments which suggested that the necessity for experience of the home country environment as a requisite to securing a senior management appointment was changing:

Senior management here used to all be staffed by corporate people but over the last few years this has changed
HR Director, German-owned, services sector MNC.

We currently have no expatriates working here although this is a recent change as from start-up until relatively recently there were five expatriates here in management positions
HR Director, US-owned, services sector MNC.

Figure 9.8 TMT Members with home country experience by country of origin

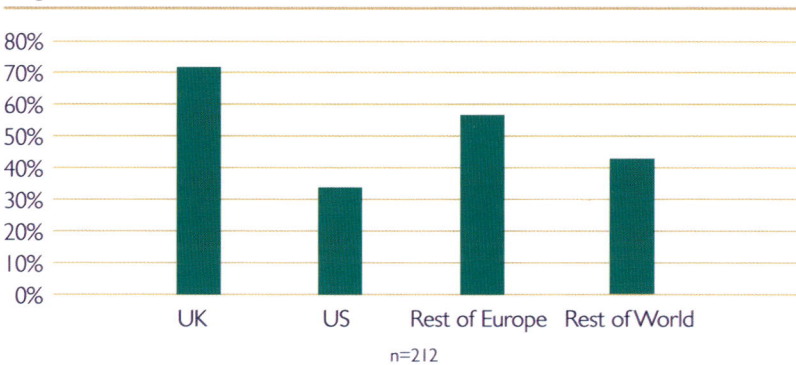

n=212

Similar to the UK findings, we found little difference in the importance of home country experience as a determinant of TMT membership across sectors. 53 per cent of multi-sector MNCs reported that at least one member of their TMT in Ireland had home country experience compared to 47 per cent of manufacturing sector organisations and 46 per cent of MNCs in the services sector.

We also looked at the number of 'third country nationals' (TCNs) in the top management team. Among foreign-owned MNCs, TCNs refer to individuals working in the host country (in this case Ireland), who are neither an Irish national nor a national of the country in which the parent company is located (Reynolds, 1997). We found that 27.5 per cent of foreign-owned MNCs reported that there was at least one TCN on the TMT - almost half the number of TMT members with home country experience. Such a finding may be categorised as relatively high, particularly when one takes into account that those with parent country experience stood at 47 per cent.

Conclusion

This chapter has reviewed evidence on the extent discretion is afforded to local management over the four substantive areas of HR that this survey has considered. The level of discretion was explored in both foreign and indigenous-owned MNCs but kept separate in our analysis because a host country management perspective was provided in the case of foreign firms. Indigenous MNCs involved a headquarters perspective whereby corporate management reported the level of discretion they afford to their foreign operations.

The extent of variation reported by local management in foreign-owned MNCs varied across each of the four substantive HR areas investigated, as well as differences within these areas with respect to the individual measures. All of the measures investigated in the pay and performance management realm reported lower levels of local managerial autonomy relative to employee representation and consultation, employee involvement and communication and training, development and organisational learning. The 'softer' HR issues such as training and development policy and the involvement of employees in the work process and so forth provided greater autonomy to local management than the 'harder' financial issues. This was also found to be the case in the parallel study of MNCs in the UK (Edwards et al., 2007).

Indigenous MNCs tended to report much lower levels of discretion being afforded to their foreign operations across each of the four substantive HR areas than the subsidiary level responses from foreign-owned MNCs. These differences are worthy of further explication because they may represent an exaggerated view of control and autonomy which may not act out in practice. At the same time, the local Irish managers of foreign-owned MNCs may have over-estimated their levels of discretion across each area. However, it may also represent the relative 'new multinational' status of indigenous MNCs. As detailed in chapters one and two, Irish-owned MNCs are 'new MNCs' due to their late internationalisation. Previous research has suggested tighter controls and lower levels of autonomy are afforded to new subsidiaries (cf. Fenton-O'Creevy et al., 2008).

Within each of the areas, we explored variations between MNCs of different nationalities and sectors. Firstly, we turn to country of origin differences. Overall, US-owned MNCs were shown to proffer lower levels of autonomy to local managers in Ireland over policies across the HR areas that were investigated. This supports the extant literature which argues that US MNCs are the more centralised, standardised and formalised in employment relations and HR policy areas (cf. Young et al., 1985; Child et al., 2000). In particular, there has been a plethora of studies that show US MNCs holding considerable control over trade union recognition, recruitment, pay, and employee communications. Furthermore, studies have shown a link between centralised policies in US MNCs and higher levels of formalisation (cf. Harzing, 1999). This can also be pointed to in this study, as the chapters to date tend to highlight US-owned MNCs as the most likely to report the use of most formalised systems and practices that we investigated. They were also found to use structural controls (e.g. shared services centres, HRIS) rather than social controls (i.e. use of parent country expatriates or senior managers with parent country work experience) which is again consistent with previous research (cf. Harzing, 1999).

Sectoral differences also emerged in parts of our analysis on the discretion afforded to subsidiary level managers on HR policies and practices. For example, multi-sector firms were shown to be less likely to report full discretion over trade union recognition compared to services and manufacturing sector MNCs. However, there were few differences with respect to the other two employee representation and consultation issues. In addition, there were minimal sectoral variations over employee involvement and communication factors. On the other hand, greater numbers of manufacturing sector firms reported higher discretion levels vis-à-vis services and multi sector MNCs over the training and development and organisation learning policies. However, overall the picture which emerged failed to show any particularly strong level of consistency with respect to the sector of operation.

This chapter involved an exploration in a descriptive manner two predictor variables, namely country of origin and sector. However, a number of other factors may account for variation in local managerial autonomy on HR policies. For example, the age of the subsidiary operations, the size of the organisation, international structures and integration, as well as the structure of the HR function.

ENDNOTE

[i] It should be noted that data is based on 'headquarter perspective' provided by senior HR practitioners/managers based in Ireland. Practice 'on the ground' may potentially differ to what is reported here. In addition some of the respondents were located at divisional, not global headquarters, of their respective firms.

CHAPTER 10
Conclusion

Jonathan Lavelle, Anthony McDonnell, & Patrick Gunnigle

Introduction

Ireland's dependence on foreign direct investment (FDI) and its success in attracting inward FDI is well established. The study upon which this volume is based represents the largest and most representative empirical investigation of human resource management (HRM) practice in MNCs in Ireland to date.

We investigated five HR areas, namely the HR function, pay and performance management, employee representation and consultation, employee communication and involvement, and training, development and organisational learning. This investigation focused on three groups of employees, (a) managers, (b) the largest occupational group (LOG) and (c) the key group. This latter category represents a major innovation in studies of this kind, concentrating on employee categories seen as particularly critical to firm performance.

In this chapter we seek to summarily highlight what we see as the selected key issues to emerge from this research.

Foreign-owned MNCs in Ireland – a diverse assemblage?

In analysing our findings, the initial - possibly most fascinating - task was to try and categorise MNCs in Ireland according to factors such as ownership and sector. The first thing that struck us as a research team was the heterogeneous nature of the MNC population in Ireland. This was particularly the case in regard to size and sector. It was interesting to find that the majority of MNCs in Ireland are located in the services sector. While manufacturing remained an important area of MNC activity, there are also a number of multi-sector MNCs.

The great majority of foreign-owned MNCs originate from three countries or regions, namely the US, continental Europe and the UK. It is evident that Ireland attracts few MNCs from outside of Europe or the US. This is quite unlike the parallel UK study which found a significant presence of MNCs from Japan and other Asian countries (Edwards et al., 2007). Among the possible reasons for the lack of Asian investment in Ireland include a relatively small domestic economy, incentive packages which fail to appeal to this type of investment, location issues and also a lack of relevant infrastructure including sub-supply, particularly in the electronics and automotive industries (Mayuya and Jacobson, 1991; Chung et al., 2006; Rios-Morales and Brennan, 2007).

Over the recent past considerable media attention has focused on the seemingly numerous cases of foreign-owned MNCs reducing employment and/or closing Irish operations. Our study presents a more nuanced picture. Approximately half of the respondent firms indicated they had established a new site or expanded an existing site within the previous five years. On the other hand, just over a fifth had closed a site during the same period. We also present a snapshot of employment patterns, where we found over six in ten MNCs reported an increase or significant increase in employment levels over the previous three years. Employment growth was particularly high among service sector MNCs. This depicts a more optimistic picture than is sometimes portrayed in the popular media. These findings indicate that we are experiencing a high level of 'job churn' among the MNC population, i.e. concurrent job loss and job creation, particularly in the manufacturing sector. It is important to note that fieldwork for this study was undertaken during the period from early Summer 2006 to February 2007 and the results must be considered in that perspective. Few, for instance, would have predicted the scale of the late-2008 worldwide economic crisis when we undertook our survey.

Irish-owned MNCs – an untold story?

Above we note that the foreign MNC population is made up of more than just US manufacturing firms, with large numbers of MNCs of other nationalities as well as service and multi-sector organisations. A particularly important sub-set of MNCs comprises indigenous (Irish-owned) MNCs, which have been somewhat neglected from a research perspective. Our findings indicate that Irish-owned MNCs comprise in excess of 10 per cent of the total MNC population. As such, the extent and growth of Irish-owned MNCs represents something akin to 'the missing chapter' in the story of MNCs in Ireland. It is also interesting to note that the scale of inward FDI is now more than rivalled by outward FDI by Irish-owned MNCs and that Ireland's stock of outward FDI is well above the EU average.

It is hardly surprising, given that industrial development did not accelerate until the turn of the 1960s, to find that Irish-owned MNCs are comparatively late internationalisers, with almost seven in ten having established foreign operations since 1980. Interestingly, they have moved quickly since then, with over eight in ten reporting operations in more than two countries.

Irish-owned MNCs are clearly very large employers by national standards. Almost two thirds (57 per cent) employ more than 1,000 workers in Ireland, substantially higher than that of foreign-owned MNCs (23 per cent). However in worldwide terms, they remain very much small to medium sized organisations, with just less than one third employing more than 5,000 people. The sectoral configuration of Irish-owned MNCs is interesting, particularly when compared to foreign-owned MNCs. A greater proportion of Irish firms operated in what are termed more 'low tech' sectors, such as 'traditional manufacturing' (e.g. food), reflecting in part Ireland's background as an agricultural country. In contrast, foreign-owned MNCs had a greater presence in 'high-tech' manufacturing and internationally traded service sectors.

Whilst the above information provides a useful picture of the size and scale of Irish-owned MNCs it is important to note how this cohort of MNCs stacks up against other MNCs when looking at HRM and employment relations (ER) practices. Given that Irish-owned MNCs are relatively new to the international scene one could plausibly hypothesise that Irish-owned MNCs would be 'behind the game' in terms of HRM structures, policies and practices. We find that the use of HRIS, international HR policy formation bodies and forms of international networking are more prevalent among foreign-owned MNCs, but in some cases the differences are relatively small. One finding of particular note here was that Irish-owned MNCs are much more likely to have shared services centres compared to foreign firms. Some potential explanations as to why this might be the case include the size of Irish-owned MNCs and the number and type of foreign locations Irish-owned MNCs have chosen to locate in. Notwithstanding this, a cursory review of the previous chapters illustrates some significant differences between Irish-owned MNCs and their foreign-owned counterparts. For instance Irish-owned MNCs are:

- less likely to report paying their LOG in the first or second quartile relative to market comparators
- the usage of performance appraisals for managers and LOG are considerably lower than MNCs of any other nationality
- indigenous MNCs tended to be the least likely to have formal training and development interventions.
- Irish-owned MNCs are much more likely to report trade union recognition but less likely to report the use of non-union structures of employee representation and European Works Councils
- formally designed teams are more likely to be found in MNCs of all other nationalities.
- less likely to use attitude or opinion surveys
- Irish-owned MNCs less likely to provide information on staffing and investment plans of the company in Ireland.

Thus when one compares Irish-owned MNCs against foreign-owned MNCs we find that there a number of differences in their approach to HRM.

US MNCs – a distinct group?

US-owned MNCs represent the largest cohort of MNCs operating in Ireland, representing 42 per cent of the total MNC population. Their scale and significance within the Irish economy has been well noted. We also find that this group of MNCs appears to be quite a distinct group with many HRM and ER practices demonstrating a US effect. Much reference has been made throughout the previous chapters in relation to US MNCs and how they approach the management of their subsidiaries and employees. The literature suggests that US MNCs tend to be much more formalised and standardised in their approach (see Ferner et al., 2004; Almond and Ferner, 2006). Indeed our findings corroborate this position, as we point towards numerous examples of where this is the case. For instance US-owned MNCs are:

- most likely to report the use of structural controls, such as shared services centres and HRIS
- most likely to report the presence of a global HR approach to the management of their employees and that the traditions of the parent company have an overriding impact on this approach
- much more likely to spent in excess of 4 per cent of their annual pay bill on T&D for the workforce as well as most likely to undertake succession planning, management development and organisational learning.
- much more likely to report lower levels of autonomy to local managers in Ireland over policies across all the HR areas investigated.

Reference was also made to the fact that US MNCs have been seen as HR innovators, particularly with regard to the management of pay and performance (see chapter 5). Our evidence suggests that US MNCs lead the way in terms of pay and performance management policies and practices. For example US-owned MNCs are much more likely to:

- report the use performance related pay
- report the use performance appraisal systems
- report the use of the performance appraisal technique of forced distribution
- use all three forms of financial incentive (employee share ownership, profit sharing and share option schemes) schemes.

US MNCs also appear to be the vanguard in relation to ER policies and practices. It is widely accepted that the American ER system is substantially different from its Irish counterpart. For example, the US system is noted for its low level of unionisation and collective bargaining coverage. This contrasts with the Irish ER system where trade unions have enjoyed quite high levels of legitimacy and influence. Our evidence suggests that across many of the ER issues investigated, US-owned MNCs differ considerably. For instance US-owned MNCs are:

- least likely to recognise trade unions
- most likely to engage in double breasting – a particular form of trade union avoidance
- more likely to report the use of non-union structures of employee representation.

Impact of sector

A number of notable differences are found according to the industrial sector. Three distinct sectors are used namely, the services, manufacturing, and multi-sector (i.e. incorporating firms which straddle both manufacturing and services).

Services sector MNCs are more likely to aim to be in the first or second quartile regarding pay for the various staff categories, when compared to manufacturing or multi-sector MNCs. The use of forced distribution for the LOG and managers is also more likely in the services sector, but the differences are slight. Multi-sector firms tend to be the most prominent users of financial incentive schemes (profit sharing, share ownership, share options). Services sector MNCs are the least likely to recognise trade unions for collective bargaining purposes. Again as expected, trade union density is higher in the manufacturing sector. Interestingly, services sector unionised firms are more likely to report the existence of a cooperative approach between management and the trade unions. In terms of pay determination, manufacturing firms are more likely to use national level pay bargaining for the LOG than service or multi-sector firms.

A marked variation was found in relation to employee involvement, with manufacturing MNCs more likely to use problem solving groups when compared to service or multi-sector firms. However formally designed teams are more commonly found in services sector MNCs. Usage of the various forms of communication are virtually identical across the three sectors. In relation to training and development spend, multi-sector firms are the most likely to report spending in excess of 4 per cent of their annual pay bill on such activities, followed by services sector firms. Multi-sector firms are also more likely to operate global succession planning and have a global management development programme. In addition multi-sector firms are more likely to report the existence of a 'key group', followed by services firms.

Manufacturing MNCs report greater discretion over pay and performance management than services or multi-sector firms. Little or no difference is found in relation to autonomy over employee representation and consultation. Manufacturing firms are also most likely to have quite 'a lot' or 'full' autonomy over the training and development, and organisational learning policies. However, services sector firms are more likely to report high discretion levels with regard to succession planning.

Further reading and analysis

This book provides a comprehensive overview of the findings from our point in time study on HR practice in MNCs in Ireland. As noted in the methodology chapter (chapter 2), these findings are presented in a largely descriptive manner, supplemented by qualitative quotes garnered during the fieldwork phase. Running descriptive analyses serves two particular purposes. First, it provides a general overview of the findings, e.g. how many MNCs have performance appraisal systems, how many MNCs recognise trade unions etc. Given the representative nature of this research project, providing such data makes an important contribution to our knowledge on HRM in MNCs. Second, descriptive analysis allows us identify particular themes or issues that are worthy of further in-depth statistical analysis. Whilst this type of analysis is beyond the remit of this volume, a number of themes have been explored through a recent and growing number of research papers, a full list of which is outlined in table 10.1, (overleaf) together with the sources.

In conclusion, this volume presents the main initial findings from Ireland's first representative survey of HR practices in MNCs. As a result, we are able to provide an unparalleled snapshot of what is happening in HR in these firms. In doing so it allows managers to benchmark their particular practices vis-à-vis the more general pattern of HR practice in the multinational sector in Ireland.

Table 10.1 Research Papers based on Irish MNC dataset

Thematic area(s)	Title	Authors	Reference/Source
Global staffing	Swimming against the tide: Outward staffing flows from Multinational subsidiaries	Collings, D. G., McDonnell, A., Gunnigle, P. and Lavelle, J. (2008)	Unpublished working paper, downloadable from: http://ssrn.com/auth or=925966
Employment relations/trade unions	Subtle but deadly - uion avoidance through 'double breasting' among multinational companies	Gunnigle, P., Lavelle, J., and McDonnell, A. (2009)	*Advances in Industrial and Labor Relations*, 16, 51-74
Employment relations/trade unions	Conceptualising 'double breasting' and its uptake in multinational companies: evidence from Ireland	Lavelle, J., Lamare, J. R., Gunnigle, P., and McDonnell, A. (2009)	Paper accepted for presentation at the 23rd *Association of Indutrial Relations Academics of Asutralian and New Zealand (AIRAANZ)* Conference, Newcastle, NSW, Australia
Employment relations/collective bargaining	Unions on the edge? Indutrial Relations in Multinational Companies in Ireland	Lavelle, J., Gunnigle, P. and McDonnell, A. (2008)	Chapter 4 in Hastings, T. (ed.) *The State of the Unions*, Dublin, The Liffey Press
Trade union recognition and avoidance	Charting the contours of union recognition in foreign-owned MNCs: survey evidence from the Republic of Ireland	Lavelle, J. (2008)	*Irish Journal of Management*, 29(1), 45-46
Employee involvement and participation	Partterning employee voice in multinational companies	Lavelle, J., Gunnigle, P., and McDonnell, A. (2009)	*Human Relations*, (forthcoming)
Training and development practices	Outward foreign direct investment and human capital development: A small country perspective	McDonnell, A. (2008)	*Journal of European Indutrial Training*, 32 (6), 452-471
Organisation learning	Learning transfer in multinational companies: explaining inter-organisation variation	McDonnell, A., Gunnigle, P. and Lavelle, J. (2009)	*Human Resource Management Journal* (forthcoming)
Global talent management	Developing Tomorrow's Leaders - Evidence of Global Talent Management in Multinational Companies	McDonnell, A., Lamare, R., Gunnigle, P., and Lavelle, J. (2008)	unpublished working paper, downloadable from: http://ssrn.com/auth or=925966
Research methods & experience of large survey research	Management research on multinational corporations: A methodological critique	Mc Donnell, A., Lavelle, J., Gunnigle P. and Collings, D.G. (2007)	*Economic and Social Review*, 38(2), 235-258

References

References

Alfaro, L. and Charlton, A. (2006). *International Financial Integration and Entrepreneurship*, available from: http://www.people.hbs.edu/lalfaro/CapitalFlowsEntrepreneurship.pdf [accessed: 01 July 2006].

Almond, P. and Ferner, A. (2006). *American Multinationals in Europe: Managing Employment Relations Across National Borders*, Oxford, Oxford University Press.

Almond, P., Edwards, T., Colling, T., Ferner, A., Gunnigle, P., Muller-Camen, M., Quintanilla, J. and Waechter, H. (2005). "Unravelling home and host country effects: an investigation of the HR policies of an American multinational in four European countries", *Industrial Relations*, 44 (2): 276-306.

Argyris, C. (1999). *On Organizational Learning*, Oxford, Blackwell.

Arrow, K. (1997). "Economic Growth Policy for a small Country" in A. W. Gray (Ed), *International Perspectives on the Irish Economy*, Dublin, Indecon.

Baddon, L. Hunter, L. Hyman, J. and Ramsay, H. (1989). *People's Capitalism ? A Critical Analysis of Profit Sharing and Employee Share Ownership*, London, Routledge.

Barney, J. (1991). "Firm resources and sustained competitive advantage", *Journal of Management*, 17 (1): 99-120.

Barney, J. (1995). "Looking inside for competitive advantage", *Academy of Management Executive,* 9 (4): 49-61.

Barney, J. (2001). "Is the Resource-Based "View" A Useful Perspective for Strategic Management Research? Yes", *Academy of Management Review*, 26 (1): 41-56.

Baron, A. and Armstrong, M. (2007). *Human Capital Management: Achieving Added Value Through People*, London, Kogan Page.

Barry, F. (2002). FDI and the Host Economy: *A Case Study of Ireland*, unpublished paper presented at Department of Management, National University of Ireland, Galway, November 8th.

Barry, F. (2004). "Export-platform foreign direct investment: the Irish experience", *European Investment Bank Papers*, 9 (2): 8-37.

Barry, F. (2007). *Foreign Direct Investment and Institutional Co-Evolution in Ireland*, Available from: http://ssrn.com/abstract=978764 [accessed: 01 July 2008].

Barry, F. and Van Welsum, D. (2005). *Services FDI and Offshoring into Ireland*, paper presented at the Organisation for Economic Co-operation and Development Directorate For Science, Technology and Industry Panel Session on Offshoring, Paris, France, 9 – 10 June.

Barry, F., Gorg, H., and McDowell, A. (2003). "Outward FDI and the Investment Development Path of a Late-industrializing Economy: Evidence from Ireland", *Regional Studies*, 37 (4): 341-349.

Bartlett, C. and Ghoshal, S. (1995). *Transnational Management, 2nd edition*. Boston, MA, Irwin.

Bartlett, C.A. and Ghoshal, S. (1989). *Managing Across Borders: The transnational solution*, Boston, MA., Harvard Business School Press.

Bartlett, K. R., Lawler, J. J., Bae, J., Chen, S.-J. and Wan, D. (2002). "Differences in International Human Resource Development Among Indigenous Firms and Multinational Affiliates in East and Southeast Asia", *Human Resource Development Quarterly*, 13 (4): 383-405.

Baruch, Y. and Holtom, B. C. (2008). "Survey response rate levels and trends in organizational research", *Human relations*, 61 (8): 1139-1160.

Beaumont, P. and Harris R. (1989). "The North–South Divide in Britain: The Case of Trade Union Recognition", *Oxford Bulletin of Economics and Statistics*, 51 (4): 413–428.

Beaumont, P. and Harris, R.I.D. (1992). "Double-breasted Recognition Arrangements in Britain", *International Journal of Human Resource Management*, 3 (2): 267-283.

Becker, B. and Gerhart, B. (1996). "The Impact of Human Resource Management on Organisational Performance", *Academy of Management Journal*, 39 (4): 779-802.

Beer, M., Spector, B., Lawrence, P., Quinn,-Mills, D. and Walton, R. (1984). *Managing Human Assets: The Groundbreaking Harvard Business School Program*, New York, The Free Press.

Begley, T.M., Delaney, E. and O'Gorman, C. (2005). "Ireland at a crossroads: still a magnet for corporate investment?", *Organizational Dynamics*, 34 (3): 202-217.

Bélanger, J., Harvey, P.-A., Jalette, P., Levesque, C. and Murray, G. (2006). *Employment Practices in Multinational Companies in Canada: Building Organizational Capabilities and Institutions for Innovation*. University of Montreal, HEC Montreal, University of Laval, Montreal and Laval: The Inter-University Research Centre on Globalization and Work (CRIMT).

Benders, J. (2005). "Team working: A tale of partial participation", in B. Harley, J. Hyman, and P. Thompson (Eds), *Participation and Democracy at Work: Essays in Honour of Harvey Ramsay*, Basingstoke, Palgrave Macmillan.

Berthoin Antal, A. (2000). "Types of Knowledge Gained by Expatriate Managers", *Journal of General Management*, 26 (2): 32-51.

Björkman, I. and Furu, P. (2000). "Determinants of variable pay for general managers of foreign-owned subsidiaries in Finland", *International Journal of Human Resource Management*, 11 (4): 698-713.

Blyton, P. and Turnbull, P. (1994). *The Dynamic at Employee Relations*, London, Macmillan.

Bomers, G. and Peterson, R. (1977). "Multinational corporations and industrial relations: the case of West Germany and the Netherlands", *British Journal of Industrial Relations*, 15 (1): 45-62.

Bonache, J. and Fernadez (1999). "Expatriate compensation and its link to the subsidiary strategic role: A theoretical analysis", *International Journal of Human Resource Management*, 8 (4): 457-475.

Boudreau, J.W. and Ramstad, P.M. (2005). "Talentship, Talent Segmentation, and Sustainability: A New HR Decision Science Paradigm for a new Strategy Definition", *Human Resource Management*, 42 (2): 129-136.

Boudreau, J.W. and Ramstad, P.M. (2007). *Beyond HR: The New Science of Human Capital*, Boston, MA, Harvard Business School Press.

Boxall, P. (1992). "Strategic human resource management: beginnings of a new theoretical sophistication", *Human Resource Management Journal*, 2 (3): 60-79.

Boxall, P. and Purcell, J. (2000). "Strategic human resource management: where have we come from and where should we be going?", *International Journal of Management Reviews*, 2 (2): 183-203.

Boxall, P. and Purcell, J. (2003). *Strategy and Human Resource Management*, Basingstoke, Palgrave.

Brady, C., Bolchover, D. and Sturgess, B. (2008). "Managing in the Talent Economy: The Football Model For Business", *California Management Review*, 50 (4): 54-73.

Brannick, T. and Coghlan, D. (2006). Quantitative and Qualitative research dichotomy, Is it a meaningless concept, paper presented at the *9th Annual Irish Academy of Management Conference*. University College Cork, Ireland.

Briscoe, D. R. and Schuler, R. S. (2004). *International Human Resource Management, Second Edition*, New York, Routledge.

Briscoe, D., Schuler, R. and Claus, L. (2008). *International Human Resource Management*, New York, Routledge.

Bryman, A. and Bell, E. (2003). *Business Research Methods*, New York, Oxford University Press.

Buckley, P. and Enderwick, P. (1985). *The Industrial Relations Practices of Foreign-Owned Firms in Britain*, London, Macmillan.

Buckley, P. J. and Ruane, F. (2006). "Foreign Direct Investment in Ireland: Policy Implications for Emerging Economies", *The World Economy*, 29 (11): 1611-1628.

Burke, L. A. (1997). "Developing High-Potential Employees In The New Business Reality", *Business Horizons*, March/April: 18-24.

Butler, R. A. (2005). *Corporations among largest global economic entities, rank above many countries*, Available from: http://news.mongabay.com/2005/0718-worlds_largest.html [accessed: 14 October 2008].

Caligiuri, P. M., Lazarova, M. and Tarique, I. (2005). "Training, learning and development in multinational organizations", in H. Scullion and M. Linehan (Eds.) *International Human Resource Management: A critical text*, Hampshire, Palgrave Macmillan.

Central Statistics Office (CSO) (2008). *Quarterly national household survey: Union membership*, Cork, Central Statistics Office.

Central Statistics Office (CSO). (2007). *Census of Industrial Production 2005*, Cork, Central Statistics Office.

CFM Capital (2008). Acquisition Survey January 2008: *A review of Mergers Acquisitions and Disposals*, Dublin, CFM Capital.

Child, J., Faulkner, D. & Pitkenthly, R. (2000). "Foreign direct investment in the UK 1985-1994: The impact on domestic", *Journal of Management Studies*, 37(1): 141-166.

Chung, L., Gibbons, P. and Schoch, H. (2006). "The management of information and managers in subsidiaries of multinational corporations", *British Journal of Management*, 17 (2): 153-166.

Colling, T., Gunnigle, P., Quintanilla, J. and Tempel, A. (2006). "Collective Representation and Participation", in P. Almond and A. Ferner (Eds.) *American Multinationals in Europe*, Oxford, Oxford University Press.

Collings, D. and Scullion, H. (2006). "Approaches to international staffing", in H. Scullion and D. G. Collings (Eds) *Global Staffing*, Abingdon (U.K), Routledge.

Collings, D. G. (2003). "HRD and labour market practices in a US multinational subsidiary: the impact of global and local influences", *Journal of European Industrial Training*, 27 (2-4): 188-200.

Collings, D.G., Gunnigle, P. and Morley, M.J. (2008a). "Boston or Berlin? American MNCs and the Shifting Contours of Industrial Relations in Ireland", *International Journal of Human Resource Management*, 19 (2): 242–263.

Collings, D. G., McDonnell, A. and Scullion, H. (2008b). "Global Talent Management: The Law of the Few", unpublished working paper.

Collings, D. G., Morley, M. J. and Gunnigle, P. (2008c). "Composing the top management team in the international subsidiary: Qualitative evidence on international staffing in U.S. MNCs in the Republic of Ireland", *Journal of World Business*, 43 (2): 197-212.

Collings, D. G., Scullion, H. and Morley, M. J. (2007). "Changing Patterns of Global Staffing in the Multinational Enterprise: Challenges to the Conventional Expatriate Assignment and Emerging Alternatives", *Journal of World Business*, 42 (2): 198-213.

Collings, D.G. (2008). "Multinational corporations and industrial relations research: a road less travelled", *International Journal of Management Reviews*, 10 (2): 173-193.

Collinson, S. and Rugman, A. (2005). *Studying the wrong firms: Selection biases in management research*, unpublished paper, University of Warwick.

Conte, M. and Tannenbaum, A. (1978). "Employee Owned Companies: is the difference measurable ?", *Monthly Labor Review*, July: 23-8.

Cooke, W.N. (2001). "Union Avoidance and Foreign Direct Investment in the USA," *Employee Relations*, 23 (6): 558–580.

Cooke, W.N. (2003a). "The influence of industrial relations systems factors on foreign direct investment" in W.N. Cooke (Ed) *Multinational Companies and Global Human Resource Strategies*, Wesport, Quorum Books.

Cooke, W.N. (2003b). "Global Human Resource Strategies: A Framework and Overview" in W.N. Cooke (Ed) *Multinational Companies and Global Human Resource Strategies*, Wesport, Quorum Books.

Crawford, R., Romiti, L., Smith, D. J. and Wilson, A. (2005). *Major Companies of Europe 2005 Volume 4,* London, Graham and Whiteside.

Creswell, J. (1994). Research Design: *Qualitative and Quantitative Approaches*, Thousand Oaks, CA, Sage Publications.

Cully, M., Woodland, S., O'Reilly, A. and Dix, G. (1999). *Britain at work as depicted by the 1998 Workplace Employee Relations Survey*, London, Routledge.

Cycyota, C. S. and Harrison, D. A. (2006). "What (not) to expect when surveying executives", *Organizational Research Methods*, 9 (2): 133-160.

Czarnecki, E. R. (1970). "Effects of Profit Sharing Plans on Union Organising Efforts", *Personnel Journal,* 49 (September): 763-773.

D'Art D. (1992). *Economic Democracy and Financial Participation; A comparative study*, London, Routledge.

D'Art, D and Turner, T. (2004). "Profit Sharing, firm performance and union influence in selected European countries", *Personnel Review*, 33 (3): 322-334.

D'Art, D. and Turner, T. (2006). "Profit Sharing and Employee Share Ownership in Ireland: A New Departure?", *Economic and Industrial Democracy*, 27 (4): 543-564.

Daniels, J. D. and Radebaugh, L. H. (1995). International Business: *Environments and Operations*, 7th edition, Reading, Massachusetts, Addison-Wesley.

De Cieri, H. and Dowling, P.J. (1999). "Strategic human resource management in multinational enterprises: Theoretical and empirical developments", in P.M. Wright, L.D. Dyer, J.W. Boudreau and G.T. Milkovich (Eds.) *Research in personnel and human resources management: Strategic human resources management in the 21st century*, Supplement 4, Greenwich, CT, JAI Press.

DeVos, T. (1981). *US Multinationals and Worker Participation in Management: The American Experience in the European Community*, London, Adwych Press.

Dixon, N. M. (1994). *Organizational Learning Cycle: How We Can Learn Collectively,* London, McGraw-Hill.

Dobbins, T (2005). "Fewer 'above the norm' Sustaining Progress deals than under PPF", *Industrial Relations News*, 3, October 4th.

Doherty, R. E (1989). *Industrial and labor relations terms: a glossary*, Ithaca, Cornell University Press.

Donnelly, S.N. (1999). *The Management of Industrial Relations and Human Resources in Irish-Owned Multinationals*, unpublished PhD thesis, Warwick Business School, University of Warwick, UK.

Dowling, P., Welch, D., and Schuler, R. (1999). *International Human Resource Management: Managing People in a Multinational Context*, 3rd Edition, Cincinnati, OH, South-Western College Publishing.

Dundon, T. (2003). "The State of Employee Information and Consultation in Ireland", *Labour Relations Commission Review*, 1 (2): 15-20.

Dundon, T., Curran, D., Maloney, M. and Ryan, P. (2006). "Conceptualising the dynamics of employee voice: evidence from the Republic of Ireland", *Industrial Relations Journal*, 37 (5): 492-512.

Dundon, T., Wilkinson, A., Marchington, M. and Ackers, P. (2005). "The management of voice in non-union organisations: managers' perspectives", *Employee Relations*, 2 (3): 307-19.

Dunning, J.H.(1998). *American Investment in British Manufacturing Industry*. (2nd ed.), London, Routledge.

Easterby-Smith, M., Thorpe, R. and Lowe, A. (2002). *Management Research An Introduction*, London, Sage Publications.

Economist (2006). "The battle for brainpower: A survey of talent", *The Economist*, October 7th.

Edstrom, A. and Galbraith, J. (1977). "Alternative policies for international transfers of managers", *Management International Review*, 17 (2): 11-22.

Edwards, P., Edwards, T., Ferner, A., Marginson, P. and Tregaskis, O. (2007). *Employment Practices of MNCs in Organisational Context: A Large-Scale Survey, Feedback report for participating companies*. Economic and Social Research Council (ESRC), De Montfort University, Kings College London & Warwick Business School.

Edwards, P., Geary, J. and Sisson, K. (2002). "New Forms of Work Organization in the Workplace", in G. Murray, J. Belanger, A. Giles and P. A. Lapointe (Eds) *Work and Employment Relations in the High-performance Workplace*. London, Continuum.

Edwards, T. and Ferner, A. (2002). "The renewed 'American Challenge': a review of employment practice in US multinationals", *Industrial Relations Journal*, 33 (2): 94-111.

Edwards, T., Treaskis, O., Edwards, P., Ferner, A. & Marginson, P. (2008). "Charting the contours of Multinationals in Britain: Methodological Challenges arising in survey-based research", published in the Leicester Business School's Occassional Paper series and Warwick Papers in Industrial Relations.

Edwards, T. and Zhang, M. (2008). "Multinationals and National Systems of Employment Relations: Innovators or Adapters?", *Advances in International Management*, 21: 33-58.

Elger, T. and Smith, C. (2005). *Assembling Work*. Oxford, Oxford University Press.

Enderwick, P. (1986). "Multinationals and Labour Relations: The Case of Ireland", *Journal of Irish Business and Administrative Research*, 8 (2): 1–11.

Enterprise Ireland (2005). *Economic Profile*, Available from: http://www.enterprise-ireland.com/NR/rdonlyres/FA1CFB86-ED2A-489C-BD46-D7D48A16C0E1/0/EconomicProfileApril2005.pdf [accessed: 4 July 2005].

European Foundation for the Improvement of Living and Working Conditions (1997). *New forms of work organisation: Can Europe realise its potential?* Dublin, European Foundation for the Improvement of Living and Working Conditions.

European Foundation for the Improvement of Living and Working Conditions (EFILWC) (2008). *Impact of the information and consultation directive on industrial relations*, Available from: http://www.eurofound.europa.eu/docs/eiro/tn0710029s/tn0710029s.pdf [accessed: September 2008].

Eurostat (2004). Eurostat Yearbook: *the Statistical Guide to Europe*, Luxembourg, Office for the Official Publications of the European Community.

Evans, P., Pucik, V. and Barsoux, J. L. (2002). *The Global Challenge: Frameworks for International Human Resource Management*, New York, McGraw-Hill.

Everett, M. (2006). "Foreign Direct Investment: An Analysis of its Significance", *The Central Bank and Financial Services Authority of Ireland Quarterly Bulletin,* 4, 93-112.

Expert Group on Future Skills Needs and Higher Education Authority (2008). *Survey of Selected Multi-National Employers' Perceptions of Certain Graduates from Irish Higher Education*, Dublin, Forfás.

Ezzamel, M. and Willmot, H. (1998). "Accounting for teamwork: A critical study group-based systems of organizational control", *Administrative Science Quarterly*, 38 (3): 358-396.

Feeney, E. (2007). "Retail sector set to stay strong", *Sunday Business Post*, 9 September 2007.

Fenton-O'Creevy, M., Gooderham, P. & Nordhaug, O. (2008). "HRM in US subsidiaries in Europe and Australia: centralization or autonomy", *Journal of International Business Studies*, 39 (1): 151-166.

Ferner, A. (1997). "Country of Origin Effects and HRM in Multinational Companies", *Human Resource Management*, 7 (1): 19-37.

Ferner, A., Almond, P., Clark, I., Colling, T., Edwards, T., Holden, L. and Muller-Camen, M. (2004). "The dynamics of central control and subsidiary autonomy in the management of human resources: case-study evidence from US MNCs in the UK", *Organization Studies*, 25 (3): 363-391.

Ferner, A., Almond, P., Colling, T., and Edwards, T (2005). "Policies on union representation in US multinationals in the UK: between micro-politics and macro-institutions", *British Journal of Industrial Relations*, 43 (4): 703-728.

Ferner, A., Edwards, P., Edwards, T., Marginson, P. & Tregaskis, O. (2007). 'The determinants of central control and subsidiary 'discretion' in HRM and employment relations policies', paper presented at the *IIRA European Regional Congress*, September 2007, Manchester.

Fitzgerald, K. (2007). "Supreme Court judgment in Ryanair Ltd and The Labour Court and IMPACT", *Industrial Relations News*, 5, 20-27.

Flint, P. (2004). "Low Cost, but Not Cheap. Budget carriers bring a new dimension to managing pilot training", *Air Transport World,* October 2004.

Flood, P. and Toner, B. (1997). "Large Non-Union Companies: How do they avoid a catch-22?" in D. D'Art and T. Turner (Eds.) *Collectivism and Individualism: Trends and Prospects.* Vol 7 of the Official Proceedings of the Fifth IIRA European Regional Industrial Relations Congress, Dublin: Oak Tree Press.

Flood, P.C., Guthric, J.P., Liu, W. and MacCurtain, S. (2005). *High Performance Work Systems in Ireland: the Economic Case.* Dublin, National Centre for Partnership and Performance.

Forfás (2003). *International Trade and Investment Report 2002,* Dublin, Forfás.

Forfás (2005). *International Trade and Investment Report 2004,* Dublin, Forfás.

Forfás (2006). *International Trade and Investment Report 2005,* Dublin, Forfás.

Forfás (2007). *Enterprise Statistics - at a glance*, 2006, Dublin, Forfás.

Foulkes, F. K. (1980). *Personnel Policies in Large Non-union Companies*, Englewood Cliffs (New Jersey), Prentice Hall.

Fox, A. (1985). *Man Mismanagement (2nd edition),* London, Hutchinson

Freeman, R.B. and Medoff, J.L. (1984). *What do unions do?* New York, Basic Books.

Frost, T. S. and Zhou, C. (2005). "R&D co-practice and 'reverse' knowledge integration in multinational firms", *Journal of International Business Studies*, 36 (6): 676-687.

Galbraith, J. R. and Edstrom, A. (1976). "International Transfer of Managers: Some Important Policy Considerations", *Columbia Journal of World Business*, 11 (2): 100-112.

Gamble, J. (2003). "Transferring human resource practices from the United Kingdom to China: the limits and potential for convergence", *International Journal of Human Resource Management*, 14 (3): 369-87.

Garavan, T. N. and Heraty, N. (2001). *Training and Development in Ireland: Results of the 2001 National Survey*, Dublin, CIPD.

Garavan, T. N., Collins, E. and Brady, S. (2003). *Results of the 2003 National Survey of Benchmarks*. Dublin, CIPD.

Garavan, T. N., Shanahan, V. and Carbery, R. (2008). *Training and Development in Ireland: Results of the 2007 National Survey of Benchmarks*, Dublin, CIPD.

Geary, J. (1996). "Working at restructuring work in Europe: The case of team-working", *Journal of Irish Business and Administrative Research*, 17: 44-57.

Geary, J. (1998). "New Work Structures and the Diffusion of Team Working Arrangements in Ireland", Paper presented at the *6th Annual John Lovett Memorial Lecture*, University of Limerick, April.

Geary, J. (2007). "Employee voice in the Irish Workplace: Status and Prospect", in R.B. Freeman, P. Boxall and P. Hayes (Eds), *What Workers Say: Employee Voice in the Anglo-American World*, Ithaca, Cornell University Press.

Geary, J. and Roche, W. (2001). "Multinationals and human resource practices in Ireland: a rejection of the 'new conformance thesis", *International Journal of Human Resource Management*, 12 (1): 109-27.

Geary, J.F. and Roche, W. K. (2005). "Anticipating the Likely Implications of the EU Employee Information and Consultation Directive in Ireland", in J. Storey, (Ed) *Adding Value Through Information and Consultation*, Basingstoke, Palgrave Macmillan.

Gennard, J. and Steuer, M.D. (1971). "The industrial relations of foreign owned subsidiaries in the United Kingdom", *British Journal of Industrial Relations*, 9 (2): 143-159

Gill, J. and Johnson, P. (2002). *Research Methods for Managers*, London, Sage Publications.

Gooderham, P. N., Nordhaug, O. and Ringdal, K. (1999). "Institutional and rational determinants of organizational practices: Human resource management in European firms", *Administrative Science Quarterly*, 44 (3): 507-531.

Gregersen, H. B., Morrison, A. J. and Black, S. J. (1998). "Developing leaders for the Global frontier", *Sloan Management Review*, 40 (1): 21-32.

Grugulis, I. (2007). *Skills, Training and Human Resource Development: A Critical Text*, Hampshire, Palgrave Macmillan.

Gunnigle, P. (1993). *"Exploring Patterns of Industrial Relations Management in Greenfield sites: Evidence from the Republic of Ireland"*, Mimeo, University of Limerick.

Gunnigle, P. (1995). *"Management Styles in Employee Relations in Greenfield Sites: Challenging a Collectivist Tradition"*, Unpublished PhD Thesis, Cranfield: Cranfield School of Management.

Gunnigle, P. (1998). "Human Resource Management and the Personnel Function" in W.K. Roche, K. Monks and J. Walsh (Eds.), *Human Resource Management Strategies: Policy and Practice in Ireland*, Dublin, Oak Tree Press.

Gunnigle, P. and McGuire, D. (2001). "Why Ireland? A Qualitative Review of the Factors influencing the Location of US Multinationals in Ireland with particular reference to the impact of labour issues", *Economic and Social Review*, 32 (1): 43-67.

Gunnigle, P., Collings, D.G., Morley, M.J. (2004), "Die Personalpolitik amerikanischer multinationaler Unternehmen in Irland", in H. Wächter and R. Peters (Eds), *Personalpolitik amerikanischer multinationaler Unternehmen in Europa*. München und Mering, Rainer Hampp Verlag.

Gunnigle, P., Collings, D. G. and Morley, M. J. (2005). "Exploring the dynamics of industrial relations in US multinationals: evidence from the Republic of Ireland", *Industrial Relations Journal*, 36 (3): 241-56.

Gunnigle, P., Collings, D. G., Morley, M., McAvinue, C., O'Callaghan, A. and Shore, D. (2003). "US Multinationals and Human Resource Management in Ireland, Towards a Qualitative Research Agenda", *Irish Journal of Management*, 24 (2): 7-25.

Gunnigle, P., Flood, P., Morley, M. J. and Turner, T. (1994). *Continuity and change in Irish employee relations,* Dublin, Oak Tree Press.

Gunnigle, P., Heraty, N., and Morley, M.J. (2006). *Human resource management in Ireland,* third edition, Dublin, Gill and Macmillan.

Gunnigle, P., Lavelle, J., and McDonnell, A. (2009). "Subtle but deadly - union avoidance through 'double breasting' among multinational companies", *Advances in Industrial and Labor Relations,* 16: 51-74.

Gunnigle, P., Morley, M. J., Clifford, N., Turner, T., Heraty, N. and Crowley, M. (1997). *Human resource management in Irish organisations: practice in perspective,* Dublin, Oak Tree Press.

Gunnigle, P., Turner, T. and D'Art, D. (1998). "Counterpoising collectivism: Performance-related pay and industrial relations in Greenfield sites", *British Journal of Industrial Relations,* 36 (4): 565-79.

Gupta, A. K. and Govindarajan, V. (1991). "Knowledge Flows and the Structure of Control within Multinational Corporations", *Academy of Management Review,* 16 (4): 768-792.

Gupta, A. K. and Govindarajan, V. (2000). "Knowledge Flows within Multinational Corporations", *Strategic Management Journal,* 21 (4): 473-496.

Harley, B. (2001). "Hope or hype? High performance work systems", in B. Harley, J. Hyman, and P. Thompson (Eds), *Participation and Democracy at Work: Essays in Honour of Harvey Ramsay,* Basingstoke, Palgrave Macmillan.

Harvey, M. G., Speier, C. and Novicevic, M. M. (2000). "Strategic Global Human Resource Management: The Role of Inpatriate Managers", *Human Resource Management Review,* 10 (2): 153-175.

Harvey, M., Speier, C., and Novicevic, M.M. (2001). "A Theory-based Framework for Strategic Global Human Resource Staffing Policies and Practices", *International Journal of Human Resource Management,* 12: 898-915.

Harzing, A-W. (1999). *Managing the Multinationals. An international study of control mechanisms,* Cheltenham, Edward Elgar.

Harzing, A.W.K. (2001). "Who's in charge: an empirical study of executive staffing practices in foreign subsidiaries", *Human Resource Management,* 40: 139-158.

Harzing, A.-W. and Sorge, A. (2003). "The Relative Impact of Country of Origin and Universal Contingencies on Internationalization Strategies and Corporate Control in MNEs", *Organization Studies*, 24 (2): 187-214.

Heenan, D.A. and Perlmutter, H.V. (1979). *Multinational Organizational Development*, Reading, MA, Addison-Wesley.

Heller, F., Pusić, E. and Strauss, G. and Wilpert, B. (1998). *Organisational participation: Myth and reality*, Oxford and New York, Oxford University Press.

Heneman, R.L. (1992). Merit pay: *Linking pay increases to performance ratings*, Reading, MA: Addison-Wesley.

Heraty, N. and Morley, M. J. (2003). "Management development in Ireland: the new organizational wealth?", *Journal of Management Development*, 22 (1): 60-82.

Higgins, C. (2004). "Unions Being Pushed Out Of Multinational Sector", *Industrial Relations News*, 9, 26 February, 22-26.

Hill, C.W. (1988). "Differentiation versus low cost or differentiation and low cost: A contingency framework", *Academy of Management Review*, 13 (3): 401-412.

Hourihan, F. (1996). "Non-union Policies on the Increase Among New Overseas Firms", *Industrial Relations News*, 4, 25 January, 17-23.

Huff, A. (2000). "Citigroup's John Reed and Standford's James March on Management Research and Practice", *Academy of Management Executive*, 14 (1): 52-64.

Huselid, M. (1995). "The Impact of Human Resource Management Practices on Turnover, Productivity and Corporate Financial Performance", *Academy of Management Journal*, 38 (3): 635-672.

Huselid, M. A., Beatty, R. W. and Becker, B. E. (2005). "A Players or A Positions? The Strategic Logic of Workforce Management", *Harvard Business Review*, 83 (12): 110-117.

IDA Ireland (2007). *Ireland: Vital Statistics*. Dublin, IDA Ireland.

IDA Ireland (2008). *Vital Statistics.*, Dublin, IDA Ireland.

Industrial Relations News (2005). "US Chamber leaves indelible stamp on Employee Consultation Bill", *Industrial Relations News*, 30, 2-3.

Industrial Relations News (2006). "Irish multinationals have 14% European Works Council compliance rate", *Industrial Relations News*, 37, October 4th.

Industrial Relations News (2007). "Apathy reigns on Information and Consultation, despite Minister's move", *Industrial Relations News*, 12, 3-4.

Ion Equity (2003). *MandA Tracker Survey Review of Irish MandA Activity 2002*, available from: http://www.ionequity.com/surveys.htm [accessed: 15 August, 2006].

Irish Business and Employers Confederation (1999). *Partnership at enterprise level: Survey results*, Dublin, IBEC Partnership Unit.

Irish Congress of Trade Unions (1999) *Sharing the Gains – Supporting Partnership*, Guideline for unions on Gainsharing, Profit Sharing and Employee *Share Ownership Plans*, Irish Congress of Trade Unions (ICTU), Dublin.

Irish Independent (2008). 'Irish based US companies have 1500 vacancies', available from: http://www.independent.ie/breaking-news/national-news/business/irish-based-us-companies-have-1500-vacancies-1507442.html [accessed: 26 Nov, 2008].

Irish Management Institute (IMI) (2008). *Survey of MNCs in Ireland 2008: Results of the 10th Anniversary Competitiveness Survey*, Dublin, IMI.

Jacoby, S. M. (1997). *Modern Manors*, Princeton, Princeton University Press.

Kamoche, K. (1997). "Knowledge creation and learning in international HRM", *International Journal of Human Resource Management*, 8(3): 213-225.

Kelly, A. and Brannick, T. (1985). "Industrial Relations Practices in Multinational Companies in Ireland", *Journal of Irish Business and Administrative Research*, 7, 98-111.

Kelly, P. (2007). "A huge one in seven works in retail sector", *Irish Examiner*, 7 September 2007.

Kerckhofs, P. (2002). *European Works Councils: Facts and Figures*, Brussels, European Trade Union Institute.

Kerin, R. A. and Peterson, R. A. (1977). "Personalization, respondent anonymity, and response distortion in mail surveys", *Journal of Applied Psychology*, 62 (1): 86-89.

Kessler, I (1995). "New Developments in Reward Systems" in J. Storey (Ed), *Human Resource Management: Critical Perspectives*, London, Routledge.

Kets De Vries, M. F. R. (1999). "High-performance Teams: Lessons from the Pygmies", *Organizational Dynamics*, 27 (3): 133-145.

Kidger, P. J. (2002). "Management structure in multinational enterprises: Responding to globalisation", *Employee Relations*, 24(1): 69-85.

Kirby, P. (2002). *The Celtic Tiger in Distress: Growth with Inequality in Ireland*, Hampshire, Palgrave.

Latta, G. (1979). *Profit Sharing, Employee Stock Ownership, Savings and Asset Formation Plans in the Western World*, University of Pennsylvania, The Wharton School Industrial Research Unit.

Lavelle, J. (2008). "Charting the contours of union recognition in foreign-owned MNCs: survey evidence from the Republic of Ireland", *Irish Journal of Management*, 29 (1): 45-64.

Lawler, E. and Mohrmen, S. (1987). "Unions and the New Management", *Academy of Management Executive*, 1 (4): 293-300.

Leavy, B. (1993). "Ireland: Managing the Economy of a Newly Independent State", in D. J. Hickson (Ed.) *Management in Western Europe: Society, Culture and Organization in Twelve Nations*, New York, Walter de Gruyter and Co.

Legge, K. (1978). Power, *Innovation and Problem-solving in Personnel Management*, London and New York, McGraw-Hill.

Lipsky, D. and Farber, H.S. (1976). "The Composition of Strike Activity in the Construction Industry", *Industrial and Labor Relations Review*, 29 (3): 388-404.

Livingston, D. and Henry, J. (1980). "The effect of Employee Stock Ownership Plans on Corporate Profits", *Journal of Risk and Insurance*, 23 (4): 491-505.

Loane, S., Morrow, T. and Bell, J. (2004). "The Role of Human Resource Policy in the Internationalization of Irish Organizations", in F. McDonald, M. Mayer and T. Buck (Eds.), *The Process of Internationalization*, Hampshire, Palgrave Macmillan.

Lowe, K. B., Milliman, J., De Cieri, H. and Dowling, P. J. (2002). "International compensation practices: a ten-country comparative analysis", Human Resource Management, 41 (1): 45-66.

Mabey, C. and Ramirez, M. (2004). *Developing Managers: A European Perspective*, London, Chartered Management Institute.

MacDuffie, J. (1995). "Human Resource Bundles and Manufacturing Performance: Organisational Logic and Flexible Production Systems in the World Auto Industry", *Industrial and Labor Relations Review*, 48 (2): 197-221.

Macharzina, K., Oesterle, M. J. and Brodel, D. (2001). "Learning in Multinationals", in M. Dierkes, A. Berthoin Antal, J. Child and I. Nonaka (Eds.), *Handbook of Organizational Learning and Knowledge*, New York, Oxford University Press.

Marchington, M. (2005). "Employee involvement: Patterns and explanations", in B. Harley, J. Hyman, and P. Thompson, (Eds.) *Participation and Democracy at Work: Essays in Honour of Harvey Ramsay*, Basingstoke, Palgrave Macmillan.

Marchington, M., Wilkinson, A., Ackers, P. and Goodman, J. (1993). "The Influence of Managerial Relations on Waves of Employee Involvement", *British Journal of Industrial Relations*, 31 (4): 543-576.

Marginson P., Hall, M and Hoffman, A. (2004). "The impact of European Works Councils on management decision-making in UK- and US-based multinationals", *British Journal of Industrial Relations,* 42 (2): 209-33.

Marginson, P. and Meardi, G. (2006). "European Union enlargement and the foreign direct investment channel of industrial relations transfer", *Industrial Relations Journal*, 37 (2): 92-110.

Marginson, P., Edwards, P., Edwards, T., Ferner, A. and Tregaskis, O. (2007). "Channels of coverage of employee voice in multinational companies operating in Britain", paper presented to the 2007 International Industrial Relations Association European Congress, Manchester, 3rd to 6th September.

Mayuya, R. and Jacobson, D. (1991). "Japanese direct investment in Ireland", *Irish Business and Administrative Research*, 12 (1): 114-123.

McBeath, G. and Ranels, N. (1989). *Salary Administration*, London, Gower.

Mc Pherson, A. H. and Roche, W. K. (1997). "Peripheral location equals localized labour? Multinationals and the internationalization of training and development in Ireland", *International Journal of Human Resource Management*, 8 (4): 369-384.

McCartney, J. and Teague, P. (1998). "Workplace innovations in the Republic of Ireland", *Economic and Social Review*, 28 (4): 381–399.

McDonnell, A., Lavelle, J., Gunnigle, P. and Collings, D. G. (2007). "Management Research on Multinational Corporations: A Methodological Critique", *Economic and Social Review*, 38 (2): 235-258.

Mendez, A. (2003). "The coordination of globalized R&D activities through project teams organization: an exploratory empirical study", *Journal of World Business*, 38 (2): 96-109.

Metzger, B. (1975). *Profit Sharing in 38 Large Companies - A Piece of the Action for 1,000,000 Participant*, Evanston Illinois, Profit Sharing Research Foundation.

Milkovich, G. (1988). "A strategic perspective on compensation management" in K. Rowland and G. Ferris (Eds.), *Research in personnel and human resources management*, Vol. 6. Greenwich, CT, JAI Press.

Millward, N., Bryson, A. and Forth, J. (2000). *All change at work*, London, Routledge.

Moingeon, B. and Edmondson, A. (1996). *Organizational Learning and Competitive Advantage*, London, Sage.

Monks, K., Scullion, H. and Creaner, J. (2001). "HRM in international firms: evidence from Ireland", *Personnel Review*, 30 (5): 536-553

Mooney, P. (1980). *An inquiry into Wage Payment Systems in Ireland*, Dublin, European Foundation for the Improvement of Living and Working Conditions.

Mooney, P.M. (1989). *"From Industrial Relations to Employee Relations in Ireland"*, Unpublished PhD Thesis, Trinity College, Dublin.

Morley, M. and Gunnigle, P. (1997). "Compensation and Benefits" in P. Gunnigle, M. Morley, N. Clifford and T. Turner (Eds), *Human Resource Management in Irish Organisations: Practice in Perspective*, Dublin, Oak Tree Press.

Morley, M., Gunnigle, P. and Turner, T. (2001). *The Cranfield Network on Human Resource Management (Cranet E) Survey: Executive Report Ireland,* Limerick: University of Limerick.

Morley, M.J., Gunnigle, P., O'Sullivan, M. and Collings, D. (2006). "New Directions in the Roles and Responsibilities of the HRM Function", *Personnel Review*, 35 (6): 609-617.

MSF (Manufacturing, Science and Finance Union) (1998). *Underpinning Partnership at the Workplace: An MSF Guide to Profit Sharing, ESOPs and Equity Paricipation*, Dublin, Manufacturing, Science and Finance Union.

Murphy, M. (1997). "Conducting Survey Research: A Practical Guide", in T. Brannick and W. Roche (Eds.), *Business Research Methods*, Dublin, Oak Tree Press.

Murray, S. (1984). *Employee Relations in Irish Private Sector Manufacturing Industry*. Dublin, Industrial Development Authority.

Northrup, H.R. (1995). "Doublebreasted operations and the decline of construction unionism", *Journal of Labor Research*, 16 (3): 379-385.

O'Malley, E. (1985). "The Performance of Irish Indigenous Industry: Some Lessons for the 1980s", in J. Fitzpatrick and J. Kelly (Eds.), *Perspectives On Irish Industry*, Dublin, Irish Management Institute.

O'Malley, E. (1992). "Problems of Industrialisation in Ireland", in J.H. Goldthorpe and C.T. Whelan (Eds.), *The Development Of Industrial Society In Ireland*, New York, Oxford University Press.

O'Malley, E. (1998). "The Revival of Irish Indigenous Industry", *Quarterly Economic Commentary*, Dublin, ESRI.

O'Sullivan, M. (2000). *Contests for Corporate Control: Corporate Governance and Economic Performance in the United States and Germany*, Oxford, Oxford University Press.

OECD (2005a). *Science, Technology and Industry Scoreboard*, Paris, OECD.

OECD (2005b). *Trends and Recent Developments in Foreign Direct Investment*, Paris, OECD.

OECD (2006). *Trends and Recent Developments in FDI*. Paris, Organisation for European Cooperation and Development.

O'Hagan, E. (2005). "Ten years of European works councils in Ireland: testing the regulatory capacity of soft-style EU directives", *Employee Relations*, 27 (4): 386-412.

Osland, J. S., Bird, A., Mendenhall, M. and Osland, A. (2006). "Developing global leadership capabilities and global mindset: a review", in G. K. Stahl and I. Bjorkman (Eds.), *Handbook of Research in International Human Resource Management*, Cheltenham, Edward Elger.

Pearce, J. (1987). "Why Merit Pay doesn't Work: Implications for Organisational Theory" in D. Balkin. and L. Gomez-Mejia (Eds), *New Perspectives on Compensation*, Englewood Cliffs, NJ, Prentice Hall.

Penrose, E. (1959). *The Theory of the Growth of the Firm*, New York, Wiley.

Perlmutter, H.V. (1969). "The tortuous evolution of the multinational corporation", *Columbia Journal of World Business*, 4 (1): 9-18.

Pfeffer, J. (1994). *Competitive Advantage Through People*, Boston Mass, Harvard Business School Press.

Poole, M. (1989). *The Origins of Economic Democracy: Profit Sharing and Employee Shareholding Schemes*, London, Routledge.

Poole, M. and Jenkins, G. (1990). *The Impact of Economic Democracy: Profit Sharing and Employee Shareholding Schemes*, London, Routledge.

Porter, M. (1985). *Competitive Advantage*, New York, Free Press.

Purcell, J. (2004). "The HRM-Performance Link: Why, How and When does People Management Impact on Organisational Performance?", Paper presented at the *12th Annual John Lovett Memorial Lecture*, University of Limerick, March.

Purcell, J., Kinnie, N., Hutchinson, S., Rayton, B. and Swart, J. (2003). *Understanding the People and Performance Link: Unlocking the Black Box*, London, Chartered Institute of Personnel and Development.

Ramsay, H. (1977). "Cycles of control: Workers participation in sociological and historical perspective", *Sociology*, 11 (3): 481-506.

Ramsay, H. (1991). "Reinventing the Wheel ? A Review of the Development and Performance of Employee Involvement", *International Journal of Human Resource Management*, 1 (4): 1-22.

Ramsay, H. and Scholarios, D. (1999). "Employee direct participation in Britain and Australia: Evidence from AWIRS95 and WERS98", Asia *Pacific Journal of Human Resources*, 38 (2): 42-53.

Reilly, P., Tamkin, P. and Broughton, A. (2007). *The Changing HR Function: Transforming HR?*, London, CIPD.

Rios-Morales, R. and Brennan, L (2007). "Ireland's Foreign Direct Investment Competitive Advantage and Japanese Outward Direct Investment", *Asia Pacific Business Review*, 13(2): 201-231.

Roche, W. and Turner, T. (1994). "Testing Alternative Models of Human Resource Policy Effects on Trade Union Recognition in the Republic of Ireland", *International Journal of Human Resource Management*, 5(3): 721-753.

Roche, W. and Turner, T. (1998). "Human Resource Management and Industrial Relations: Substitution, Dualism and Partnership", in W.K. Roche, K. Monks and J. Walsh (Eds.), *Human Resource Strategies: Policy and Practice in Ireland*. Dublin, Oak Tree Press.

Roche, W. K. (2001). "Accounting for the trend in trade union recognition in Ireland", *Industrial Relations Journal*, 32 (1): 37-54.

Roche, W. K. (2008). "The trend of unionisation in Ireland since the mid-1990s", in T. Hastings (Ed.), *The state of the unions: challenges facing organised labour in Ireland*, Dublin, The Liffey Press.

Roche, W.K. and Geary, J. (1996). "Multinational Companies in Ireland: Adapting to or diverging from national industrial relations practices and traditions", *Irish Business and Administrative Review*, 17 (1): 14-31.

Roche, W.K. and Geary, J. (2002). "Collaborative production and the Irish boom: work organisation, partnership and direct involvement in the Irish workplace", in D. D'Art and T. Turner (Eds), *Irish Employment Relation in the New Economy*, Dublin, Blackhall Publishing.

Roche, W.K. and Geary, J.F. (1999). "Collaborative production and the Irish boom: Work organisation, partnership and direct involvement in Irish workplaces", *The Economic and Social Review*, 31 (1): 1-36.

Roehling, M.V., Cavanaugh, M.A., Moynihan, L. M. and Boswell, W.R. (2000). "The nature of the new employment relationship: A content analysis of the practitioner and academic literatures", *Human Resource Management*, 39 (4): 305–320.

Rollinson, D. (1993). *Understanding Employee Relations*, Wokingham (U.K.), Addison-Wesley.

Rose, M. (1978). *Industrial Behaviour: Theoretical Development since Taylor*, Harmondsworth (U.K.), Penguin.

Rosenzweig, P.M. and Nohria, N. (1994). "Influences on Human Resource Management Practices in Multinational Corporations", *Journal of International Business Studies*, 25 (2): 229-242.

Ruane, F. and Uğur, A. (2005). "Trade and Foreign Direct Investment in Manufacturing and Services", in J. O'Hagan and C. Newman (Eds.), *The Economy of Ireland: National and Sectoral Policy Issues*, Dublin, Gill and Macmillan Ltd.

Russ-Eft, D., Preskill, H. and Sleezer, C. (1997). *Human resource development review: Research and implications*, Thousand Oaks, CA, Sage.

Saka-Helmhout, A. (2007). "Unravelling learning within Multinational Corporations", *British Journal of Management*, 18 (3): 294-310.

Sargent, A. (1990). *Turning People On: The Motivational Challenge*, London, Institute of Personnel Management.

Saunders, M., Lewis, P. and Thornhill, A. (2007). *Research methods for business students*, 4th edition, Harlow, Financial Times Prentice Hall.

Saunders, P. and Harris, C. (1994). *Privatization and Popular Capitalism*, Buckingham (UK), Open University Press.

Schlegelmilch, B. B. and Diamantopoulos, A. (1991). "Prenotification and mail surveys response rates: a quantitative integration of the literature", *Journal of the Market Research Society*, 33 (3): 243-255.

Schuler, R.S., Dowling, P.J. and De Cieri, H. (1993). "An Integrative Framework of Strategic International Human Resource Management", *Journal of Management*, 19 (2): 419-459.

Scullion, H. (1994). "Staffing Policies and Strategic Control in British Multinationals", *International Studies of Management and Organization*, 24 (3): 86-104.

Scullion, H. (1999). "International HRM in medium-sized MNEs: evidence from Ireland", in C. Brewster and H. Harris (Eds.), *International HRM: Contemporary issues in Europe*, London, Routledge.

Scullion, H. and Collings, D. G. (2006). *Global Staffing*, Abingdon, Routledge.

Scullion, H. and Donnelly, N. (1998). "International Human Resource Management: Recent Developments in Irish Multinationals", in W. Roche, K. Monks and J. Walsh (Eds.) *Human Resource Strategies: Policy and Practice in Ireland*, Dublin, Oak Tree Press.

Scullion, H. and Starkey, K. (2000). "In search of the changing role of the corporate human resource function in the international firm", *International Journal of Human Resource Management*, 11 (6): 1061-1081.

Shaked, I. (1986). "Are Multinational Corporations Safer?", *Journal of International Business*, 17 (1): 83-106.

Sheehan, B. (1996). MComm Thesis, Graduate School of Business, University College Dublin.

Sloan, E. B., Hazucha, J. F. and Van Katwyk, P.T. (2003). "Strategic Management of Global Leadership Talent", in W. H. Mobley and P.W. Dorfman (Eds.), *Advances in Global Leadership,* Volume 3, Oxford, Elsevier Science.

Solomon, C. (1995). "Learning to manage host-country nationals", *Personnel Journal,* 74 (3): 60-66.

Sparrow, P. (2007). "Globalization of HR at function level: four UK-based case studies of the international recruitment and selection process", *International Journal of Human Resource Management,* 18 (5): 845-867.

Sparrow, P. and Hiltrop, J.-M. (1994). *European Human Resource Management in Transition,* Hemel Hempstead, Herts., (U.K.), Prentice-Hall.

Sparrow, P., Brewster, C. and Harris, H. (2004). *Globalizing Human Resource Management,* London, Routledge.

Spreitzer, G.M. and Mishra, A.K. (1999). "Giving up control without losing control: Trust and its substitutes' effects on managers' involving employees in decision making", *Group and Organization Management,* 24 (2): 155-187.

Stahl, G. K., Bjorkman, I., Farndale, E., Morris, S. S., Stiles, P., Trevor, J. and Wright, P. M. (2007). *Global Talent Management: How Leading Multinationals Build and Sustain Their Talent Pipeline,* Faculty & Research Working Paper, Fontainebleau, France, INSEAD.

Stiles, P., Wright, P., Paauwe, J., Stahl, G., Trevor, J. Farndale, E., Morris, S. and Bjorkman, I. (2006). *Best practice and key themes in global human resource management: project report,* Global Human Resource Research Alliance (GHRRA).

Sturgeon, T. (2001). "How do we define value chains and production networks", Globalization Working Paper 00-010, Industrial Performance Center, Massachusetts Institute of Technology.

Suutari, V. (2002). "Global leader development: an emerging research agenda", *Career Development International,* 7 (4): 218-233.

Tansey, P. (1998). *Ireland at Work: Economic growth and the Labour Market 1987 – 1997*, Dublin, Oak Tree Press.

Taylor, S. (2006). "Emerging motivations for global HRM integration", in A. Ferner J. Quintanilla and J. I. Sanchez (Eds.), *Multinationals and the Construction of Transnational Practices: Convergence and Diversity in the Global Economy*, London, Palgrave.

Thompson, K. and Keating, M. (2004). "An Empirical Study of Executive Nationality Staffing Practices in Foreign-Owned MNC Subsidiaries in Ireland", *Thunderbird International Business Review*, 46 (6): 771-797.

Tiernan, S., Morley, M. J. and Foley, E. (2006). *Modern Management*, Third edition, Dublin, Gill & Macmillan.

Tregaskis, O., Edwards, T., Edwards, P., Ferner, A. and Marginson, P. (2008). "Transnational learning capability in multinational firms: mediated country of origin effects", *unpublished working paper*.

Tregaskis, O., Glover, L. and Ferner, A. (2005). *International HR Networks in Multinational Companies*, Chartered Institute of Personnel and Development Research Report, London, Chartered Institute of Personnel and Development.

Tregaskis, O., Heraty, N. and Morley, M. (2001). "HRD in multinationals: the global/local mix", *Human Resource Management Journal*, 11 (2): 34-56.

Turner, T., D'Art, D. and Gunnigle, P. (1997a). "Pluralism in retreat: A comparison of Irish and multinational manufacturing companies", *International Journal of Human Resource Management*, 8 (6): 825-840.

Turner, T., D'Art, D. and Gunnigle, P. (1997b). "US Multinationals: changing the framework of Irish industrial relations?" *Industrial Relations Journal*, 28 (2): 92-102.

Turner, T., D'Art, D. and Gunnigle, P. (2001). "Multinationals and human resource practices in Ireland: a rejection of the 'new conformance thesis': a reply", *International Journal of Human Resource Management*, 12 (1): 128-33.

Turner, T., D'art, D. and Gunnigle, P. (2002). "Multi-National Corporations: A Challenge to European Trade Unions?" *Irish Journal of Management*, 23 (1): 125-141.

UNCTAD (2001). *World Investment Report 2001. Promoting Linkages*, New York and Geneva, United Nations.

UNCTAD (2004). *World Investment Report 2004. The Shift Towards Services*, New York and Geneva: United Nations.

UNCTAD (2005). *Foreign Direct Investment Statistics 2005*, Available from: http://www.unctad.org/Templates/StartPage.asp?intItemID=2527andlang=1 [accessed: 25 May 2006].

UNCTAD (2006). *World Investment Report 2006. FDI from Developing and Transition Economies: Implications for Development*, New York and Geneva, United Nations.

UNCTAD (2007). *World Investment Report 2007: Transnational Corporations, Extractive Industries and Development*, New York and Geneva, United Nations.

UNCTAD (2008). *World Investment Report 2008. Transnational Corporations and the Infrastructure Challenge*, New York and Geneva, United Nations.

te Velde, D.W. (2001). *Policies towards foreign direct investment in developing countries: emerging best practices and outstanding issues*, Report presented at the Conference held at the Overseas Development Institute, London, 16 March 2001.

Vernon, R. and Wells, L.T. (1986). *Manager in the International Economy*, Englewood Cliffs, Prentice Hall.

Visser, J. (2006). "Union Membership Statistics in 24 Countries", *Monthly Labor Review*, 129 (1): 38–49.

Von Prondzynski, F. (1998). "Ireland: Corporatism Revisited", in A. Ferner and R. Hyman (Eds.), *Changing Industrial Relations* in Europe, Oxford, Blackwell.

Wallace, J., Gunnigle, P. and Mc Mahon, G. (2004). *Industrial Relations in Ireland: Third edition,* Dublin, Gill and Macmillan.

Welch, D. (1994). "Determinants of international human resource management approaches and activities: a suggested framework", *Journal of Management Studies*, 31 (2): 139-164.

Wernerfelt, B. (1984). "A Resource-based View of the Firm", *Strategic Management Journal*, 5 (2): 171-180.

Whitfield, K. and Poole, M. (1977). "Organising Employment for High Performance", *Organization Studies*, 18 (5): 745-764.

Wilkinson, (1998). "Empowerment: Theory and practice", *Personnel Review*, 27 (1): 40-56.

Williams, J. (1997). "The Sampling Process", in T. Brannick and W. Roche (Eds.), *Business Research Methods*, Dublin, Oak Tree Press.

Willman, P., Bryson, A., and Gomez, R. (2006). "The sound of silence: Which employers choose no employee voice and why?", *Socio-Economic Review*, 4 (2): 283-99.

Windolf, P. (1986). "Recruitment, selection and internal labour markets in Britain and Germany", *Organizational Studies*, 7 (3): 235-254.

Wong, J. and Chan, S. (2003). "China's Outward Direct Investment: Expanding Worldwide", *China: An International Journal*, 1 (2): 273-301.

Wood, G., Martin, G. and Collings, D. (2008). "Institutions, HR Strategies and the Adoption and Exploitation of e-HR", unpublished working paper, Sheffield, University of Sheffield Management School.

Wood, S.J. and Fenton-O'Creevy, M.P. (2005). "Direct Involvement, Representation and Employee Voice in UK Multinationals in Europe", *European Journal of Industrial Relations*, 11 (1): 27-50.

Wrynn, J. (1997). "Foreign Direct Investment to a peripheral country: The case for Ireland" in B. Fynes and S. Ennis (Eds.) *Competing from the periphery*, Dublin, Oak Tree Press.

Young, S., Hood, N. & Hamill, J. (1985). "Decision-Making in Foreign-Owned Multinational Subsidiaries in United Kingdom", ILO Working Paper, no. 35, Geneva: ILO.

Yu, J. and Cooper, H. (1983). "A quantitative review of research design effects on response rates to questionnaires", *Journal of Marketing Research*, 20 (1): 36-44.